The series Lecture Notes in Computer Science (LNCS), including its subseries Lecture Notes in Artificial Intelligence (LNAI) and Lecture Notes in Bioinformatics (LNBI), has established itself as a medium for the publication of new developments in computer science and information technology research, teaching, and education.

LNCS enjoys close cooperation with the computer science R & D community, the series counts many renowned academics among its volume editors and paper authors, and collaborates with prestigious societies. Its mission is to serve this international community by providing an invaluable service, mainly focused on the publication of conference and workshop proceedings and postproceedings. LNCS commenced publication in 1973.

Daniel Balouek · Antonio Filograna ·
Omer Rana · Stefan Schulte · Massimo Villari
Editors

Service-Oriented and Cloud Computing

12th IFIP WG 6.12 European Conference, ESOCC 2026
Bolzano, Italy, September 7–8, 2026
Proceedings

Springer

Editors
Daniel Balouek
IMT Atlantique
Nantes, France

Antonio Filograna
Engineering Ingegneria Informatica Spa
Lecce, Italy

Omer Rana
Cardiff University
Cardiff, UK

Stefan Schulte
TU Berlin
Berlin, Germany

Massimo Villari
Università degli Studi di Messina
Messina, Italy

ISSN 0302-9743 ISSN 1611-3349 (electronic)
Lecture Notes in Computer Science
ISBN 978-3-032-37830-9 ISBN 978-3-032-37831-6 (eBook)
https://doi.org/10.1007/978-3-032-37831-6

This Springer imprint is published by the registered company Springer Nature Switzerland AG
The registered company address is: Gewerbestrasse 11, 6330 Cham, Switzerland

Preface

The European Conference on Service-Oriented and Cloud Computing (ESOCC) is the premier European forum on advances in the state of the art and practice of Service-Oriented Computing and Cloud Computing. Since its inception in 2012, ESOCC has provided a venue for presenting innovative research on Cloud Computing, Service-Oriented Computing, Edge Computing, Data-Intensive Systems, and emerging computing paradigms that shape the future of digital infrastructures.

As distributed systems continue to evolve toward increasingly decentralized, heterogeneous, and AI-enabled computing environments, the challenges faced by software and systems engineers have expanded significantly. Nowadays, Cloud-Edge Continuum Computing is the mainstream approach to building large-scale distributed systems and delivering software services to end users. Cloud-Edge-native software is pervading the delivery of enterprise applications, which are comprised of microservices. Microservices can be independently developed and deployed by exploiting multiple heterogeneous technologies. These characteristics make Service-Oriented Computing and Cloud-Edge Continuum Computing the natural answers to the industry's need for flexibly scalable and maintainable enterprise applications that can be delivered through state-of-the-art methodologies like DevOps and more. Considering this basis, the evolution of distributed systems is going towards supporting AI and Machine Learning, specifically in Workflow Domains, Agentic AI, and AIOps. ESOCC brings together contributions spanning these research directions, fostering collaboration between academia and industry and encouraging interdisciplinary approaches to the design and operation of next-generation service-based systems.

The 2026 edition of ESOCC continued this tradition by providing a high-quality international forum to facilitate exchanges between researchers and practitioners in these areas. The conference accepted nine full research papers, four short research papers, and ten project papers from 40 submissions. Each submission underwent a rigorous single-blind peer-review process conducted by the members of the Program Committee. Every paper received at least three independent reviews, ensuring a thorough evaluation based on originality, technical quality, significance, and relevance to the conference scope.

The end result was a very promising ESOCC 2026 program. We thank all PC members and additional reviewers for taking part in the reviewing and selection process. Our gratitude extends to the chairs and organizers of the projects track and PhD symposium. We thank the invited speakers for their valuable contribution to the program.

We are especially grateful to the organizers of the 20th European Conference on Software Architecture (ECSA), which was co-hosted with ESOCC 2026. Special thanks go to Andrea Janes and his team for help in the local and financial organization of the conference. Last, but not least, we want to thank the International Federation for Information Processing (IFIP) for their support of ESOCC since its inception, and for the granting of a travel grant for ESOCC 2026 authors.

Finally, we thank all authors of technical papers and those who presented their research for contributing to this successful conference. With their work and dedication, ESOCC continued its tradition of advancing the field of Service-Oriented Computing and Cloud Computing.

July 2026

Daniel Balouek
Antonio Filograna
Omer Rana
Stefan Schulte
Massimo Villari

Organization

Steering Committee

Antonio Brogi	University of Pisa, Italy
Schahram Dustdar	TU Wien, Austria
Paul Grefen	Eindhoven University of Technology, Netherlands
Einar Broch Johnson	University of Oslo, Norway
Kyriakos Kritikos	ICS-FORTH, Greece
Winfried Lamersdorf	University of Hamburg, Germany
Flavio de Paoli	University of Milano-Bicocca, Italy
Ernesto Pimentel	University of Málaga, Spain
Pierluigi Plebani	Politecnico di Milano, Italy
Ulf Schreier	Hochschule Furtwangen University, Germany
Stefan Schulte	TU Berlin, Germany
Massimo Villari	University of Messina, Italy
Olaf Zimmermann	Eastern Switzerland University of Applied Sciences, Switzerland
Wolf Zimmermann	Martin Luther University Halle-Wittenberg, Germany

General Chair

Stefan Schulte	TU Berlin, Germany

Program Chairs

Daniel Balouek	Inria, France
Antonio Filograna	Engineering Ingegneria Informatica S.p.A., Italy
Omer Rana	Cardiff University, UK
Massimo Villari	University of Messina, Italy

Program Committee

Nour Ali	Brunel University of London, UK
Vasilios Andrikopoulos	University of Groningen, Netherlands

Raadesh Gupta Balanarasimmagupta	Oracle America Inc., USA
Luciano Baresi	Politecnico di Milano, Italy
Uwe Breitenbücher	Reutlingen University, Germany
Antonio Brogi	Università di Pisa, Italy
Lorenzo Carnevale	University of Messina, Italy
Marco Comuzzi	Ulsan National Institute of Science and Technology, South Korea
Amr Elsayed	Meta Platforms, USA
Matteo Esposito	University of Oulu, Finland
Jonas Fritzsch	University of Stuttgart, Germany
Ilche Georgievski	University of Stuttgart, Germany
Indika Kumara	Tilburg University, Netherlands
Francesco La Rosa	University of Messina, Italy
Xiaozhou Li	Free University of Bozen-Bolzano, Italy
Jacopo Massa	Università di Pisa, Italy
José Merseguer	Universidad de Zaragoza, Spain
Phu Nguyen	SINTEF, Norway
Claus Pahl	Free University of Bozen-Bolzano, Italy
Adam Przybylek	Lero, University of Galway, Ireland
Larisa Safina	INRIA Lille - Nord Europe, France
Jacopo Soldani	University of Pisa, Italy
Davide Taibi	University of Southern Denmark, Denmark and University of Oulu, Finland
Md Arfan Uddin	University of Arizona, USA
Gianluigi Zavattaro	Università di Bologna, Italy
Olaf Zimmermann	Eastern Switzerland University of Applied Sciences, Switzerland
Christian Zirpins	Karlsruhe University of Applied Sciences, Germany

Edge-Cloud Continuum in the URBREATH Project

Giuseppe Ciulla and Roberto Di Bernardo

Engineering Ingegneria Informatica S.p.A., Piazzale dell'agricoltura 24, 00144 Rome, Italy
{giuseppe.ciulla,roberto.dibernardo}@eng.it

Abstract. URBREATH develops a cloud-native framework that combines Nature-Based Solutions, citizen participation, and Local Digital Twins to support climate-neutral urban transformation. Real-time sensing, data harmonization, and microservice orchestration enable inclusive planning processes. Future integration of Large Language Models will enhance accessibility, narrative generation, and community engagement.

Keywords: Local Digital Twins · Nature Based Solutions · Large Language Models

1 Introduction

The Horizon Europe URBREATH project, develops and validates a new paradigm for urban revitalization driven by Nature-Based Solutions (NBS) and community participation. The project enhances social interactions, inclusion, and liveability while steering cities toward climate neutrality and resilience. URBREATH implements hybrid solutions that integrate "grey" infrastructure with natural elements, placing local communities at the heart of the decision-making process [1, 2]. The methodology is operationalized through Urban Living Labs in Madrid, Leuven, Tallinn, Cluj-Napoca, Athens, Parma, Aarhus, Pilsen and Kajaani. Local Digital Twins supports this vision by managing the entire data value chain and supporting end-users in the co-design of NBS.

2 URBREATH Toolbox

URBREATH is architected as Cloud-native highly modular, service-oriented system designed to manage complex urban data flows, providing scalable services for urban planning and citizen engagement, where Edge-Cloud Continuum optimizes data processing and resource allocation. **Edge Components (Data Ingestion & Real-Time Sensing):** operating over IoT networks, edge computing is prioritized for real-time sensor data coming from urban NBS sites. Sensors monitor critical environmental variables (e.g., PM2.5, NO_2, temperature, humidity), ensuring low-latency responses and immediate data validation by processing this data at the Edge via IoT Connectors. **Cloud**

Components (Big Data & 3D Visualization): manage heavy computational tasks. The 3D Digital Twin leverages Cloud resources for rendering CityGML data. The Digital Enabler, a cloud-native platform, serves as data harmonisation hub for scattered sources and cross-domain analytics. Orchestration and Microservices: built on built on Apache Kafka and Airflow, Orion-LD, and NGSI-LD and OGC standards, the "orchestration middleware", ensures data integrity and automated execution of analytical pipelines. The Edge-Cloud Continuum is prodromal to feed participatory process enabled by the URBREATH dedicated e-participation platform.

3 Conclusions and Future Perspectives

URBREATH leverages the Edge-Cloud Continuum to transform urban planning from an administrative task into a collaborative data-driven process. URBREATH defines a roadmap for integrating Large Language Models (LLMs) within the e-participation platform. With LMMs, the platform will lower the threshold for participation, ensuring that complex data are accessible for all. This innovative framework provides a scalable, Cloud-native solution for European cities aiming to achieve climate neutrality through inclusive and technologically advanced renaturing strategies. The LLMs will act as an interface layer allowing non-technical users to explore complex datasets and simulations using natural language queries, to automated "storytelling" and knowledge generation, generate descriptive summaries that explain the "why" behind specific design choices (e.g. from Digital Twin 3D visualisations), translating technical KPIs into understandable narratives. To complement the architectural framework, ongoing validation activities in URBREATH Living Labs are generating quantitative evidence on system performance (latency, scalability, and user engagement metrics); LLM integration will be operationalised through pilot studies that explicitly address data quality, privacy compliance, and long-term maintainability considerations.

Acknowledgments. This work is co-funded by the European Union under grant agreement ID 101139711.

Disclosure of Interests. The authors have no competing interests to declare that are relevant to the content of this article.

References

1. Ciulla, G., et al.: Urban greening and renaturing towards climate neutrality: the URBREATH approach. In: Proceedings EGOV-CeDEM-ePart conference, 1–5 September 2024. Ghent University and KU Leuven, Ghent/Leuven, Belgium. https://ceur-ws.org/Vol-3737/paper44.pdf
2. Giest, S., Klievink, B.: Data for Policy CIC. Data for Policy 2025 (DfP'25) - Europe Book of Abstracts. Data for Policy 2025 - Europe, Leiden University, The Hague, The Netherlands, 6 June 2025. CONFERENCE 2016, LNCS, vol. 9999, pp. 1–13. Springer, Heidelberg (2016). https://doi.org/10.5281/zenodo.15625131

TEMA – Trusted Extremely Precise Mapping and Prediction for Emergency Management

Aikaterini Beli[1], Alessandro Paciaroni[1], Mpampis Chatzimallis[1], Vasileios Mygdalis[22], and Antonio Filograna[3]

[1] The Lisbon Council Asbl, Brussels, Belgium
{aikaterini.beli,alessandro.paciaroni}@lisboncouncil.net, mygdalisv@csd.auth.gr
[2] Aristotle University of Thessaloniki, Thessaloniki, Greece
[3] Engineering Ingegneria Informatica S.p.A, Lecce, Italy

Abstract. TEMA (Trusted Extremely Precise Mapping and Prediction for Emergency Management) is a Horizon Europe project (GA No. 101093003) developing an AI-driven decision-support platform for Natural Disaster Management as a Service (NDM-aaS). Combining trustworthy AI, digital twin modelling, and extended reality visualisation across the edge-to-cloud continuum, TEMA supports civil protection authorities in real-time emergency response. Now in its final year, the project has validated its platform through four pilot exercises across Finland, Italy, Greece, and Germany, integrating 22 technologies at TRL 5. This paper reports on pilot validation, impact, policy alignment with the EU Preparedness Union Strategy, and clustering activities through the AI.BIG Cluster.

Keywords: Natural disaster management · Trustworthy AI · Pilot validation · EU civil protection · Clustering

1 Introduction

Climate-related emergencies across Europe demand advanced decision-support systems. TEMA[1] is a four-year Horizon Europe project (Dec. 2022 – Nov. 2026, GA No. 101093003) that develops an NDM-as-a-Service (NDM-aaS) platform enabling civil protection authorities to process and act upon heterogeneous extreme data in near real-time. The platform integrates 22 technologies, spanning DNN-based fire/smoke/flood detection, geo-social media analysis, federated edge-cloud orchestration, and digital-twin-based Extended Reality (XR) visualisation through the SmartDesk dashboard [1]. All AI components embed explainability mechanisms aligned with the EU AI Act [2].

---

[1] TEMA project website: https://tema-project.eu.

2 Pilot Trials and Validation

TEMA's validation strategy follows the Trial Guided Methodology (TGM), a structured approach in which each pilot is governed by a Trial Action Plan (TAP) that defines operational scenarios, stakeholder roles, data flows, KPIs, and evaluation criteria. Four pilot campaigns, executed between May and November 2025, reconstructed or simulated a real disaster event with operational end users.

KAHY1 – Forest Fire, Finland (May 2025). In Finland, TEMA was evaluated through a wildfire-response simulation in a realistic control-room environment. End users highlighted improved situational awareness, faster access to integrated information, and the usefulness of fire-spread simulations and drone imagery for operational planning, while identifying the need for improved interface usability and clearer visualization of critical infrastructure and water resources.

RAS1 – Prescribed Fire, Italy (June 2025). In Italy, TEMA was validated during a large-scale prescribed fire experiment with real-time drone and ground sensor streams feeding the TEMA analytics. Participants positively assessed the platform's support for shared situational awareness and coordination between field teams and command centres, while also highlighting challenges related to simulator reliability, wildfire-specific operational constraints and predictive accuracy.

D.MALIAN1 – Flash Flood, Greece (October 2025). In Greece, TEMA supported a flash-flood command-and-control scenario using historical flood data, satellite imagery, drone feeds, hydrodynamic simulations, and geo-social media analysis. First responders highlighted improved inter-agency situational awareness and operational decision-making, while stressing the need for better meteorological integration and clearer visualization of vulnerable infrastructure.

BRK1 – Regional Flood, Germany (November 2025). The German pilot reproduced the 2021 Ahr Valley floods in a realistic command-centre environment. End users positively assessed TEMA's information-fusion capabilities, flood simulation tools, and geo-social media analysis, particularly for evacuation planning and rapid damage assessment, while also emphasized the need for improved interface clarity, multilingual support, better integration with existing command systems, and increased trustworthiness of automated flood predictions in high-risk scenarios.

Across all pilots, first responders valued TEMA's support for situational awareness and operational coordination, while identifying the need for simpler interfaces, stronger system integration, and more trustworthy AI-assisted outputs. The TAP methodology constitutes a reusable procedural output for the broader NDM research community, enabling reproducible trial design and cross-pilot benchmarking.

3 Impact, Policy Alignment and Clustering

Scientific and societal impact. As of M36, TEMA has produced 104 publications across AI, remote sensing, and emergency management venues, with three journal special issues under preparation. The TEMA Wallet provides a unified entry point to the data catalogue,

NDM-aaS platform, and technological assets. A policy brief on AI in European civil protection is also being prepared.

Policy alignment and standardisation. TEMA's design supports the EU Preparedness Union Strategy by enhancing cross-border interoperability and early warning capabilities. The project aligns with ISO 19115 and OGC SensorThings API standards and supports the European Green Deal Data Space by generating FAIR-compliant geospatial datasets for disaster monitoring.

European clustering. TEMA co-founded the AI.BIG Cluster with CREXDATA, ExtremeXP, and PANTHEON, enabling joint dissemination and technology benchmarking on AI-driven Big Data analytics for extreme events. TEMA also engages with the EU Civil Protection Knowledge Network (UCPKN) and has established collaboration with civil protection authorities in all four pilot countries.

4 Conclusion and Outlook

TEMA demonstrates how AI-driven, service-oriented architectures across the edge-to-cloud continuum can advance operational emergency management, through improved situational awareness and inter-agency coordination. With 104 publications, policy engagement, TEMA contributes to Europe's resilience against climate-related disasters. In its final year, the consortium focuses on cross-pilot validation, platform consolidation, and sustainability of exploitable results through the TEMA Wallet.

Acknowledgment. This work has been supported by the European Union's Horizon Europe research and innovation programme under grant agreement No. 101093003 (TEMA).

References

1. TEMA Consortium. Deliverable D2.2 – Report on TEMA platform design, data models and architecture. Horizon Europe Project TEMA (Grant Agreement No. 101093003) (2023)
2. European Parliament and Council: Regulation (EU) 2024/1689 laying down harmonised rules on artificial intelligence (AI Act). Official Journal of the EU, L series (2024)

Adaptive Grid-Interactive Edge Datacenter Fleets with AEGIS

Paul Pop[1], Stefan Schulte[2], and Gopika Premsankar[3]

[1] Danmarks Tekniske Universitet, Denmark
paupo@dtu.dk
[2] Technische Universität Berlin, Germany
schulte@tu-berlin.de
[3] Aalto University, Finland
gopika.premsankar@aalto.fi

Abstract. The establishment of at least 10,000 edge nodes by 2030 has been named as one of the core digital targets of the European Union (EU). To make these nodes climate-neutral, the basic idea is to power them with green energy. However, if combined into Edge Data Centers (EDCs) and considering energy grid data, these edge nodes may play an even more important role in the EU's carbon-neutral future.

Instead of operating as passive loads in the energy grid, EDCs and the grid may exchange data in order to take into account the real-time needs of the energy grid and of services running at the edge. However, making edge nodes a grid-interactive asset has received little attention so far. The recently accepted Horizon Europe Marie Skodowska-Curie Action Doctoral Network Adaptive Grid-Interactive Edge Datacenter Fleets (AEGIS) aims at changing this by bringing together 15 doctoral candidates from seven universities all over Europe.

Keywords: Edge Data Centers · Edge Computing · Smart Grids

1 Overview

Edge Data Centers (EDCs) are often presented as an alternative to cloud data centers because they provision compute resources close to end users. Frequently cited advantages of edge computing include reduced bandwidth consumption, potentially higher reliability under weak or intermittent connectivity, improved data locality, and low-latency processing [4]. The European Union (EU) has defined the deployment of "at least 10,000 climate-neutral highly secure edge nodes" by 2030 as a key digital target [1], where an edge node is understood as compute capacity located near a data source. Such nodes can vary widely in capacity, ranging from lightweight endpoints such as microcontroller units and single-board computers (e.g., Raspberry Pis), to cloudlets, up to full-fledged EDCs with powerful server-grade resources [2, 3].

Especially the latter can play an important role in balancing the needs of the energy grid. By monitoring the current and future demands of services running in EDCs and the state of the energy grid, it is possible to identify opportunities to not only run edge services in a carbon-efficient way, but also help to establish grid stability and energy security. For this, however, it is necessary to overcome the barrier that EDCs are currently merely passive loads in the energy grid: Physically connected to the grid, but blind to its real-time needs. This can be traced back to two challenges: First, the lack of EDC-internal means to safely coordinate energy-consuming subsystems (servers, networking equipment, cooling, batteries) to provide the verifiable performance the grid requires. And, second, the absence of EDC fleet coordination mechanisms: Individual EDCs lack sufficient power capacity to meet the minimum bid thresholds of European energy markets, which typically require between 0.5 and 3MW of dispatchable capacity.

The recently accepted Marie Skodowska-Curie Action Doctoral Network Adaptive Grid-Interactive Edge Datacenter Fleets (AEGIS) aims at addressing these barriers by providing the means to transform EDCs into grid-interactive assets. To reach this goal, the researchers involved in AEGIS provide a software-defined platform for EDC and grid flexibility. This platform is made up of three layers: (i) The foundational cyber-physical layer provides runtime-verified control to unlock safe, quantifiable flexibility in energy consumption within an EDC, (ii) The intelligence layer uses carbon-aware forecasting and control, enabling service workloads to dynamically adapt their behavior and resource consumption in response to real-time grid signals, and (iii) The orchestration layer enables trusted, EDC fleet-scale coordination using privacy-preserving mechanisms to create a unified energy grid resource.

AEGIS is coordinated by Danmarks Tekniske Universitet and brings together 15 doctoral candidates from seven universities in the EU and affiliated countries. The doctoral candidates and their supervisors provide expertise from computer science, electrical engineering, energy systems, telecommunications, and sustainability, thus covering all the fields necessary for the success of the doctoral network.

Acknowledgments. This project has received funding from the European Union's Horizon Europe Marie Skodowska-Curie Action programme under grant agreement No 101311399.

References

1. European Commission: Decision (EU) 2022/2481 of the European Parliament and the Council of 14 December 2022 establishing the Digital Decade Policy Programme 2030 (2022). https://eur-lex.europa.eu/eli/dec/2022/2481/oj
2. Jansen, M., Al-Dulaimy, A., Papadopoulos, A.V., Trivedi, A., Iosup, A.: The SPECRG reference architecture for the compute continuum. In: 2023 IEEE/ACM 23rd International Symposium on Cluster, Cloud and Internet Computing (CCGrid), pp. 469–484. IEEE (2023). https://doi.org/10.1109/CCGrid57682.2023.00051

3. Ren, J., Zhang, D., He, S., Zhang, Y., Li, T.: A survey on end-edge-cloud orchestrated network computing paradigms: transparent computing, mobile edge computing, fog computing, and cloudlet. ACM Comput. Surv. **52**(6), 125:1–125:36 (2019). https://doi.org/10.1145/3362031
4. Satyanarayanan, M.: The emergence of edge computing. IEEE Comput. **50**(1), 30–39 (2017). https://doi.org/10.1109/MC.2017.9

Urgency Meets Uncertainty Across the Computing Continuum: The QUICK Project

Maryam Masoumi, Kawther Tlili, Maphineth Ung, Nancy Victor, and Daniel Balouek

IMT Atlantique, Inria, LS2N, UMR CNRS 6004, 44307 Nantes, France
daniel.balouek@inria.fr

Abstract. The QUICK project investigates the scientific foundations of Urgent Computing across the Computing Continuum, addressing the challenge of enabling geo-distributed infrastructures to sustain critical computations under dynamic and hardly predictable conditions. By bridging edge computing, artificial intelligence, and chaos engineering, QUICK aims to develop software abstraction and resource management policies that enable resiliency, adaptation, and timely response to urgency.

Keywords: Urgent Computing · Computing Continuum · Chaos Engineering · Multi-Agent systems · Agentic AI

1 Introduction

Societal resilience increasingly depends on large-scale cyber-physical ecosystems spanning sensors, edge, cloud, and scientific instruments, *the Computing Continuum*, that must sustain observation, coordination, and decision support during extreme events such as natural disasters and infrastructure failures [1].

Two research communities have addressed computing continuum challenges from complementary perspectives. In summary, the distributed systems community have developed mechanisms for optimizing cloud-edge infrastructures [2, 3], while the cyber-physical systems and sensing community have developed closed-loop analytics for large-scale monitoring [4]. However, a key question remains: *how to coordinate computation, observation, and decision-making when infrastructure is uncertain, partially observable and intermittently available?*

The QUICK project investigates decision-making policies under uncertainty by combining chaos theory and multi-agent systems within an experimental platform. Rather than relying on fixed scheduling or orchestration policies, autonomous agents will continuously generate, evaluate, compose, and adapt resource-management heuristics when resources, observations, and environmental conditions cannot be assumed stable, fully observable, or continuously available.

2 Project Overview

Ongoing work involves emulating different urgent-computing scenarios and injecting chaos into the system, such as node failures, network disruptions, congestion, resource overload, and cascading failures over the SLICES-FR testbed [5]. Observing system behavior under these conditions, a portfolio of policies can be developed, including optimization-based methods, heuristic and metaheuristic approaches, backup strategies, and approximate computing.

The core methodological contribution is a data-driven policy adaptation approach, where the orchestrator dynamically selects, combines, or adjusts policies instead of relying on a one-size-fits-all strategy. This adaptation is guided by real-time factors such as workload, resource availability, network conditions, task priority, and deadline constraints. The specific objectives are as follows:

Agentic AI for managing uncertainty: This proposes a multi-agent decision-making framework emulating continuum orchestration under uncertainty. Agents adaptively select policy classes based on probabilistic system-state and execution-context indicators, balancing decision quality with performance [6].

Translating crisis management scenarios into system scenarios: This studies earthquake early warning over an edge-cloud infrastructure using traces of 200+ events. It simulates seismic stations, edge resources, cloud monitors, and operators to evaluate fallback and recovery under degraded conditions [7].

Federated Learning for Distributed Control: Hierarchical FL (HFL) uses multi-level edge aggregation to reduce communication overhead. We combine HFL with dynamic adaptation to train a global disaster management model on a continuum-native platform [8].

Acknowledgments. This project is funded within the program *Etoiles Montantes* (Rising Stars), id. 175045-2024, by the Region Pays de la Loire, France. We also thank Chihab Hanachi for its various inputs on crisis management.

References

1. Balouek-Thomert, D., et al.: Harnessing the computing continuum for urgent science. ACM SIGMETRICS **48**(2), 41–46 (2020)
2. Dustdar, S.: Edge intelligence: the confluence of edge computing and artificial intelligence. ACM Trans. Internet Things (2020)
3. Singh, H., et al.: Metaheuristics for scheduling of heterogeneous tasks in cloud computing environments: Analysis, performance evaluation, and future directions. Simul. Model. Pract. Theory (2021)
4. Beckman, P., et al.: Harnessing the computing continuum for programming our world. Fog Comput. Theory Pract. 215–230 (2020)
5. Balouek, D., et al.: Adding virtualization capabilities to the grid'5000 testbed. In: Ivanov, I.I., van Sinderen, M., Leymann, F., Shan, T. (eds.) CLOSER 2012. CCIS,

vol. 367, pp. 3–20 (2013). Springer, Cham. https://doi.org/10.1007/978-3-319-04519-1_1
6. Powell, W.B.: From reinforcement learning to optimal control: a unified framework for sequential decisions. In: Vamvoudakis, K.G., Wan, Y., Lewis, F.L., Cansever, D. (eds.) Handbook of Reinforcement Learning and Control. Studies in Systems, Decision and Control, vol. 325, pp. 29–74 (2021). Springer, Cham. https://doi.org/10.1007/978-3-030-60990-0_3
7. Bénaben, F., et al.: A metamodel and its ontology to guide crisis characterization and its collaborative management. In: ISCRAM (2008)
8. Prigent, C., et al.: Enabling federated learning across the computing continuum: Systems, challenges and future directions. FGCS (2024)

Towards Trustworthy AI Use for Software Architecture

Klara Borowa[1], Matteo Esposito[2,3], Valentina Lenarduzzi[2,3], and Davide Taibi[2,3]

[1] Warsaw University of Technology, Institute of Control and Computation Engineering, Poland
klara.borowa@pw.edu.pl
[2] University of Oulu, Finland
matteo.esposito@oulu.fi, {lenarduzzi,taibi}@imada.sdu.dk
[3] University of Southern Denmark, Denmark

Abstract. Generative AI for software architecture (GenAI4SA) adoption is connected to ethical concerns. These can be tackled by Trustworthy AI use, development, and deployment. This project investigates which considerations practitioners and researchers consider as the most critical for GenAI4SA through a mixed-methods approach. Preliminary findings show that key concerns include AI use for safety-critical systems impacting human health, and securely handling sensitive data.

Keywords: Generative AI · Trustworthy AI · Software architecture · Safety-critical systems for health

1 Introduction

Research on Generative AI for software architecture (GenAI4SA) is currently growing swiftly [2]. Yet, it seems that unresolved ethical concerns are a key challenge in GenAI4SA adoption. These issues could possibly be addressed by Trustworthy AI (TAI), which should be (1) lawful, (2) ethical, and (3) robust by definition [3]. Additionally, according to the ICSE FOSE community survey, a particularly insufficiently addressed and crucial issue is not only TAI development and deployment, but also its trustworthy use [1]. As such, the goal of this project is to find ethical, regulatory, and robustness considerations that should guide GenAI4SA. This will lead to a set of requirements and guidelines useful for designing service oriented and cloud native architectures. To do so, we are currently performing a mixed-methods study focusing on the perspectives of software practitioners and software architecture researchers.

2 Method and Current Status

Our approach focuses on a set of subsequent steps. Firstly, we submitted the project plan and obtained **ethical approval** from the Warsaw University of Technology's ethics committee. Then, we conducted 19 interviews with practitioners (with an average of 16 years of industrial experience) from Poland, Denmark, Germany, and Finland to elicit their perspectives on TAI4SA, focusing on the three TAI dimensions, how they can be achieved, and their opinions on GenAI4SA. We analyzed interview transcripts through structural, descriptive, and value coding [4]. After initial coding, we reached code saturation, and we are currently refining the results through iterative review and discussion.

Based on the interviews, we will prepare a **questionnaire for practitioners**. In particular, we will focus on closed-ended ordinal-scale questions about participants' agreement with the interview results. These will be distributed at on-site events and online through social media. The questionnaire will be analyzed through descriptive statistics and statistical hypothesis testing, in order to define findings that are generally agreed upon by practitioners.

Finally, we will show the practitioners' perspective on TAI4SA to software architecture researchers during a **working session** at the 2026 International Conference of Software Architecture, which has already been accepted. Through this, we will compare and integrate data from both practitioners and researchers.

Emerging Results

Practitioners' opinions on AI4SA vary greatly, ranging from fear, uncertainty, and distrust to excitement and the belief that it improves their workflow. Ethical concerns focused mainly on: (1) safety-critical systems, with particular focus on ones impacting human health and well-being, (2) security and handling sensitive data (e.g., personal data, company secrets), (3) efficient architecting systems for malevolent purposes (e.g., botnets). The main law-related suggestion was to regulate which LLMs can be used in what contexts, and to specify which kinds of data can be used as AI input (e.g., avoiding sharing company secrets).

Acknowledgments. This work has been funded by the National Science Centre, Poland (grant 2025/09/X/ST6/00901).

References

1. Borowa, K., Esposito, M., Lenarduzzi, V., Taibi, D.: Too much AI, too little trust: what the software engineering community really thinks. In: Proceedings of the 2026

IEEE/ACM 48th International Conference on Software Engineering: Future of Software Engineering (ICSE-FoSE), pp. 1–5. Association for Computing Machinery, Rio de Janeiro, Brazil, April 2026. https://doi.org/10.1145/3793657.37
2. Bucaioni, A., Weyssow, M., He, J., Lyu, Y., Lo, D.: Artificial Intelligence for Software Architecture: Literature Review and the Road Ahead (2025). https://doi.org/10.48550/arXiv.2504.04334
3. Independent high-level expert group on artificial intelligence set up by the European Commission: Ethics Guidelines For Trustworthy AI (2019)
4. Saldaña, J.: The coding manual for qualitative researchers, pp. 1–440 (2021)

SIZ-MSH: Development of an Interdisciplinary Software Integration Center in Medical and Nursing Care Facilities, with a Particular Focus on the Mansfeld-Südharz District

Wolf Zimmermann[1], Daniel Gompf[2], Clemens Wagner[3], Andreas Claus[4], and Anita Köhler[4]

[1] Martin-Luther-Universität Halle-Wittenberg, Institut für Informatik, Germany
wolf.zimmermann@informatik.uni-halle.de
[2] EDV Baumgarten, Germany
daniel.gompf@edv-baumgarten.de
[3] Eigenbetrieb Rettungsdienst MSH, Germany
cwagner@rettungsdienst-msh.de
[4] DRK Kreisverband Sangerhausen, Germany
{a.claus,a.koehler}@drk-sangerhausen.de

The digitization of intersectoral processes in the nursing and healthcare sectors has received little attention to date. Nursing and medical staff still transmit emergency and care data verbally or on paper. This type of communication is time-consuming and prone to errors. One obstacle to digitization is the existing software used by individual facilities (nursing homes, emergency centers, ambulance services, etc.), as the interfaces are generally not designed for intersectoral communication. Therefore, direct interfaces are needed to transmit only relevant information, bridging inconsistencies and incompatibilities.

The various interfaces are to be bridged using adapters. However, the number of necessary adapters increases exponentially with the number of communication partners. The idea is therefore to design a central interface so that only two adapters are required. This approach is analogous to a compiler architecture, where the source program is first translated into an intermediate language and then into a machine language (or other programming languages). The central communication interface to be developed corresponds to the intermediate language, as shown in Fig. 1. The translation of the interfaces should be defined using a domain-specific interface description language. This language must include semantic concepts so that the consistency and correctness of the adapters can be formally defined. To this end, an extensible type system is constructed from the application domain. An ontology, such as the one described in [3], can be used as a starting point.

There are no existing solutions for intersectoral digitalization in the nursing and healthcare sectors. In [5], Zaha et al. present a method for generating adapters to bridge type incompatibilities in interfaces. Their work does not examine dynamic processes or the semantics of the interfaces. In [4], Yellin and Strom consider processes in the form of protocols to which interfaces are assigned. On this basis, the compatibility of interfaces is defined. Interface incompatibilities can be bridged by specifying the mapping between

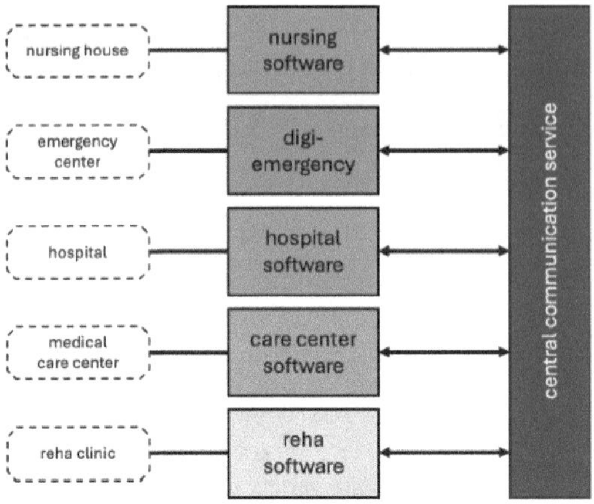

Fig. 1. Reducing complexity through a central communication service

them. In [3], Chouali et al. extend protocols to include preconditions and postconditions. When mapping interfaces, not only 1-1 mappings (one action to one action) but also n-1 and 1-n mappings are considered. Zimmermann and Schaarschmidt demonstrated in [6] that protocol violations, and thus interface incompatibilities, go undetected if recursive callbacks exist within the component system. As a representative example of research in the field of artificial intelligence (AI), we cite the work [1], which builds adapters on large language models. The general problem with AI-based adapters is that they are inherently prone to errors, whereas the classical methods discussed here are at least verifiable in principle.

Acknowledgments. The Federal Ministry of Research, Technology and Space (BMFTR) is funding this project within the framework of its funding priority "Innovationsregion für die digitale Transformation von Pflege und Gesundheit". BMFTR funding code: "SIZ-MSH: Entwicklung eines interdisziplinären Softwareintegrationszentrums in Medizin- und Pflegeeinrichtungen mit Schwerpunktwirkung im Landkreis Mansfeld-Südharz" (16SV9645).

References

1. Altin, M., Mutlu, B., Kilinc, D., Cakir, A.: Automated testing for service-oriented architecture: Leveraging large language models for enhanced service composition. IEEE Access **13**, 89627–89640 (2025). https://doi.org/10.1109/ACCESS.2025.3571994
2. Chouali, S., Mouelhi, S., Mountassir, H.: Component design and adaptation based on behavioral contracts. In: Abdelwahed, E., et al. (eds.) MEDI 2018. CCIS, vol. 929, pp. 217–230. Springer, Cham (2018). https://doi.org/10.1007/978-3-030-02852-7_19

3. Goyer, F., Fabry, P., Barton, A., Ethier, J.F.: An ontology for healthcare systems. In: International Conference on Biomedical Ontology: Lessons from Ontologies in Diverse Domains (ICBO 2022). pp. paper–5498. Ann Arbor, USA (2022)
4. Yellin, D.M., Strom, R.E.: Protocol specifications and component adaptors. ACM Trans. Program. Lang. Syst. (TOPLAS) **19**(2), 292–333 (1997). https://doi.org/10.1145/244795.244801
5. Zaha, J.M., Geisenberger, M., Groth, M.: Compatibility test and adapter generation for interfaces of software components. In: Ghosh, R.K., Mohanty, H. (eds.) ICDCIT 2004. LNCS, vol. 3347, pp. 318–328. Springer, Heidelberg (2004). https://doi.org/10.1007/978-3-540-30555-2_37
6. Zimmermann, W., Schaarschmidt, M.: Automatic checking of component protocols in component-based systems. In: Löwe, W., Südholt, M. (eds.) SC 2006. LNCS, vol. 4089, pp. 1–17. Springer, Heidelberg (2006). https://doi.org/10.1007/11821946_1

COAGENT: Cognitive Computing Continuum for Large-Scale Distributed GenAI Agents

Massimo Mecella[1,2], Maria Fazio[1,3], Flavia Monti[1,2], Dumitru Roman[4], Hui Song[4], Massimo Villari[1,3], and Radu Prodan[5]

[1] Consorzio Interuniversitario Nazionale per l'Informatica, Italy
[2] Sapienza Università di Roma, Italy
[3] Università degli Studi di Messina, Italy
[4] SINTEF Digital, Norway
[5] University of Innsbruck, Austria

Abstract. CoAgent Horizon Europe project, starting on 1 October 2026, 22 partners from Europe and Korea, in the context of HORIZON-CL4-2025-04-DATA-02: Empowering AI/generative AI along the Cognitive Computing Continuum (RIA).

Keywords: Computing Continuum · Generative Artificial Intelligence · Cognitive Agents · Large-scale Distributed Systems and HPC

1 Motivations

Although Generative AI (GenAI) today is powerful in conversation, content creation, and reasoning, the future of GenAI applications lies in agents that act, decide, and collaborate for themselves to solve real-world problems. However, infrastructure capacity is a decisive factor for adopting GenAI agents at scale. Real-world scenarios like traffic management and telecom operation may require thousands of concurrently operating agents interacting with numerous real-world elements. Using GenAI services like ChatGPT to power these agents would generate enormous costs for European companies. On the other hand, self-deploying GenAI models currently rely on scarce, expensive, and energy-consuming resources, either from high-performance datacentres or on-premises GPU servers. To break this resource bottleneck, the EU's AI Continent action plan will not only build AI factories and gigafactories for AI training, but also support leveraging all resources along the cloud-edge continuum for AI inference applications, such as agentic AI applications. At the same time, the attention in GenAI is shifting from a few Large Language Models to many Small Language Models. These challenges lead to three essential research questions: *(1)* How can many agents operate seamlessly on cloud and edge, with diverse and even unconventional resources, at affordable cost and energy? *(2)* How can the many distributed agents scattered across the continuum connect one another for collaborative real-world task-solving with advanced emergent intelligence? and *(3)* How can real-world connected agents ensure trustworthiness and align behaviour with human intents?

2 The Proposal

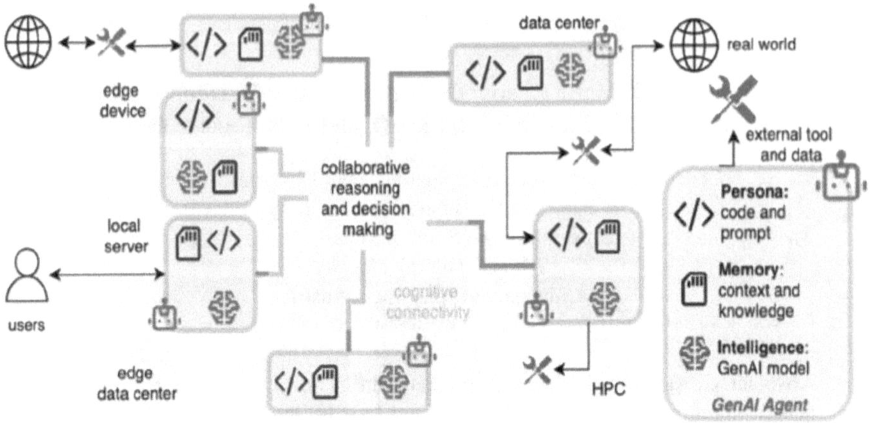

Fig. 1. The CoAgent framework.

CoAgent will implement a novel concept of agent continuum, in two complementary dimensions: *(1)* Continuum-native AI agents encompassing novel architectures, models, and operational paradigms for GenAI agents capable of leveraging the full spectrum of resources across the continuum; and *(2)* Agent-oriented cognitive continuum encompassing advanced agent-driven resource management and allocation for efficient, energy-aware, and trustworthy large-scale deployment.

Specifically, these are the highlights of the project (also schematically shown in Fig. 1):

- GenAI models and agents run seamlessly across the entire computing continuum, from High-Performance Computing (HPC) to edge;
- Hyper distributed agent collaboration and decision making with emergent intelligence; Trustworthy agents, aligned with human values;
- Innovative enablers, powered by agentic GenAI themselves, to manage the continuum, achieving agentic cognitive continuum to empower AI agents;
- Brain-inspired theories for cutting edge AI research;
- Full coverage of supply chain of computing continuum and GenAI, made in Europe;
- EU LLM (i.e., Velvet) and agent framework (i.e., AIWave);
- Four pilots demonstrate agentic GenAI at scale across the continuum, solving real-world problems in transportation, medical devices, drones, and telecom;
- Green GenAI via small models, optimized operation, smart connectivity, and neuromorphic hardware;
- Shift of EU business's GenAI workload from US hyperscalers to edge, EU cloud and EU models.

A Joint Federated Edge Intelligence Framework for Battery Monitoring: The NEUROKIT2E Perspective

Pierluigi Dell'Acqua[1], Francesco La Rosa[1], Lorenzo Carnevale[1], Massimo Villari[1], Fabian Chersi[2], Mattia Antonini[3], Massimo Vecchio[3], and Fabio Antonelli[3]

[1] MIFT Department, University of Messina, Messina, Italy
{pidellacqua,flarosa,lcarnevale,mvillari}@unime.it
[2] Laboratory of Embedded Artificial Intelligence, CEA-LIST, Paris-Saclay, France
fabian.chersi@cea.fr
[3] OpenIoT Research Unit, DI Center, Fondazione Bruno Kessler, Trento, Italy
{m.antonini,mvecchio,fantonelli}@fbk.eu

Abstract. As Electric Vehicles (EVs) demand real-time monitoring under strict privacy and resource constraints, the NEUROKIT2E project proposes a decentralized AI ecosystem. This report details the joint effort between the University of Messina, Fondazione Bruno Kessler, and CEA-LIST in developing an evolving Federated Learning (FL) architecture. We transition from a general-purpose Edge Intelligence model to a specialized, Quantization-aware, and Knowledge-Distilled framework tailored for Lithium-ion (Li-ion) battery State-of-Health (SoH) estimation.

Keywords: Edge Intelligence · Federated Learning · Knowledge Distillation · Battery Management Systems · NEUROKIT2E

1 The NEUROKIT2E Edge Intelligence Ecosystem

1.1 Context and Motivation

Accurate SoH estimation for Li-ion batteries is vital for electric mobility, optimizing battery life, and enabling second-life applications. While deep learning models degradation effectively, its practical automotive application is constrained by microcontrollers (MCUs) limits, strict data privacy regulations, and unacceptable cloud latency. To address these critical gaps, the NEUROKIT2E project develops AIDGE [6], an open-source Edge Intelligence (EI) framework enabling a decentralized, secure ecosystem for advanced battery management.

1.2 Architectural Evolution

NEUROKIT2E's multi-layered EI architecture decouples physical sensing from orchestration. This modularity allows raw telemetry filtering at the vehicle level while offloading complex coordination tasks to edge nodes [1]. To handle hardware heterogeneity, we introduce a TinyMLOps framework [2] that evaluates candidate models across cloud sandboxes and physical devices, using direct hardware metrics (e.g., latency, memory) to guide refinement. This lifecycle is supported by a serverless Quantization-as-a-Service (QaaS) [3] built on OpenFaaS, which automates Quantization-Aware Training to tailor precision for automotive MCUs, and mPickle [4] for seamless model serialization between CPython and MicroPython targets.

Prioritizing data sovereignty and privacy, we integrate a hybrid FL and Knowledge Distillation paradigm [5]. This allows fleets of EVs to act as local learners sharing only distilled knowledge rather than sensitive raw data, eliminating the need for a centralized teacher model. Furthermore, the framework bridges numerical predictions with physical explainability by transforming Electrochemical Impedance Spectroscopy into structured symbolic representations. Here, Large Language Models constrained by an electrochemical Knowledge Graph provide interpretable SoH diagnostics, explicitly identifying degradation phenomena like active material loss or lithium plating. These advancements are operationalized via AIDGE [6], which serves as the comprehensive industrial backbone. Integrating the entire DNN pipeline, from data pre-processing and topology prototyping to performance benchmarking, AIDGE ultimately exports optimal networks to diverse targets (CPU, GPU, FPGA) for seamless industrial automotive deployment.

Acknowledgments. This work is partially supported by the Horizon Europe "Open source deep learning platform dedicated to Embedded hardware and Europe" project (Grant Agreement, project 101112268 - NEUROKIT2E)

References

1. Dell'Acqua, P., Carnevale, L., Villari, M.: Edge Intelligence Architecture for Distributed and Federated Learning Systems, pp. 65–87 (2025). https://doi.org/10.1201/9788743808862-3
2. Antonini, M., Vecchio, M., Antonelli, F.: A TinyMLOps framework for real-world applications. In: Charting the Intelligence Frontiers – Edge AI Systems Nexus, pp. 255–265. River Publishers, New York (2025)
3. De Novi, D., et al.: A serverless quantization-as-a-service model to run compression jobs for edge intelligence. In: 2025 IEEE Symposium on Computers and Communications (ISCC), pp. 1–7 (2025). https://doi.org/10.1109/ISCC65549.2025.11326460
4. Antonini, M., Vecchio, M., Antonelli, F.: mPickle: Pickle for MicroPython. J. Open Res. Softw. **14** (2026). https://doi.org/10.5334/jors.587

5. Dell'Acqua, P., et al.: Knowledge distillation and federated learning for data-driven monitoring of electrical vehicle li-battery. In: 2024 IEEE Symposium on Computers and Communications (ISCC), pp. 1–5 (2024). https://doi.org/10.1109/ISCC61673.2024.10733629
6. Chersi, F., et al.: AIDGE: A framework for deep neural network development, training and deployment on the edge. In: Beyond Horizons–The Rise of the Edge AI Processing Paradigm, pp. 41–54 (2025)

rAIdD: A Federated AI Platform for the Multi-domain Diagnosis of Chronic and Neurological Diseases

Roberto Marino[1], Rossella Laudani[2], and Massimo Villari[1]

[1] Department of Mathematics, Computer Science, Physics and Earth Science, University of Messina, Messina, Italy
{roberto.marino,rossella.laudani}@unime.it
[2] Department of Engineering, University of Messina, Messina, Italy
massimo.villari@unime.it

Abstract. National health systems are increasingly strained by the simultaneous burden of chronic and neurodegenerative conditions, whose clinical complexity demands analytics at a scale that no single institution can sustain alone.

The rAIdD project addresses this challenge by designing a federated, AI-enabled eHealth infrastructure connecting nine Italian institutions across eight regions. This report outlines the architectural evolution of the platform—from an Edge/Cloud orchestration backbone to a privacy-preserving learning ecosystem—covering federated deep learning, foundation-model-based lesion segmentation, and miniaturised biosensing, all applied concurrently across six target pathologies: Parkinson's disease, Alzheimer's disease, Multiple Sclerosis, liver cirrhosis, type 2 diabetes mellitus, and chronic kidney disease.

Keywords: eHealth infrastructure · Distributed Learning · Medical Internet of Things · Chronic disease diagnostics · Support Decision Systems

1 Clinical Need, Project Scope, and Consortium

Six high-burden pathologies—Parkinson's, Alzheimer's, Multiple Sclerosis, liver cirrhosis, type 2 diabetes, and chronic kidney disease—share a common analytical demand: longitudinal, multimodal datasets spanning many centres. Deep learning can exploit such data, but two barriers persist: GDPR prohibits centralising patient records, and hospital computing ranges from GPU clusters to low-power ward devices, resisting uniform deployment [2].

The rAIdD project (*Rete eHealth: AI e strumenti ICT innovativi orientati alla Diagnostica Digitale*), funded by the Italian Ministry of Health (FSC 2014–2020, CUP J43C22000380001), tackles both barriers through a federated national platform. The consortium pairs four ICT institutions—University of Messina (lead), University of

Catania, Fondazione Bruno Kessler (FBK), and University of Siena—with five clinical partners across eight regions: University of Trieste, AO S. Camillo Forlanini, AO Riuniti di Foggia, ASL5 Spezzino, and AOU San Luigi Gonzaga di Orbassano.

2 A Layered Ecosystem for Data-Driven Clinical Intelligence

Layered infrastructure. The platform is structured as a stack of specialised tiers, each containerised with Docker and orchestrated by Kubernetes, enabling transparent workload migration across Edge and Cloud nodes as computational demand varies. At the base, a Medical IoT abstraction layer unifies signals from heterogeneous wearables—commercial fitness trackers, custom Arduino-based demonstrators, and VR peripherals—behind a single REST API, shielding clinical applications from device-level heterogeneity. Near-source pre-processing at the Edge reduces network load and allows near-real-time feedback to operators. The federated private Cloud spans two primary nodes at UniME and UniCT; the UniCT node hosts four NVIDIA H100 SXM5 GPUs (80 GB HBM3, NVLink-connected) and over 60 TB of NVMe storage, provisioned for large-scale model training. MongoDB stores structured EHRs, DICOM imaging, wearable time-series, and ontology-annotated bibliographic data in a single flexible schema. All curated datasets receive DataCite DOIs and will be published in a FAIR-compliant digital archive to ensure reproducibility.

Privacy-preserving learning. Since patient records cannot be centralised under GDPR, the platform adopts Federated Learning [3]: each partner site trains a local model on its own data and submits only model parameters to a coordinator node, which aggregates them into a global update without ever accessing raw records. To further reduce communication overhead and improve convergence across heterogeneous clinical environments, Knowledge Distillation is integrated into the federated pipeline [1]: local models transfer compressed "soft" representations rather than full gradient updates, enabling efficient aggregation even when sites differ greatly in dataset size or hardware capability. Where individual cohorts are small, GAN-based data augmentation is applied locally before training to alleviate the non-IID distribution that typically degrades federated model quality.

Foundation models for neuroimaging. Automated lesion segmentation in Multiple Sclerosis MRI is clinically essential yet labour-intensive and prone to inter-rater variability, especially on the small, spatially diffuse lesions most predictive of long-term disability. UniCT addresses this with a two-stage, Explainable-AI architecture. During training, the Segment Anything Model (SAM) [4]—a vision foundation model pre-trained on over one billion masks—supervises a dense prompt-learner that extracts task-specific embeddings from brain MRI volumes without manual prompts. At inference, SAM is replaced by a lightweight convolutional decoder mapping these embeddings to binary lesion masks, eliminating the foundation model's memory and latency cost and making the pipeline deployable on standard clinical hardware. The broader AI layer (AT13–AT14) further employs 3D convolutional networks with self-attention and dynamic routing (Capsule Networks) to quantify disease progression from multimodal data, with decisions made interpretable via NLP-based explanation. All models are trained in PyTorch and exported to ONNX for REST API deployment. Validated on the MSLesSeg benchmark [5], the pipeline achieves state-of-the-art performance, excelling on the small, irregular lesions classical methods most often miss.

Point-of-care biosensing. Continuous glycaemic monitoring typically relies on implanted electrodes or finger-prick sampling, both limiting long-term compliance. FBK developed a self-contained alternative that samples interstitial fluid through near-painless microneedles, housed in a single 3D-printed PMMA cartridge integrating two complementary transducers. The first is an electrochemical microneedle array functionalised with enzymatic layers via inkjet microdispensing, quantifying both glucose and glycated albumin directly from the extracted fluid. The second is a miniaturised silicon gas sensor measuring exhaled-breath acetone as a non-invasive proxy for ketone production [7], adding a screening dimension without sample collection. A custom Bluetooth readout board streams both signals to a companion smartphone application, closing a fully portable diagnostic loop that needs no laboratory or clinical setting.

Telemedicine: an end-to-end Parkinson's use case. A single scenario shows the layers acting in concert. An early-stage Parkinson's patient, followed by one of the consortium's neurology teams, dons a Meta Quest 3 headset, a BLE-sensorised wristband, and the UniSI BEETLE wearable (ESP32, vibrotactile motors, IMU), then performs Unity3D scenarios reproducing activities of daily living. The Medical IoT layer captures the IMU and kinematic streams; the home Edge node filters and segments them in near-real time, discarding raw traces so that only feature vectors reach the federated Cloud. There the local model scores motor performance against the Unified Parkinson's Disease Rating Scale (UPDRS), sharing parameters—never patient data—with the coordinator at the next federated round. The treating neurologist reviews an interpretable, NLP-generated report on a clinical dashboard and can immediately trigger a vibrotactile rehabilitation routine through the same wearable, closing assessment and therapy in one session. This single workflow exercises every tier of the stack and engages the platform's full stakeholder community: patients and caregivers, neurologists and rehabilitation specialists, hospital IT and data-protection officers, and the ICT partners operating the federated coordinator. By SAL2 (February 2024) progress spanned all six domains: 470 cirrhosis patients at UniME with early mortality-risk models; 45 MCI subjects with PET amyloid imaging and U-Net-based classification at ASL5 Spezzino; 250 MS patients stratified by subtype in Rome with wearable biomarker extraction underway; nephrology and diabetology datasets of ~800 and 5,000+ visits/year respectively feeding AI-driven prognostic score development—collectively confirming the operational viability of a national federated eHealth platform.

Acknowledgments. This work is funded by the Italian Ministry of Health, Piano Sviluppo e Coesione (FSC 2014–2020), Traiettoria 2 "E-Health, diagnostica avanzata, medical devices e mini invasività", Linea di azione 2.1, Convenzione n. 4990 del 05/12/2022 (CUP J43C22000380001).

References

1. Hinton, G., Vinyals, O., Dean, J.: Distilling the knowledge in a neural network. arXiv: 1503.02531 (2015)
2. Zhou, Z., et al.: Edge intelligence: paving the last mile of AI with edge computing. Proc. IEEE **107**(8), 1738–1762 (2019)
3. Nguyen, D.C., et al.: Federated learning for smart healthcare: a survey. ACM Comput. Surv. **55**(3), 1–37 (2022)
4. Ma, J. et al.: Segment anything in medical images. Nat. Commun. **15**, 654 (2024)
5. Rondinella, A., et al.: ICPR 2024 competition on MS lesion segmentation (MSLesSeg). arXiv:2410.07924 (2024)
6. Wang, Y., Wu, Y., Lei, Y.: Microneedle-based glucose monitoring: a review from sampling methods to wearable biosensors. Biomater. Sci. **11**, 5727–5757 (2023)
7. Yin, S., et al.: Wearable microneedle sensor for continuous glucose monitoring. Biosens. Bioelectron. **244**, 115822 (2024)
8. McMahan, H.B., et al.: Communication-efficient learning of deep networks from decentralized data. In: AISTATS 2017, PMLR, vol. 54, pp. 1273–1282 (2017)
9. Rieke, N., et al.: The future of digital health with federated learning. NPJ Digit. Med. **3**(1), 119 (2020)

Contents

Research Track

Research Track

Comparative Analysis of Lightweight Kubernetes Distributions for Edge Computing: CPU Microarchitecture and Energy Efficiency

Diyaz Yakubov(✉), Sergio Moreschini, and David Hästbacka

Tampere Software Engineering Research Centre (TASE), Tampere University, 33014 Tampere, Finland
{diyaz.yakubov,sergio.moreschini,david.hastbacka}@tuni.fi

Abstract. Energy consumption is a critical yet under-studied dimension of container orchestration selection for edge computing, that is on the rise with edge intelligence and edge AI. While prior analyses of Kubernetes distributions (KDs) have measured CPU utilisation, they have not translated those metrics into power and energy estimates. This paper applies a Dynamic Voltage and Frequency Scaling (DVFS) power model to CPU microarchitecture telemetry (frequency scaling, interrupt profiling, and thermal throttling) collected from five KDs, namely k0s, k3s, k8s, KubeEdge, and OpenYurt. We study these on a Raspberry Pi 4 cluster with ARM Cortex-A72 workers. We report three findings. First, power draw is nearly uniform across distributions under the same workload (3.62–3.83 W for control-plane operations), so energy efficiency is determined by the interplay of power draw and operation speed: k8s achieves the lowest energy per operation (10.18 J/pod, 0.249 mJ/op) through lower power draw on the control plane and highest throughput on the data plane, while KubeEdge is 4.0× less efficient on the data plane. Second, interrupt rates differ significantly across KDs (Kruskal–Wallis $p < 0.01$ for all workloads), with KubeEdge producing the highest amplification under control-plane load (3.39×). Third, no statistically detectable link exists between CPU frequency and orchestration performance (all Spearman correlations $p > 0.05$), consistent with performance differences being predominantly software-architectural. Zero thermal throttling was observed, validating the thermal stability of the testbed. Within the limits of the DVFS model and the experimental scope, these findings indicate that energy efficiency in edge orchestration is dominated by software-architectural factors rather than hardware-level differences, informing distribution selection for resource-constrained deployments.

Keywords: Kubernetes · Edge Computing · Energy Efficiency · DVFS · CPU Microarchitecture · ARM Cortex-A72 · Power Modeling · Container Orchestration

D. Balouek et al. (Eds.): ESOCC 2026, LNCS 16834, pp. 3–19, 2027.
https://doi.org/10.1007/978-3-032-37831-6_1

1 Introduction

Edge computing is shifting workloads from centralised cloud data centres to resource-constrained devices at the network periphery [11]. Unlike cloud servers backed by virtually unlimited power budgets, edge nodes frequently operate under strict energy constraints: battery power, solar harvesting, or metered electricity in remote deployments. For a fleet of thousands of edge devices running continuously, even modest per-node power differences translate into substantial operational costs.

Container orchestration platforms, primarily based on Kubernetes, have become the standard for managing workloads at the edge. However, the choice of Kubernetes distribution introduces a software-level overhead that directly affects energy consumption. Lightweight distributions such as k3s and k0s were designed to minimise this overhead, while edge-specific extensions like KubeEdge and OpenYurt add capabilities for disconnected operation at the cost of additional components.

Prior comparative studies, including our own empirical benchmarks of performance, security, resilience, and maintainability [16,17], have measured CPU utilisation as a percentage. However, CPU utilisation alone is an incomplete proxy for energy consumption. Two distributions operating at 10% CPU may consume different power if their frequency governors, interrupt handling patterns, or idle-state behaviours differ. To date, no study has applied CPU microarchitecture-level analysis (frequency scaling, interrupt profiling, and thermal throttling) to compare Kubernetes distributions on edge hardware.

This paper addresses that gap with three analysis pillars applied to the same experimental infrastructure and data as [16,17]:

1. **DVFS energy modelling:** A power model calibrated to the ARM Cortex-A72 estimates per-distribution energy consumption from CPU frequency and activity ratio time series.
2. **Interrupt storm analysis:** Cross-distribution statistical comparison of hardware and software interrupt rates under idle, control-plane, and data-plane workloads.
3. **Thermal stability and frequency–latency correlation:** Verification that no thermal throttling occurred, and that CPU frequency does not predict orchestration performance.

We pose three research questions:

- **RQ1 (Energy Efficiency):** How does energy consumption per orchestration operation differ across five Kubernetes distributions on resource-constrained ARM edge hardware?
- **RQ2 (Interrupt Overhead):** Do Kubernetes distributions produce statistically different interrupt loads under identical workloads, and what is the associated CPU overhead?
- **RQ3 (Hardware–Software Decoupling):** Does CPU frequency or thermal throttling predict Kubernetes distribution performance differences, or are the differences purely software-level?

The contributions of this paper are: (1) the first CPU microarchitecture-level energy comparison of Kubernetes distributions on real edge hardware; (2) statistical evidence that interrupt overhead is distribution-dependent; and (3) evidence that performance differences are predominantly software-architectural rather than hardware-determined.

The remainder of this paper is organised as follows. Section 2 presents background on CPU power modelling and related work. Section 3 describes the methodology. Section 4 presents results across the three analysis pillars. Section 5 discusses the implications. Section 6 addresses threats to validity, and Sect. 7 concludes.

2 Background and Related Work

2.1 CPU Power Modelling for Edge Devices

Dynamic Voltage and Frequency Scaling (DVFS) [13] is the primary mechanism by which modern processors regulate power consumption. The dynamic power of a CMOS circuit is given by [15]:

$$P_{\text{dynamic}} = C_{\text{eff}} \times V^2 \times f \times \alpha \tag{1}$$

where C_{eff} is the effective switched capacitance, V is the supply voltage, f is the clock frequency, and α is the activity ratio [18]. On ARM Cortex-A72 processors [2] such as those in the Raspberry Pi 4's BCM2711 SoC [10], the Linux `cpufreq` subsystem [14] governs frequency scaling between 600 MHz and 1800 MHz, with supply voltage ranging approximately from 0.8 V to 1.0 V.

Total board power includes a static component that persists regardless of CPU activity:

$$P_{\text{total}} = P_{\text{static}} + \sum_{i=0}^{N_{\text{cores}}-1} P_{\text{dynamic},i} \tag{2}$$

The activity ratio α is derived from the aggregate CPU utilisation reported by the Linux kernel via `system.cpu`. Yassin et al. [18] demonstrated that this DVFS formulation achieves less than 4% deviation from physical measurements on an ARM Cortex-M4 edge platform.

Three alternative approaches exist. First, **direct power measurement** using USB power meters provides ground-truth accuracy but requires physical instrumentation not available in our retrospective analysis. Second, **RAPL (Running Average Power Limit) counters** [4] provide hardware-level power readings but are Intel-specific and unavailable on ARM SoCs. Third, **linear regression models** trained on hardware performance counters [12] offer simplicity but require a calibration phase. Our DVFS approach combines physical grounding with the practical advantage of requiring only CPU frequency and utilisation telemetry, both universally available on Linux ARM platforms.

2.2 Energy Studies of Container Orchestration

Koziolek and Eskandani [7] benchmarked MicroK8s, k3s, k0s, and MicroShift on a Raspberry Pi cluster, reporting CPU and memory utilisation but not translating to power or energy units. Our prior work [16,17] extended this comparison to include KubeEdge and OpenYurt but likewise did not address energy consumption.

Amaral et al. [1] introduced Kepler, a Kubernetes-native framework estimating per-container power consumption using RAPL counters and eBPF-based regression models, achieving mean squared error as low as 0.010. However, RAPL is unavailable on ARM platforms. Subedi et al. [12] demonstrated that a lightweight energy- and latency-aware scheduler on an RPi4 cluster reduces energy per request by 32%, confirming that scheduling policy significantly affects energy on this hardware.

The present study fills the cross-distribution gap by applying a DVFS power model directly to CPU microarchitecture telemetry, enabling per-distribution energy estimates in Watts and Joules.

2.3 Kubernetes Distributions Under Test

This study evaluates the same five distributions benchmarked in [16,17]: **k8s** (v1.29), the full-featured upstream Kubernetes; **k3s** (v1.27.4), a CNCF-certified lightweight distribution; **k0s** (v1.28.4), a zero-friction distribution; **KubeEdge** (on k8s v1.29), a CNCF edge/IoT extension; and **OpenYurt** (on k8s v1.29), extending upstream Kubernetes with edge capabilities.[1] All used containerd v1.7.11 as the container runtime.

3 Methodology

3.1 Experimental Setup

The experimental infrastructure is shared with [16,17]. Table 1 summarises the hardware configuration: an Intel NUC serves as the master node, while three Raspberry Pi 4 boards act as ARM-based edge workers. The DVFS-capable frequency range of the RPi4 workers (600–1800 MHz) is central to the energy model developed in Sect. 3.3.

A sidecar NUC ran Netdata [9] v1.42 for monitoring, streaming metrics at per-second granularity to MongoDB 7.0 ($\sim$1.9 billion documents, 140 GB).

3.2 Data Collection and Test Protocol

All nodes used Ubuntu 22.04.2's default `schedutil` cpufreq governor, which adjusts CPU frequency based on scheduler-provided utilisation signals. No governor overrides were applied, ensuring identical DVFS behaviour across distributions.

[1] Project websites: https://kubernetes.io, https://k3s.io, https://k0sproject.io, https://kubeedge.io, https://openyurt.io.

Table 1. Experimental node configuration.

Feature	Master (NUC)	Workers (RPi4 ×3)
CPU	Intel i7-10710U (6C/12T @ 1.10 GHz)	ARM Cortex-A72 (4C @ 1.8 GHz)
RAM	64 GB DDR4	4 GB LPDDR4
Storage	1 TB NVMe	64 GB microSD
OS	Ubuntu 22.04.2	Ubuntu 22.04.2
Freq range	400–4700 MHz	600–1800 MHz
DVFS	Intel SpeedStep	ARM cpufreq

Each distribution was tested with three workload types: **Idle** (baseline, no user workloads), **CP Heavy** (12 concurrent clients creating/deleting 120 pods via k-bench), and **DP Redis Density** (Redis pods with memtier_benchmark v2.0.0). Each test type was repeated 5 times with 30-minute stabilisation periods, yielding 75 runs total. The six metric contexts used in the analysis are listed in Table 2, showing per-core and system-aggregate availability across all five distributions.

Table 2. Data availability matrix.

Metric Context	k0s	k3s	k8s	KubeEdge	OpenYurt	Granularity
`cpufreq.cpufreq`	All	All	All	All	All	Per-core
`cpu.core_throttling`	Master	Master	Master	Master	Master	Per-core
`system.interrupts`	All	All	All	All	All	Aggregate
`system.softirqs`	All	All	All	All	All	Aggregate
`system.softnet_stat`	All	All	All	All	All	Aggregate
`system.cpu`	All	All	All	All	All	Aggregate

Data Gap Note: Worker cpufreq data is missing for all 5 k0s `dp_redis_density` runs due to a Netdata collector state change during a 3-day pause between k0s test phases. All affected tables mark this gap as "N/A."

3.3 DVFS Power Model

We apply the DVFS power model from Eq. (1) and Eq. (2) to decompose Raspberry Pi 4 board power into a fixed static component and a frequency-dependent dynamic component. Reference measurements using USB-C power meters report approximately 2.7 W at idle and 6.4 W under full CPU stress for a bare RPi4 [5].

Voltage–Frequency Relationship

$$V(f) = V_{\min} + \frac{f - f_{\min}}{f_{\max} - f_{\min}} \times (V_{\max} - V_{\min}) \tag{3}$$

where $V_{\min} = 0.8\,\text{V}$, $V_{\max} = 1.0\,\text{V}$, $f_{\min} = 600\,\text{MHz}$, $f_{\max} = 1800\,\text{MHz}$.

Power Decomposition: $P_{\text{static}} = 2.7\,\text{W}$ (bare-board idle [5]). At full load, the CPU dynamic budget is $P_{\text{dynamic}} = 6.4 - 2.7 = 3.7\,\text{W}$ for 4 cores, yielding:

$$C_{\text{eff}} = \frac{3.7}{1.0^2 \times 1.8 \times 10^9 \times 4} \approx 5.14 \times 10^{-10}\,\text{F} \tag{4}$$

Per-Core Dynamic Power

$$P_{\text{dynamic},i}(t) = C_{\text{eff}} \times V(f(t))^2 \times f(t) \times \alpha(t) \tag{5}$$

where $\alpha(t) = 1 - \text{idle\%}/(N_{\text{cores}} \times 100)$.

Energy Estimation: Total energy is computed by trapezoidal integration of $P_{\text{total}}(t)$ over the test duration, averaged across 3 worker nodes and 5 experimental runs.

Efficiency Metrics: $E_{\text{pod}} = E_{\text{total}}/N_{\text{pods}}$ (J/pod) and $E_{\text{op}} = (P_{\text{mean}}/\text{throughput}) \times 10^3$ (mJ/op).

Table 3. Idle power consumption (RPi4 workers, mean ± std).

Distribution	Mean Power (W)	Std (W)	Mean Freq (MHz)
k0s	3.430	0.009	701
k3s	3.394	0.014	674
k8s	3.397	0.010	677
KubeEdge	3.444	0.010	709
OpenYurt	3.430	0.007	698

3.4 Interrupt Overhead Estimation

Hardware interrupts (IRQs) and software interrupts (softirqs) are the two interrupt processing layers in the Linux kernel [8]. Hardware interrupts are raised by peripheral devices (timers, network controllers, block devices) and handled in a minimal top-half handler. Softirqs are deferred bottom-half handlers for categories including `NET_RX/TX` (network packet processing), `SCHED` (scheduler load balancing), `BLOCK` (block device completions), `TIMER` (kernel timers), and `RCU` (read-copy-update synchronisation). Both types impose CPU overhead through context save/restore, cache line eviction, and TLB pollution.

We estimate the per-interrupt handling cost at ~3 µs for the ARM Cortex-A72 [3]. The aggregate CPU overhead is:

$$\text{CPU overhead (\%)} = \frac{\text{irqs/s} \times 3 \times 10^{-6}}{N_{\text{cores}}} \times 100 \tag{6}$$

3.5 Statistical Methods

Kruskal–Wallis H-Test: Non-parametric test for differences across $k = 5$ groups with $n = 5$ observations per group [6]. **Spearman rank correlation (ρ):** For monotonic relationships between CPU frequency and performance metrics [6]. Significance levels: * $p < 0.05$, ** $p < 0.01$, *** $p < 0.001$.

4 Results

4.1 Pillar 1: DVFS Energy Modelling (RQ1)

Idle Power Consumption. Table 3 shows that idle power varies by only 1.5% across distributions (3.394–3.444 W). k3s and k8s have nearly identical idle power (within 3 mW), while KubeEdge draws the highest (3.444 W). The orchestration-attributable overhead above bare-board idle ranges from 0.69 W (k3s) to 0.74 W (KubeEdge). Figure 1 confirms that idle frequencies cluster in the 674–709 MHz range, well below the 1800 MHz maximum, which explains why the dynamic power component is modest.

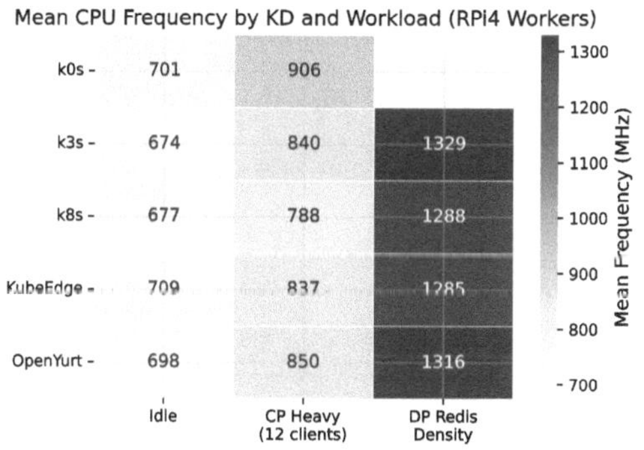

Fig. 1. CPU frequency heatmap across distributions and test types.

Control-Plane Energy. As shown in Table 4, k8s achieves the lowest energy per pod lifecycle (10.18 J), despite being the "heaviest" distribution. KubeEdge consumes 20.58 J per pod, 102% more than k8s, driven primarily by its 2.0× longer duration (669 s vs. 338 s). The power overhead from idle to CP heavy

Table 4. CP Heavy (12 clients) power and energy estimates.

Dist.	Power (W)	Overhead (W)	Energy (J)	J/Pod	Duration (s)
k0s	3.826	0.396	1,263	10.52 ± 1.28	330
k3s	3.715	0.321	1,233	10.28 ± 1.29	332
k8s	3.618	0.221	1,222	10.18 ± 1.08	338
KubeEdge	3.694	0.250	2,469	20.58 ± 1.34	669
OpenYurt	3.746	0.316	1,398	11.65 ± 1.24	374

is modest across all distributions (0.22–0.40 W), as visualised in Fig. 2. For the KubeEdge outlier, its 2.0× longer duration clearly dominates energy; among the remaining four distributions, where durations are within 13% of each other, the smaller power draw differences also contribute, a point we return to in Sect. 5.

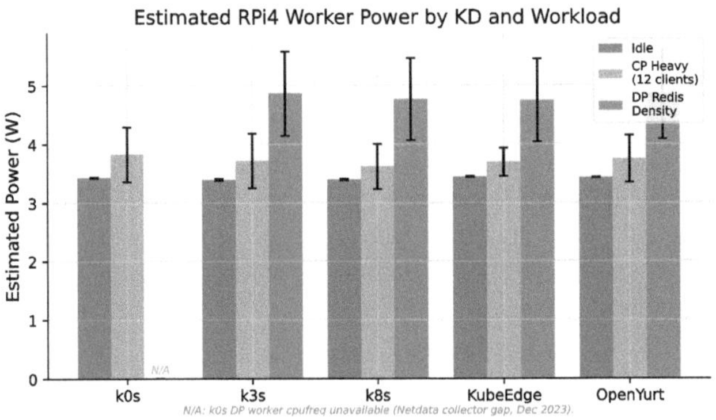

Fig. 2. Estimated power per distribution and workload type.

Data-Plane Energy. *Note:* k0s DP data unavailable due to a Netdata collector gap (Sect. 3).

Table 5 shows that k8s is the most energy-efficient at 0.249 mJ per operation, while KubeEdge requires 0.992 mJ, a 4.0× penalty. Under data-plane load, power ranges from 4.75 to 4.86 W across distributions, an even narrower spread than under CP load. The efficiency difference is therefore entirely determined by throughput: KubeEdge achieves only 4,750 ops/s versus 19,000 for k8s [16]. Figure 3 summarises both CP and DP efficiency metrics, highlighting KubeEdge as the outlier in both dimensions.

Table 5. DP Redis density power and energy per operation.

Dist.	Power (W)	Std (W)	mJ/op	Throughput (ops/s)
k3s	4.864	0.721	0.282 ± 0.042	17,200
k8s	4.767	0.704	0.249 ± 0.037	19,000
KubeEdge	4.748	0.708	0.992 ± 0.149	4,750
OpenYurt	4.850	0.766	0.267 ± 0.042	18,200

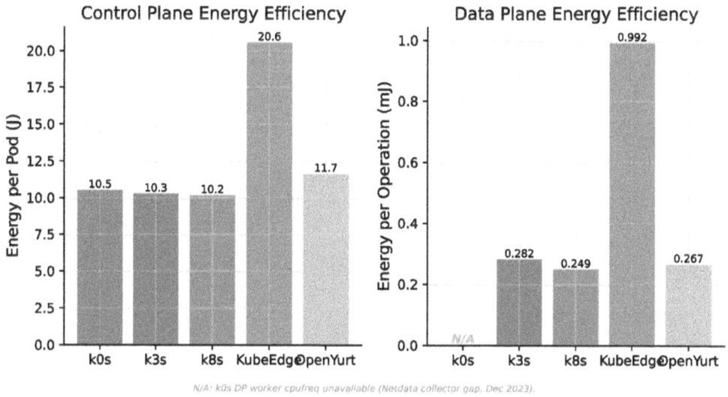

Fig. 3. Energy efficiency: J/pod (CP, left) and mJ/op (DP, right).

4.2 Pillar 2: Interrupt Storm Analysis (RQ2)

Table 6. Hardware interrupt rates on workers (irqs/s, mean ± std over 5 runs).

Dist.	Idle	CP Heavy	DP Redis
k0s	$1{,}176 \pm 8$	$3{,}329 \pm 18$	$2{,}142 \pm 127$
k3s	993 ± 16	$3{,}152 \pm 38$	$2{,}147 \pm 138$
k8s	937 ± 4	$2{,}663 \pm 25$	$1{,}964 \pm 24$
KubeEdge	$1{,}240 \pm 7$	$4{,}200 \pm 278$	$2{,}275 \pm 53$
OpenYurt	$1{,}310 \pm 5$	$3{,}812 \pm 74$	$2{,}252 \pm 4$

Cross-Distribution Interrupt Rates. Table 6 reports the mean hardware interrupt rates across all distributions and workloads. The Kruskal–Wallis test confirms significant differences for all three workload types: Idle ($H = 23.08$, $p = 1.22 \times 10^{-4}$, ***), CP Heavy ($H = 22.46$, $p = 1.63 \times 10^{-4}$, ***), and DP Redis ($H = 15.32$, $p = 4.08 \times 10^{-3}$, **). As Fig. 4 illustrates, k8s consistently generates the lowest interrupt rate across all workloads, while KubeEdge and OpenYurt cluster at the top.

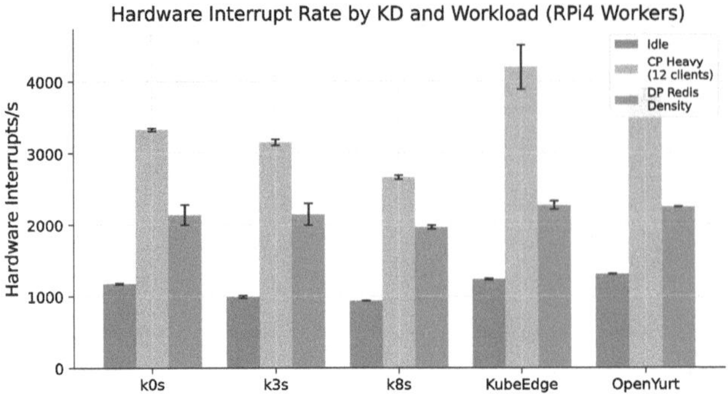

Fig. 4. Hardware interrupt rates by workload type.

Table 7. Interrupt amplification factors (loaded / idle rate).

Dist.	CP Heavy	DP Redis
k0s	2.83×	1.82×
k3s	3.17×	2.16×
k8s	2.84×	2.10×
KubeEdge	3.39×	1.83×
OpenYurt	2.91×	1.72×

Load Amplification. Table 7 quantifies the amplification factors. KubeEdge exhibits the highest control-plane amplification (3.39×) and the highest absolute rate (4,200 irqs/s under CP Heavy, Table 6), correlating with its worst test duration and highest energy per pod (Table 4). k3s shows the second-highest amplification (3.17×) despite its lightweight design, suggesting that control-plane interrupt scaling is not simply a function of distribution complexity. One hypothesis is that k3s's single-binary architecture consolidates all control-plane components (API server, scheduler, controller manager) into one process, concentrating interrupt-generating activity into fewer scheduling contexts and amplifying per-context interrupt rates under concurrent load. By contrast, k8s distributes these across separate processes, spreading interrupt generation more evenly. Confirming this would require process-level interrupt attribution (e.g., via eBPF tracing), which is beyond the scope of this retrospective analysis and is left as future work.

Softirq Category Breakdown. Under DP Redis, `NET_RX` dominates across all distributions (96–97%), consistent with memtier's network-intensive workload pattern. Under CP Heavy, the composition is more balanced (Table 8).

KubeEdge shows the highest SCHED (31.2%) and BLOCK (11.9%) proportions, suggesting its EdgeHub/EdgeController components generate additional scheduling and I/O overhead. The elevated BLOCK softirqs indicate more fre-

Table 8. Softirq composition under CP Heavy (% of total).

Category	k0s	k3s	k8s	KubeEdge	OpenYurt
RCU	39.4	44.1	43.4	36.5	42.4
SCHED	21.1	22.0	25.3	31.2	25.0
NET_RX	19.2	14.5	9.5	7.5	12.3
TIMER	9.5	10.5	11.4	11.5	11.0
BLOCK	5.3	7.1	8.2	11.9	7.7
NET_TX	5.0	1.3	1.7	1.2	1.1

quent block device completions, likely from the MQTT-based message persistence layer.

CPU Overhead from Interrupts. At observed rates and 3 µs per interrupt, direct CPU overhead is 0.07–0.10% (idle), 0.20–0.32% (CP Heavy), and 0.15–0.17% (DP Redis). While the direct overhead is small, the significance of differing interrupt profiles extends beyond raw CPU time. Each interrupt forces a context switch that evicts L1/L2 cache lines, pollutes the TLB, and disrupts branch predictor state. On the Cortex-A72's 48 KB L1I + 32 KB L1D caches [2], even modest cache pollution from 4,200 irqs/s (KubeEdge under CP) can measurably degrade instruction throughput for latency-sensitive API server paths. Furthermore, the Kruskal–Wallis significance ($p < 0.001$) establishes that interrupt load is a genuine *distribution-dependent* system characteristic, not random variation; it can therefore serve as a diagnostic signal for architectural differences between orchestration implementations.

No network softnet drops or flow limit events were recorded across any distribution (`system.softnet_stat`), confirming that interrupt rate differences reflect genuine orchestration overhead rather than packet-loss-induced retransmission.

4.3 Pillar 3: Thermal Stability and Frequency–Latency Correlation (RQ3)

Table 9. Thermal stability summary.

Dist.	Master Throttle	Mean Freq (MHz)	Min Freq (MHz)	Runs
k0s	0	801	663	10
k3s	0	947	640	15
k8s	0	917	651	15
KubeEdge	0	937	639	15
OpenYurt	0	955	669	15

Thermal Stability. As Table 9 shows, zero CPU throttling events were recorded on the master node across all distributions and workloads (70 runs analysed). Worker frequencies ranged from 639 to 955 MHz under DVFS governor control, with no anomalous drops. This validates both the thermal stability of the testbed and the reliability of the performance benchmarks in [16,17].

Frequency–Latency Correlation. Table 10 reports all four Spearman correlation tests; none reaches significance ($p > 0.05$). Figure 5 visualises the frequency–latency relationship, showing no discernible trend. At this sample size ($n = 4$–5), no statistically detectable relationship exists between CPU frequency and orchestration performance. While the limited sample precludes definitive claims, these results, combined with the power uniformity observed in Tables 4 and 5, suggest that the performance differences reported in [16] are predominantly software-architectural rather than driven by hardware-level frequency scaling.

5 Discussion

5.1 Key Findings

RQ1 (Energy Efficiency): k8s is the most energy-efficient distribution per operation (10.18 J/pod, Table 4; 0.249 mJ/op, Table 5). KubeEdge is 102% worse on CP and 4.0× on DP. The dominant energy factor differs by workload: on the data plane, throughput variation (4×) dwarfs the narrow power spread (2.4%), making speed decisive; on the control plane, where durations are more comparable, power draw differences also contribute (Sect. 5.2).

RQ2 (Interrupt Overhead): Interrupt rates differ significantly across distributions ($p < 0.01$ for all workloads, Table 6). KubeEdge generates both the highest absolute rate under CP load (4,200 irqs/s) and the highest amplification (3.39×, Table 7). Direct CPU overhead is negligible (<0.32%); however, the statistically significant differences across distributions establish interrupt profiles as a diagnostic signal for software-architectural divergence rather than a direct cause of the performance gaps.

RQ3 (Hardware–Software Decoupling): No statistically detectable relationship exists between CPU frequency and performance ($p > 0.05$ for all correlations, Table 10), though the small sample size ($n = 4$–5) limits statistical power. Zero thermal throttling was observed (Table 9). Combined with the power uniformity finding, these results are consistent with performance differences being predominantly software-architectural rather than hardware-frequency-driven, within the limits of the DVFS model and experimental scope (Sect. 6).

5.2 Power Uniformity and the Speed–Energy Link

Power draw is *nearly uniform* across distributions under the same workload type: 3.62–3.83 W for CP Heavy, 4.75–4.86 W for DP Redis. Since $E = P \times t$, the dominant energy factor depends on which of the two terms, P or t, varies more for a given workload. On the **data plane**, power varies by only 2.4% (4.75–4.86 W) while throughput varies 4×, so *speed entirely determines DP energy efficiency.* On the **control plane**, the top four distributions complete within 13% of each other (330–374 s), but power varies by 5.5% (3.618–3.826 W). Here, both factors contribute: k8s achieves the lowest J/pod (10.18) not because it is fastest (k3s completes in 332 s vs. 338 s for k8s), but because its lower power draw (3.618 W vs. 3.715 W) more than compensates for the 6 s longer duration. KubeEdge remains the clear outlier in both regimes, with 2.0× the CP duration and 4.0× the DP energy penalty.

Table 10. Spearman rank correlations between CPU frequency and performance.

Comparison	ρ	p-value	n	Significant?
CP freq vs pod-startup latency	+0.10	0.873	5	No
DP freq vs DP latency	−0.20	0.800	4	No
DP freq vs throughput	+0.20	0.800	4	No
CP freq CV vs pod-startup latency	−0.70	0.188	5	No

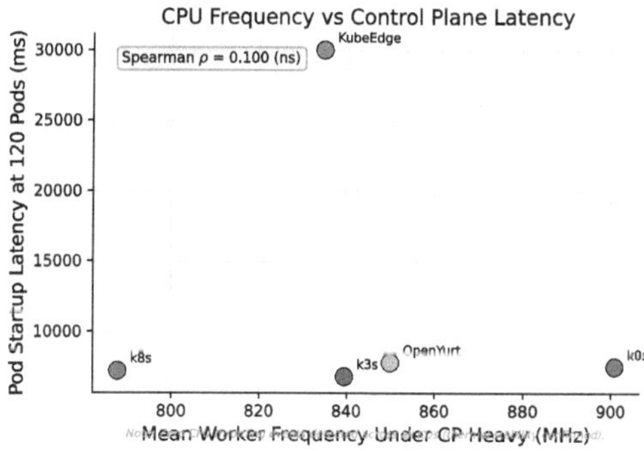

Fig. 5. CPU frequency vs. pod-startup latency ($\rho = +0.10$, $p = 0.873$, not significant).

k8s thus achieves the lowest energy per operation despite being the "heaviest" distribution with the highest idle CPU (5.2% [16]). This finding is corroborated by Subedi et al. [12], who showed on identical RPi4 hardware that a latency-optimising scheduler simultaneously reduced energy per request by 32%, precisely because faster completion shortens the integration window in $E = \int P\,dt$.

Two practical implications follow: for **throughput-dominated workloads** (data plane), the fastest distribution is the most energy-efficient; for **latency-comparable workloads** (control plane), minor power draw differences become the deciding factor. In both cases, distribution choice, a purely software-level decision, determines energy efficiency.

5.3 KubeEdge's Energy Tax

KubeEdge's 4.0× DP energy penalty is software-driven. Under DP Redis, KubeEdge draws 4.75 W (the lowest power) but achieves only 4,750 ops/s versus 19,000 for k8s. Its softirq composition shows elevated SCHED activity (31.2% vs. 21–25%) and BLOCK I/O (11.9% vs. 5–8%), suggesting EdgeHub/EdgeController generate additional scheduling and disk persistence overhead.

5.4 Idle Power at Fleet Scale

The idle power variation is 1.5% (3.394–3.444 W). For 1,000 devices operating 24/7: k3s consumes 29,731 kWh/year versus KubeEdge at 30,169 kWh/year, a 438 kWh annual delta from distribution choice alone. More significantly, KubeEdge's CP energy (2,469 J per test run) is 2.0× that of k8s (1,222 J), compounding for deployments with frequent pod churn.

6 Threats to Validity

Internal Validity. The DVFS model uses a linear V-f approximation and single C_{eff} across workloads. Yassin et al. [18] showed C_{eff} varies by ∼10% between compute- and memory-dominated workloads; their validation was performed on an ARM Cortex-M4 microcontroller, and accuracy on the Cortex-A72's out-of-order pipeline may differ. The activity ratio is a system-level aggregate. Absolute power values should be interpreted cautiously; cross-distribution ratios are more reliable. Our bare-board baseline of 2.7 W [5] is consistent with Subedi et al. [12], who measured 2.8857 W bare idle on RPi4; the 0.69–0.74 W we observe above bare idle is attributable to Kubernetes components.

Data Collection Limitations. Worker cpufreq data is missing for k0s DP tests due to a Netdata collector state change. System-level aggregates remained unaffected.

External Validity. Single hardware platform (RPi4 workers, NUC master). Tested versions (k8s v1.29, k3s v1.27.4, k0s v1.28.4) represent stable releases from the period of the experiment; the energy and interrupt patterns reflect the software architectures of those versions. Single-cluster topology (1 master + 3 workers). The Cortex-A72 is representative of the class of low-power ARM cores used in current edge devices; the cross-distribution ratios reported here are expected to transfer more reliably than the absolute values to newer ARM SoCs (e.g., A76, A78) or x86-based edge platforms, where the same software-architectural differences would manifest against a different power baseline.

Statistical Validity. $n = 5$ per configuration limits power for Spearman correlations (4–5 data points). Non-significant results indicate "no evidence" rather than "proven independence." Kruskal–Wallis results are robust (all $p < 0.01$).

7 Conclusion and Future Work

This paper presents the first CPU microarchitecture-level energy comparison of Kubernetes distributions on edge hardware.[2] By applying a DVFS power model to frequency scaling, interrupt profiling, and thermal throttling data from five distributions on a Raspberry Pi 4 cluster, we establish three findings:

1. **Power draw is nearly uniform across distributions** under the same workload, so **energy efficiency is governed by the interplay of power draw and operation speed**: k8s achieves the lowest energy per operation (10.18 J/pod, 0.249 mJ/op) through lower power draw on the control plane and highest throughput on the data plane.
2. **KubeEdge pays a 4.0× data-plane energy penalty**, driven by low throughput (4,750 ops/s) rather than high power draw.
3. **No statistically detectable link between CPU frequency and orchestration performance** ($p > 0.05$), consistent with distribution differences being predominantly software-architectural rather than hardware-frequency-driven.

Zero thermal throttling was observed across all 70 analysed runs (75 total minus 5 k0s DP runs lacking cpufreq data), validating testbed stability. Across both workload types, **k8s emerges as the most energy-efficient distribution**, an outcome that runs counter to the common assumption that lightweight distributions are inherently more efficient. Its maturity translates into lower power draw and higher throughput, outweighing its larger component footprint. KubeEdge, by contrast, pays the steepest energy tax in both regimes. Energy efficiency in edge orchestration is thus dominated by software-architectural factors rather than hardware-level differences, and distribution maturity is a relevant criterion for resource-constrained deployments.

Future work includes direct power measurement using USB power meters, extension to other ARM SoCs and RISC-V platforms, dynamic workload profiling during scaling events, and integration of per-distribution energy profiles into workload placement decisions.

Acknowledgement. This work is supported by Business Finland in projects Industry X and DAZE.

[2] Analysis pipeline and data: https://github.com/DiyazY/kd-edge-internals. Experimental infrastructure: https://github.com/DiyazY/iot-edge.

References

1. Amaral, M., et al.: Kepler: a framework to calculate the energy consumption of containerized applications. In: 2023 IEEE 16th International Conference on Cloud Computing (CLOUD), pp. 69–71 (2023). https://doi.org/10.1109/CLOUD60044.2023.00017
2. ARM Ltd: ARM Cortex-A72 Technical Reference Manual (2015). https://developer.arm.com/documentation/100095/latest/, revision r0p3
3. ARM Ltd: ARM Generic Interrupt Controller Architecture Specification (GICv3/GICv4) (2017). https://developer.arm.com/documentation/ihi0069/latest/
4. David, H., Gorbatov, E., Hanebutte, U.R., Khanna, R., Le, C.: RAPL: memory power estimation and capping. In: Proc. ACM/IEEE Int. Symp. on Low Power Electronics and Design (ISLPED '10), pp. 189–194. ACM (2010). https://doi.org/10.1145/1840845.1840883
5. Geerling, J.: Raspberry Pi dramble: power consumption benchmarks (2024). https://www.pidramble.com/wiki/benchmarks/power-consumption
6. Hollander, M., Chicken, E., Wolfe, D.A.: Nonparametric statistical methods. In: Wiley Series in Probability And Statistics, John Wiley & Sons, Inc., Hoboken, New Jersey, third edition. edn. (2014)
7. Koziolek, H., Eskandani, N.: Lightweight Kubernetes distributions: a performance comparison of MicroK8s, k3s, k0s, and MicroShift. In: Proceedings of the ACM/SPEC International Conference on Performance Engineering (ICPE '23), pp. 17–29. ACM, New York (2023)
8. Love, R.: Linux Kernel Development, 3rd edn. Addison-Wesley (2010)
9. Netdata Inc.: Netdata: real-time performance and health monitoring (2024). https://www.netdata.cloud/
10. Raspberry Pi Ltd: Raspberry Pi 4 Model B Datasheet (2019). https://datasheets.raspberrypi.com/rpi4/raspberry-pi-4-datasheet.pdf
11. Shi, W., Cao, J., Zhang, Q., Li, Y., Xu, L.: Edge computing: vision and challenges. IEEE Internet Things J. **3**(5), 637–646 (2016). https://doi.org/10.1109/JIOT.2016.2579198
12. Subedi, S., Kumar, S., Jawad, N., Kor, A.L.: Energy-aware latency optimization for scheduling serverless workload in edge computing environment. In: Proceedings of the 18th IEEE/ACM International Conference on Utility and Cloud Computing (UCC '25), pp. 1–10. Nantes, France (2025). https://doi.org/10.1145/3773274.3774276
13. Le Sueur, E., Heiser, G.: Dynamic voltage and frequency scaling: the laws of diminishing returns. 2010 HotPower (2010)
14. The Linux Kernel Documentation: CPU performance scaling (CPUFREQ) (2024). https://docs.kernel.org/admin-guide/pm/cpufreq.html
15. Weste, N.H.E., Harris, D.M.: CMOS VLSI Design: A Circuits and Systems Perspective. Addison-Wesley, 4th edn. (2010)
16. Yakubov, D., Hästbacka, D.: Comparative analysis of lightweight Kubernetes distributions for edge computing: performance and resource efficiency. In: Pahl, C., Janes, A., Cerny, T., Lenarduzzi, V., Esposito, M. (eds) Service-Oriented and Cloud Computing (ESOCC 2025), LNCS, vol. 15547, pp. 81–95. Springer, Cham (2025). https://doi.org/10.1007/978-3-031-84617-5_7

17. Yakubov, D., Hästbacka, D.: Comparative analysis of lightweight Kubernetes distributions for edge computing: security, resilience and maintainability. In: Pahl, C., Janes, A., Cerny, T., Lenarduzzi, V., Esposito, M. (eds) Service-Oriented and Cloud Computing (ESOCC 2025), LNCS, vol. 15547, pp. 96–104. Springer, Cham (2025). https://doi.org/10.1007/978-3-031-84617-5_8
18. Yassin, Y.H., Jahre, M., Kjeldsberg, P.G., Aunet, S., Catthoor, F.: Fast and accurate edge computing energy modeling and DVFS implementation in GEM5 using system call emulation mode. J. Sign. Proces. Syst. **93**, 33–48 (2021). https://doi.org/10.1007/s11265-020-01544-z

Self-adaptive Microservice Systems Using Dynamic Software Product Lines and Deep Reinforcement Learning

Ezdehar Jawabreh[1,2](✉) and Adel Taweel[1]

[1] Department of Computer Science, Birzeit University, Birzeit, Palestine
{eajawabreh,ataweel}@birzeit.edu, ezdehar@ppu.edu
[2] Palestine Polytechnic University, Hebron, Palestine

Abstract. Microservice-based systems (MSS) operate in dynamic environments, where contextual changes can degrade Quality of Service (QoS) and affect user experience (UX). While self-adaptive approaches can mitigate these challenges, existing solutions often focus on infrastructure level mechanisms, such as autoscaling, which provide limited support for reasoning over application-level configuration alternatives and their QoS–UX trade-offs. This paper presents an application-level self-adaptation approach that combines Dynamic Software Product Lines (DSPL) with Deep Reinforcement Learning (DRL). DSPL defines the valid configuration space of the MSS, while a Double Deep Q-Network (DDQN) agent learns workload-aware reconfiguration decisions using a performance prediction model (PPM) as a surrogate environment. The proposed approach is evaluated on BookLib, a real microservice-based case study, through trace-driven workload emulation and compared against a genetic algorithm (GA) baseline and an oracle upper bound. Results show that the approach achieves near-oracle decision quality and better decision quality than a budgeted GA baseline on the same evaluation states. Under trace-driven emulation with workload stress and recovery periods, the DDQN agent protects end-to-end latency during stress while maintaining competitive UX under relaxed workload. The results also show that DDQN enables substantially faster runtime decision-making than GA under the same per-trigger budget, supporting timely adaptation in dynamic MSS environments.

Keywords: Self-Adaptive Systems · Microservice-based Systems · Dynamic Software Product Lines · DDQN · Quality of Service · UX

1 Introduction

Microservice-based systems (MSS) have emerged as a prominent architectural style for developing modern software applications. Rather than structuring an application as a monolith, this style decomposes functionality into small, loosely coupled, independently deployable services. This modular organization improves

Published by Springer Nature Switzerland AG 2027
D. Balouek et al. (Eds.): ESOCC 2026, LNCS 16834, pp. 20–35, 2027.
https://doi.org/10.1007/978-3-032-37831-6_2

maintainability, supports rapid evolution, and enables flexible deployment and scaling in distributed environments. Consequently, MSS are increasingly adopted in diverse domains, including web and mobile applications, cyber-physical systems, and Internet of Things (IoT) systems. Yet MSS typically operate in highly dynamic environments: sudden shifts in workload, usage patterns, and resource availability are common and cannot be fully anticipated due to design-time uncertainty. As a result, maintaining Quality of Service (QoS) across fluctuating operating conditions remains challenging.

A second challenge concerns application-level trade-offs that directly affect user experience (UX) delivered through application functionality [28]. To illustrate this, consider our case-study system BookLib [13], a microservice-based website where users browse and purchase books. In this system, UX-enhancing services refer to optional or richer microservices/variants, such as personalized recommendations, detailed reviews, or richer content presentation, which improve the user experience but are not always critical for the core transaction. Under high workload e.g., flash-sale-like conditions, keeping all these services active may increase processing and communication overhead, leading to higher end-to-end latency and possible Service Level Objectives (SLO) violations. We therefore focus on response time as the operational QoS metric, since it reflects the user-perceived delay of a request in latency-sensitive MSS. The goal is thus not only to reduce latency, but also to preserve UX-enhancing functionality when workload conditions allow it.

Self-Adaptive Systems (SAS) have emerged as a promising solution to these challenges. Equipping MSS with self-adaptation capabilities enables them to dynamically adjust their behavior under varying workloads and operating conditions. However, most existing MSS self-adaptation approaches still rely primarily on infrastructure-level mechanisms, such as horizontal or vertical auto-scaling and microservice placement, typically driven by rule-based engines [12,14,20,27]. Although these mechanisms are effective for resource management, they have two fundamental limitations. First, they are resource-bounded: when resources are saturated or quotas are reached, scaling actions become ineffective or fail, yet performance violations may persist [1,23]. Second, autoscaling primarily changes resource allocation, not the application-level functionality; it does not directly decide which UX-enhancing microservices should be enabled or disabled to keep QoS within bounds. As a result, infrastructure-centric adaptation may be insufficient to maintain acceptable QoS under sustained stress, and it does not provide a principled mechanism for negotiating the QoS-UX trade-off at runtime.

To address these challenges, we adopt an application-level self-adaptation strategy that builds on previous work on Dynamic Software Product Line (DSPL)-based adaptability in MSS [11]. In this approach, an MSS is modeled as a configurable set of microservices, explicitly capturing variability across both functional and non-functional features. To select suitable configurations at runtime, we integrate the DSPL framework with a Deep Reinforcement Learning (DRL) agent [26], specifically a Double Deep Q-Network (DDQN). The DDQN agent is designed to balance QoS objectives and user experience under dynamic workload conditions. In this paper, QoS is operationalized using end-to-end response time (RT), i.e., latency, as the primary QoS metric. By combining structured variability modeling with data-driven decision-making, the proposed approach supports runtime selection of configurations that better balance the RT–UX trade-off.

This paper presents the proposed DSPL–DRL approach and evaluates it on a real microservice-based case study (BookLib) under trace-driven workloads. The results show that the approach makes configuration decisions that closely match the oracle and achieves better decision quality than a budgeted GA baseline on the same evaluation states. Under trace-driven emulation with workload stress and recovery periods, the DDQN agent protects end-to-end latency during stress while maintaining competitive UX under relaxed workload. The results also show that DDQN enables substantially faster runtime decision-making than GA under the same per-trigger budget, supporting timely adaptation in dynamic MSS environments.

2 Related Work

We review prior work relevant to our study in two main research streams: (i) self-adaptation in microservice systems (MSS), and (ii) DSPL-based self-adaptation. Table 1 compares these works in terms of adaptation scope, supported actions, use of explicit variability models, and decision-making mechanisms.

MSS Self-Adaptation. Research on MSS self-adaptation covers a broad range of scopes and techniques. Some studies extend orchestration frameworks with explicit adaptation actions and architectural support. For instance, Zhang et al. [29] extend Kubernetes with rule-based actions such as adding, deleting, or upgrading services, while Liu et al. [17] propose a multi-layer reference architecture that separates infrastructure-level scaling from higher-level application adaptation. However, both mainly rely on predefined rules or architectural guidance, without systematically constraining application-level decisions through an explicit variability model. Other works move toward service selection based on user needs, as in Santi'c/De Sanctis et al. [5,6], but the focus remains on service composition rather than runtime reconfiguration of a predefined configuration space. He et al. [10] support application-level refactoring actions, such as switching, splitting, and merging microservices, and combine heuristic reasoning with GA-based search under SLA constraints, which may introduce search overhead at runtime. In parallel, another line of work emphasizes infrastructure elasticity, including improved autoscaling control in Kubernetes [1], learning-based threshold policies for scaling [22], and runtime microservice evolution to cope with workload shifts [21]. Overall, MSS self-adaptation research either focuses on infrastructure-level elasticity or considers application-level changes without using an explicit DSPL/feature model to constrain valid runtime reconfigurations.

DSPL-Based Self-Adaptation. DSPL-based approaches explicitly use feature and variability models to support safe runtime adaptation. Alférez et al. [2] employ DSPL models to guide service composition reconfiguration under SLA triggers. Mousa et al. [19] combine DSPL workflow variability with multi-objective optimization and QoS prediction. Metzger et al. [18] integrate DSPL with reinforcement learning and feature-model-guided exploration to address large discrete configuration spaces. In contrast, our approach provides a fully implemented application-level DSPL adaptation for MSS, where the agent selects valid microservice configurations and variants under observed workload, guided by a workload-aware RT–UX trade-off, and is evaluated against a budgeted GA baseline.

Table 1. Comparison of related work

Work	Scope	Action	Objective(s)	FM	Decision-making
Zhang et al. [29]; Liu et al. [17]	App./orch. level	Rule-based service actions; architectural guidance	QoS,RT/SLA	No	Rules/architecture
Santić / De Sanctis et al. [5,6]	Composition	Service selection/composition	User requirements + partial QoS	No	Goal/model driven
He et al. [10]	App. level	Switch/split/merge services	QoS with SLA constraints	No	Heuristic + GA
Ahmad et al. [1]	Infra. level	Autoscaling/resource management	QoS + efficiency	No	Controller/heuristic
Rossi et al. [22]	Infra. level	Threshold-based scaling	QoS + resource metrics	No	RL-based policy
R.-Filho et al. [21]	Service impl.	Runtime microservice evolution	QoS under workload shifts	No	Learning driven
Alférez et al. [2]	DSPL composition	DSPL-guided reconfiguration	SLA/QoS	Yes	Rule/model driven
Mousa et al. [19]	DSPL workflow	Context-aware reconfiguration	QoS + cost	Yes	NSGA-II
Metzger et al. [18]	DSPL cloud configs	Runtime configuration selection	QoS(RT/energy)	Yes	Online RL
Our Work	**App.-level DSPL**	**Configuration/variant switching**	**Workload-aware RT–UX trade-off**	**Yes**	**DDQN + GA baseline**

3 The Proposed Approach: Overview

The proposed approach combines DSPL and DRL to enable intelligent self-adaptation in MSS. DSPL defines the valid adaptation space as a set of configurations with different QoS and UX characteristics, while the DRL implemented as DDQN agent learns to select the configuration that best fits the current context. By combining structured variability modeling with adaptive decision-making, the approach supports QoS-compliant and workload-aware adaptation under dynamic conditions. The following subsections describe the DSPL and DRL components in detail.

3.1 Dynamic Software Product Line Feature Model

From a DSPL perspective, a running MSS can be viewed as a collection of features that can be dynamically enabled or disabled in response to changes in the operating context. DSPL employs a runtime variability model, most commonly a feature model (FM) that captures the variation points and the constraints among features [9]. Currently, our approach supports two types of variability points: *alternative* (XOR), where exactly one variant (feature) is selected from a set of alternatives, and *optional*, where a feature may be either included or omitted.

In our design, each feature in the FM, particularly the leaf features, is uniquely mapped to a specific microservice implementation within the system. This mapping establishes a clear one-to-one correspondence between the feature model and the deployed architecture. The DSPL component in our work is responsible for realizing runtime variability by generating valid combinations of microservices that conform to the constraints of the FM. Each combination represents an alternative system architecture, or more precisely, a distinct configuration of the MSS.

Variability at the user-experience level is defined at the granularity of individual microservices. In the current approach, we associate each concrete feature (microservice variant) with a UX contribution value that reflects its expected impact on the end-user experience. At design time, the software engineer can estimate these UX contributions based on domain knowledge (e.g., whether a variant provides richer content, more accurate recommendations, or more detailed feedback). These contributions are represented as mean-value estimates and are later aggregated to compute a configuration-level UX score, which is used by the decision-making component. While this paper uses static UX contribution estimates for our case study, as described later, the same formulation can be instantiated using real user-interaction signals when available. For example, UX contributions can be derived from operational logs using metrics such as click-through rate (CTR) and dwell time [28], either directly or through a learned mapping that relates observed engagement to the corresponding microservice variants.

We illustrate our approach using the *BookLib* MSS case study. Figure 1 shows the FM of this system, while Table 2 lists the system features, the names of their variants, and their descriptions. The last column of the table provides static values at the variant level for end-user experience (UX). Consider the two valid configurations of *BookLib* highlighted in Fig. 1[1]. From the figure, Configuration X attains a higher total UX score S_{ux} because it includes features with strong positive impact on user satisfaction, such as the *Accurate Recommender* and *Detailed Review* services. In contrast, Configuration Y attains a lower S_{ux} by selecting lighter variants, such as a *lower-quality recommender* and a *Review Summary* service, which may reduce user interactions but can help protect response time under high workload.

Alongside these UX-based scores, each configuration is also associated with configuration-level QoS attributes, particularly response time (RT), as described later in Sect. 4. By jointly modeling UX levels and QoS attributes for each configuration, the DSPL component of our approach defines a structured adaptation space that captures both functional and non-functional trade-offs. Selecting

[1] The depicted configurations respect all FM constraints. For example, in an XOR relationship, selecting a variant implies that its parent feature is also selected. In each configuration, an active (selected) feature is indicated with a binary value of 1, whereas an inactive (unselected) feature is assigned 0. The *user experience score* S_{ux} of a configuration is obtained by summing the UX contributions of all its active features.

the most suitable configuration under dynamic conditions requires an intelligent reasoning mechanism; this is provided by the DRL component, which performs data-driven decision-making over the DSPL-defined adaptation space.

Table 2. Details of microservices and variants in the BookLib FM

Service	Variant	Description	UX
DisplayBook (DB)	DB-Text	Text-based display with rich details, faster loading in low-bandwidth settings, and accessibility support.	0.7
	DB-Image	Image-based display with stronger visual appeal and marketing potential.	0.2
Inventory (Inven)	Inven-Light	Lightweight inventory service showing basic stock information.	0.3
	Inven-Enhanced	Enhanced inventory service showing richer details, e.g., stock count, best-selling items, and notifications.	0.8
Recommender (Recom)	Recom-Light	Lightweight recommender with lower accuracy.	0.2
	Recom-Accurate	Personalized recommender with higher accuracy using advanced algorithms.	0.8
Review (Rev)	Rev-Summary	Top-five reviews or a short review summary for faster display.	0.2
	Rev-Detailed	Richer review presentation with filtering/personalization, requiring more computation.	0.7
Advertisement	–	Promotional or book-related advertisements.	0.1

3.2 Deep Reinforcement Learning-Based Decision Making

A self-adaptive MSS relies on an adaptation management component capable of monitoring the target system and its external context, analyzing changes, planning suitable adaptation actions, and applying them. These steps follow the well-known MAPE (Monitor-Analyze-Plan-Execute) reference model proposed in autonomic computing paradigms [16]. In our approach, the Analyze and Plan phases are driven by a trained DDQN agent. The agent is trained offline using an offline dataset together with a performance prediction model (PPM) that estimates the end-to-end response time (RT) of candidate configurations under the observed context. In general, the context in MSS can include operating-environment conditions, system-level signals from the managed microservices, and user-behavior indicators. In our current implementation, however, the context is primarily captured by the external workload experienced by the system.

To illustrate how the basic DDQN components are mapped to our approach, we formalize them as a Markov Decision Process (MDP) defined by the tuple (S, A, R, T):

- S: The set of states, combining the external workload context (requests per minute RPM) with internal system performance (end-to-end response time

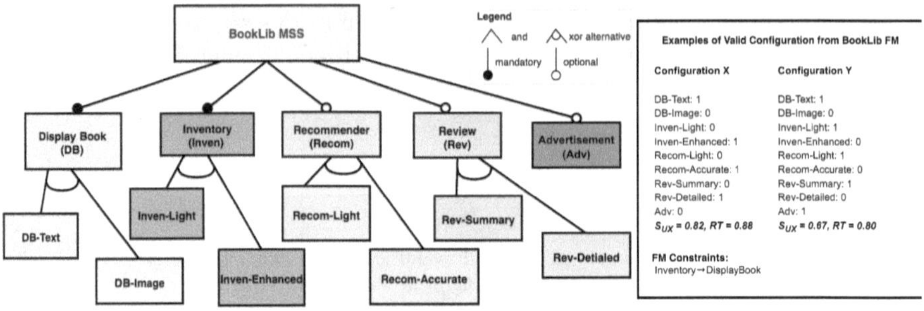

Fig. 1. Feature Model (FM) of the *BookLib* MSS with example valid configurations X and Y.

RT), represented as:

$$\text{State} = [\text{RPM}, \text{RT}]$$

- A: The set of actions, corresponding to configuration indices generated by the DSPL component, where each index represents a unique configuration.
- $R : S \times A \rightarrow \mathbb{R}$: The reward function, designed to promote configuration decisions that protect RT under high workload while preserving UX when workload is relaxed. Reward details are shown in the next section.
- $T : S \times A \rightarrow S'$: The transition function, describing how the system state evolves as the workload progresses over the trace and as the selected configuration affects the predicted response time.

Using this formalism, the agent learns a policy $\pi : S \rightarrow A$ that adapts configuration decisions to the current workload conditions. The policy aims to protect QoS during high-load periods by reducing response time, while preserving higher UX when the workload is relaxed, according to the workload-aware reward design.

3.3 Reward Function: Workload-Aware RT–UX Trade-Off

The reward function reflects a workload-aware trade-off between RT protection and UX. Under high workload, the reward emphasizes minimizing RT to keep the system within the SLO threshold τ. Under relaxed workload, it shifts emphasis toward preserving UX by favoring configurations with higher UX value.

At each control interval, the agent selects a valid DSPL configuration as an action a and receives a reward as represented in equation below:

$$R = -\omega(\text{RPM}) \cdot \widehat{RT} + \big(1 - \omega(\text{RPM})\big) \cdot \widehat{S}_{ux}(a) - \lambda_{SLO}\, \mathbb{I}[RT > \tau]. \quad (1)$$

where

- R is the scalar reward.
- RT is the observed end-to-end response time under configuration a.

- $\widehat{RT}$ is the normalized response time.
- $S_{ux}(a)$ is the UX value of configuration a, computed as:

$$S_{ux}(a) = \sum_{i=1}^{n} UX_i \cdot f_i(a), \qquad f_i(a) \in \{0, 1\},$$

  where n is the number of features in the feature model, UX_i is the utility contribution of feature i (higher is better UX), and $f_i(a) = 1$ if feature i is enabled in configuration a, and 0 otherwise.
- $\widehat{S}_{ux}(a)$ is the normalized UX utility (normalization reported in the experimental settings).
- RPM is the observed request rate (requests per minute).
- $\omega(\text{RPM}) \in [0, 1]$ is a workload-dependent trade-off weight (Eq. (2)).
- τ is the response-time SLO threshold (ms).
- $\mathbb{I}[RT > \tau]$ equals 1 if the SLO is violated and 0 otherwise.
- $\lambda_{SLO} > 0$ is a constant penalty applied when the SLO is violated.

Workload-Aware Weight. We compute the trade-off weight from the current request rate:

$$\omega(\text{RPM}) = \text{clip}\left(\frac{\text{RPM} - \text{RPM}_{low}}{\text{RPM}_{high} - \text{RPM}_{low}}, 0, 1\right). \qquad (2)$$

where

- RPM_{low} is a relaxed-load anchor.
- RPM_{high} is a high-load anchor.
- $\text{clip}(\cdot, 0, 1)$ bounds the value to $[0, 1]$.

Finally, $\omega(\text{RPM}) \to 1$ as the workload approaches RPM_{high}, increasing the emphasis on RT minimization, while $\omega(\text{RPM}) \to 0$ as the workload approaches RPM_{low}, increasing the emphasis on UX preservation.

4 Operational Framework of the Approach

The operational framework instantiates the DSPL and DRL components of the proposed approach as a complete self-adaptation workflow for MSS. It comprises two tightly connected phases: an offline data collection and training phase, where the PPM and DDQN policy are learned, and a trace-driven emulation phase, where the learned policy is evaluated under evolving workload conditions through emulated configuration switching. The following subsections describe these phases in detail.

4.1 Offline Data Collection and Training Phase

This phase aims to construct a surrogate training setting that reflects the behavior of the target MSS under dynamic workload conditions. As illustrated in Fig. 2, the process begins with a software engineer populating the approach's knowledge

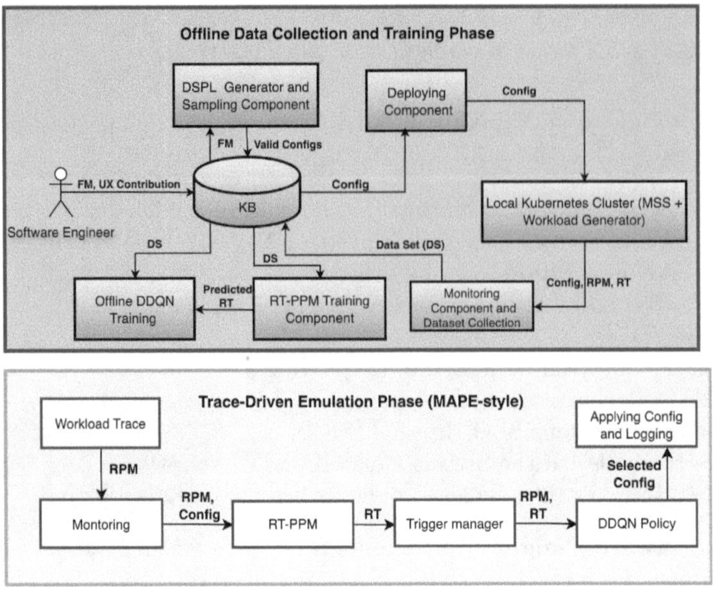

Fig. 2. Operational Framework of the DSPL–DRL Approach.

base (KB) with the FM of the MSS and the UX contributions of its microservices/variants. This initial knowledge establishes the adaptation space and links each valid configuration to a corresponding UX value.

A fundamental element of this phase is the DSPL component, which interprets the FM to generate the set of valid configurations. Since the full adaptation space may be large, a sampling technique can be used to select a representative subset of configurations for data collection. The sampled configurations are then executed under trace-driven workloads, and the monitoring component records key QoS properties(e.g., RT in our case) for each deployed configuration.

The collected measurements form an offline dataset that captures how the MSS behaves across the sampled adaptation space under varying workload levels. This dataset becomes the foundation for training a performance prediction model (PPM) [25] that generalizes system behavior to unseen configuration–workload pairs. By integrating the trained PPM into a dedicated surrogate environment, the approach enables the DDQN agent to explore a broad range of configuration decisions without incurring the cost, risk, or delay of live executions. Within this safe but representative environment, the agent learns a policy that maximizes long-term reward by balancing predicted RT with UX values according to the workload-aware reward design.

4.2 Trace-Driven Emulation Phase

In the trace-driven emulation phase, the DDQN agent is evaluated by replaying a workload trace and emulating configuration switching decisions over time. This phase is designed to approximate the behaviour of runtime MAPE loop [16] in a controlled and repeatable setting: instead of monitoring and reconfiguring a live deployment, we iterate over trace steps (e.g., minutes), observe the current workload (RPM), and estimate the RT of the currently active configuration using the trained PPM. This provides a lightweight proxy for the Monitor and Analyze steps, while enabling the Plan step to invoke the DDQN policy whenever an adaptation trigger is met.

When a trigger occurs, the DDQN policy selects a new configuration based on the current workload-RT state. The selected configuration is then applied within the emulation by updating the active configuration identifier, and subsequent trace steps proceed from this updated setting. Throughout the replay, we log the workload level, the selected configuration, the predicted RT, the corresponding UX value, and the achieved reward, producing a complete time series that supports subsequent analysis of RT protection under stress periods and UX preservation under relaxed periods. The emulation includes separate triggers for RT protection and UX upgrading, which are defined in Sect. 5.2.

5 Evaluation and Experiments

To evaluate the effectiveness of the DSPL–DRL approach, we define the following research questions (RQs):

- **RQ1:** *How close is the learned DDQN policy to the oracle, compared with a budgeted GA baseline, on the same evaluation dataset?*
- **RQ2:** *Under trace-driven emulation, can the learned DDQN policy balance RT protection and UX preservation, compared with a budgeted GA baseline?*
- **RQ3:** *How fast is runtime decision-making for DDQN compared with GA under the same per-trigger budget?*

5.1 Experiments Setup

The evaluation was conducted on the BookLib MSS introduced in Sect. 3 and implemented in Java Spring Boot; the full replication package is publicly available [13]. BookLib was designed and developed to expose explicit DSPL variability, including optional and alternative microservice variants, a capability not commonly supported by existing MSS benchmarks. This makes it suitable for evaluating application-level configuration adaptation and for studying clear RT–UX trade-offs. Using the feature model shown in Fig. 1 and the Sat4j reasoner [24], BookLib has a total of 72 valid configurations. To reduce deployment effort, we used 3-wise sampling with SPLCATool [15] to select 24 representative configurations. The 24 sampled configurations were used only for offline measurement and PPM training, whereas DDQN, GA, and the oracle operate over all 72 valid DSPL configurations. The configuration sample was then deployed on a local Kubernetes cluster running on a Windows machine with a 2.4 GHz CPU and 12 GB RAM. For data collection, a compressed FIFA 1998 World Cup workload trace [3] was replayed using k6 load-testing tool [7], while end-to-end RT was recorded at one-minute granularity. The resulting dataset, collected in approximately 12 h, was used to train an XGBoost-based PPM [4], selected for its strong predictive accuracy and efficiency in configurable systems [8]. The PPM achieved $R^2 = 0.8917$ on a held-out split and was shared by both DDQN and the GA baseline for fair comparison. The DDQN hyperparameters were selected as the best-performing setting among multiple experimental configurations, as summarized in Table 3. Training was performed on a Mac device with 8 GB RAM and an Apple M2 chip (8-core CPU, 3.49 GHz maximum clock speed), and the learned DDQN policy was finally assessed through trace-driven emulation on the same PPM-based environment.

Table 3. Key parameters used in the reward formulation (Eqs. (1)–(2)) and DDQN training setup

Parameter	Description	Value
τ	Response-time SLO threshold in the indicator term $\mathbb{I}[RT > \tau]$ (Eq. (1)), defined as $P_{0.95}$(RT) in the offline DS.	4600 ms
τ_{low}	Relaxed threshold used in the trigger logic (e.g., Upgrade-UX), defined as 0.8τ.	3680 ms
λ_{SLO}	Constant penalty when the SLO is violated in Eq. (1).	1.2
RPM_{low}	Relaxed-load anchor in ω(RPM) (Eq. (2)), set to the 10th percentile of the observed RPM distribution in the training dataset, $P_{0.10}$(RPM).	388
RPM_{high}	High-load anchor in ω(RPM) (Eq. (2)), set to the 90th percentile of the observed RPM distribution in the training dataset, $P_{0.90}$(RPM).	752
norm(·) (RT)	Normalization used for $\widehat{RT}$.	RunningMeanStd
norm(·) (UX)	Normalization used for $\widehat{S}_{ux}(a)$.	Min–max
N	Protect persistence Number of consecutive minutes with $RT > \tau$ required to trigger RT-protection adaptation	2 min
M	Upgrade persistence Number of consecutive minutes with $RPM \leq RPM_{low}$ and $RT \leq \tau_{low}$ required to trigger UX upgrade adaptation	2 min
W / Cooldown window	Number of minutes during which no new adaptation trigger is allowed after a reconfiguration, to prevent oscillations.	3 min
η (learning rate)	Learning rate used to train the Q-network (DDQN).	1×10^{-4}
γ	Discount factor in DDQN.	0.90
Optimizer	Optimizer used for DDQN training.	Adam
Total training steps	Maximum number of offline DDQN training steps.	120,000
Start ϵ	Initial exploration rate in ϵ-greedy during offline training.	1.0
End ϵ	Final exploration rate after decay in offline training.	0.05
Decay steps (ϵ)	Steps over which ϵ decays linearly in offline training.	50,000

5.2 Evaluation

We now report the experimental findings of our DSPL–DRL approach, organized around the research questions defined earlier.

RQ1. Decision quality against the oracle. For RQ1, we assess the decision quality of the learned DDQN policy and a budgeted GA baseline by comparing both methods against the optimal oracle reference. We used an evaluation dataset of 100 points sampled from the original offline dataset. Each evaluation point corresponds to a workload–performance state $s = \langle RPM, RT \rangle$ for the currently active configuration under that workload.

The evaluation dataset is constructed to explicitly include two categories of trigger-relevant states. First, *Protect-SLO* points represent stress conditions, selected under high workload (near/above the 90th Percentile $P90(RPM)$) and high RT ($RT \geq \tau$), where τ is set to the dataset-derived $P95$ RT threshold ($\tau = 4600$ ms) as shown in Table 3. Second, *Upgrade-UX* points represent relaxed conditions, selected under low workload ($RPM \leq P10(RPM)$) and low RT ($RT \leq 0.8 \cdot \tau$), i.e., 3680 ms. In addition, we include a small number of mid-range points (between $P10$ and $P90$) to avoid restricting the evaluation to extremes, while maintaining emphasis on these two categories.

To obtain the *oracle* decision for each evaluation state, we perform an exhaustive brute force search over all DSPL-derived configuration set A and select the configuration that maximizes the same reward function used by the agent:

$$a^*(s) = \arg\max_{a \in A} R(s, a).$$

This oracle acts as an upper-bound reference under our reward definition and the considered configuration space.

We report two complementary metrics. *Match rate* measures the percentage of evaluation states for which the agent selects the same configuration as the oracle. *Regret* quantifies the loss when the agent deviates from the oracle, computed per state as $\Delta(s) = R(s, a^*) - R(s, a_{\text{agent}})$ and summarized over all 100 states. Together, these metrics capture both how often the DDQN reproduces oracle decisions and how costly the remaining mismatches are, particularly in stress states near τ and relaxed states eligible for UX upgrading.

Table 4 summarizes the results. DDQN achieves a higher oracle match rate (94%) than the budgeted GA baseline (90%), indicating that the learned policy more consistently selects the same configurations as the oracle under the same evaluation states. Moreover, DDQN yields a lower mean regret (0.0001 vs. 0.0002), showing that when mismatches occur, the resulting reward loss is smaller. Although GA optimizes the same workload-adaptive reward (including the SLO penalty), it is a stochastic search under a limited budget and may stop at near-optimal configurations, which explains its lower match rate and higher regret compared to DDQN.

Table 4. Decision quality against the oracle on evaluation dataset (100 states).

Method	Oracle Match rate	Mean regret
DDQN	94.00%	0.0001
GA	90.00%	0.0002

Table 5. Trace-driven emulation results under workload stress and recovery

Metric	DDQN	GA
SLO triggers	1	1
Upgrade-UX triggers	1	1
Mean RT (ms)	1921.59	1951.62
Mean UX	0.6948	0.7620

RQ2. Balancing RT protection and UX preservation. For RQ2, we compare the learned DDQN policy against the budgeted GA baseline using a trace-driven emulation that includes explicit workload stress and recovery periods. Over the 35-minute trace, the controller triggered one RT protection adaptation during stress and one UX upgrade adaptation during relaxed conditions, reflecting its dual operational objectives.

In the trace-driven emulation, the DDQN agent is invoked only when an adaptation condition is met. We use two categories of triggers (with a cooldown to prevent oscillations): (i) a *protect* trigger, raised when the predicted response time of the active configuration exceeds the SLO threshold τ for a set of N consecutive minutes; and (ii) an *upgrade_UX* trigger, raised in a relaxed regime when $RPM \leq RPM_{\text{low}}$ and the predicted response time remains below τ_{low} for M consecutive minutes. Table 3 shows the values derived for these parameters. When either trigger fires, the emulator queries the learned DDQN policy using the current state $\langle RPM, RT \rangle$ and applies the selected configuration for subsequent trace steps, subject to a cooldown window. Table 5 summarizes the results. Both DDQN and the budgeted GA exhibit stable behavior, requiring only two configuration switches over the entire trace, indicating that the selected configurations remain effective until the workload regime changes. In terms of RT, DDQN achieved a slightly lower mean response time than GA (1921.59 ms vs. 1951.62 ms), suggesting slightly stronger RT stabilization under fluctuating workload. In the relaxed regime (low RPM), GA achieved higher average UX than DDQN (0.7620 vs. 0.6948), indicating a more aggressive UX preference when slack was available. Nevertheless, DDQN maintained competitive UX while preserving lower average RT. Overall, these results indicate that the proposed DDQN policy provides a balanced RT–UX trade-off in trace-driven emulation, with performance comparable to the budgeted GA baseline while relying on fast policy inference.

Table 6. Decision-making time per trigger on evaluation dataset (100 states)

Method	Mean (ms)	Median (ms)
DDQN (policy inference)	0.0670	0.0624
GA (budgeted search)	31.3565	31.6481

RQ3. Decision-making time (DDQN vs GA). To answer RQ3, we measure the time required to select the next DSPL configuration once a trigger occurs in the trace-driven emulation. The GA baseline uses a practical budget of *pop*=20 and *gens*=10, chosen to keep per-trigger latency low, resulting in at most 200 candidate evaluations per trigger, while DDQN selects a configuration using a single forward pass (policy inference). We report the mean and median decision time across 100 decision points.

Table 6 shows that DDQN is below 0.1 ms per decision, while GA requires about 31 ms. This difference is expected because DDQN shifts exploration offline and uses one runtime policy inference, whereas GA searches online at each trigger, evaluating up to 200 candidates with PPM-based RT prediction and reward computation. Thus, DDQN better supports timely adaptation when triggers are frequent.

Summary of the Findings. Overall, the results indicate that the proposed DSPL–DRL approach achieves strong decision quality, balanced RT–UX behavior in trace-driven emulation, and clear runtime efficiency advantages over the budgeted GA baseline. These findings support the feasibility of application-level DSPL–DRL adaptation for dynamic MSS.

Threats and Limitations. The findings should be interpreted with some limitations. First, both offline training and trace-driven evaluation rely on a PPM-based surrogate environment, so prediction errors may affect the learned policy and the GA baseline, although the same validated PPM ($R^2 = 0.8917$) was used for fair comparison. In addition, the evaluation focuses mainly on response time and configuration-level UX scores, which do not capture all QoS dimensions or real user behavior. Finally, the study is based on a single case study, a sampled subset of configurations, and one workload source, so broader validation on additional systems, workloads, and deployment environments is needed.

6 Conclusion

This paper presented a DSPL–DRL approach for self-adaptation in microservice systems, where the feature model defines the valid configuration space and a DDQN agent learns workload-aware reconfiguration decisions using a PPM-based surrogate environment. Using the BookLib case study, the results showed that the approach achieved near-oracle decision quality, remained competitive with a budgeted GA baseline under trace-driven emulation, and enabled very fast runtime decisions. Future work will focus on live online deployment, evaluation on additional MSS and workload traces, richer QoS and cost metrics, and robustness under workload drift and PPM updates.

Disclosure of Interests. The authors have no competing interests to declare that are relevant to the content of this article.

References

1. Ahmad, H., Treude, C., Wagner, M., Szabo, C.: Towards resource-efficient reactive and proactive auto-scaling for microservice architectures. J. Syst. Softw. **225**, 112390 (2025)
2. Alférez, G.H., Pelechano, V., Mazo, R., Salinesi, C., Diaz, D.: Dynamic adaptation of service compositions with variability models. J. Syst. Softw. **91**, 24–47 (2014)
3. Arlitt, M., Jin, T.: A workload characterization study of the 1998 world cup web site. IEEE Netw. **14**(3), 30–37 (2000)

4. Chen, T., Guestrin, C.: XGBoost: a scalable tree boosting system. In: Proceedings of the 22nd ACM SIGKDD International Conference on Knowledge Discovery and Data Mining, pp. 785–794 (2016). https://doi.org/10.1145/2939672.2939785
5. De Sanctis, M., Muccini, H., Vaidhyanathan, K.: Data-driven adaptation in microservice-based IoT architectures. In: 2020 IEEE International Conference on Software Architecture Companion (ICSA-C), pp. 59–62. IEEE (2020)
6. De Sanctis, M., Muccini, H., Vaidhyanathan, K.: A user-driven adaptation approach for microservice-based IoT applications. In: Proceedings of the 11th International Conference on the Internet of Things, pp. 48–56 (2021)
7. Grafana Labs: K6. https://grafana.com/docs/k6/latest/. Accessed 14 Feb 2026
8. Grebhahn, A., Siegmund, N., Apel, S.: Predicting performance of software configurations: there is no silver bullet. arXiv preprint arXiv:1911.12643 (2019)
9. Hallsteinsen, S., Hinchey, M., Park, S., Schmid, K.: Dynamic software product lines. Computer **41**(4), 93–95 (2008)
10. He, X., Tu, Z., Xu, X., Wang, Z.: Programming framework and infrastructure for self-adaptation and optimized evolution method for microservice systems in cloud-edge environments. Futur. Gener. Comput. Syst. **118**, 263–281 (2021)
11. Jawabreh, E., Taweel, A.: Self-adaptation in microservice systems: a dynamic software product line approach. In: International Conference on Service-Oriented Computing, pp. 195–201. Springer (2024)
12. Jawabreh, E., Taweel, A.: Self-adaptation in microservice systems: a literature review. In: International Conference on Service-Oriented Computing, pp. 28–40. Springer (2024)
13. Jawabreh, E., Taweel, A.: Booklib DSPL self-adaptation replication package (2026). https://github.com/ezdehar1/booklib-dspl-self-adaptation. Accessed 03 June 2026
14. Jawabreh, E., Taweel, A.: Self-adaptation in microservice systems: literature review informed classification taxonomy. Inf. Softw. Technol. (2026). https://doi.org/10.1016/j.infsof.2026.108135
15. Johansen, M.F., Haugen, Ø., Fleurey, F.: An algorithm for generating t-wise covering arrays from large feature models. In: Proceedings of the 16th International Software Product Line Conference-Volume 1, pp. 46–55 (2012)
16. Lalanda, P., McCann, J.A., Diaconescu, A.: Autonomic Computing: Principles, Design and Implementation. Springer, London (2013). https://doi.org/10.1007/978-1-4471-5007-7
17. Liu, P., Mao, X., Zhang, S., Hou, F.: Towards reference architecture for a multi-layer controlled self-adaptive microservice system. In: SEKE, pp. 236–241 (2018)
18. Metzger, A., Quinton, C., Mann, Z.Á., Baresi, L., Pohl, K.: Feature model-guided online reinforcement learning for self-adaptive services. In: International Conference on Service-Oriented Computing, pp. 269–286. Springer (2020)
19. Mousa, A., Bentahar, J., Alam, O.: Context-aware composite SaaS using feature model. Futur. Gener. Comput. Syst. **99**, 376–390 (2019)
20. Pimentel, E., Pereira, W., Maia, P.H.M., Cortés, M.I.: Self-adaptive microservice-based systems-landscape and research opportunities. In: 2021 International Symposium on Software Engineering for Adaptive and Self-Managing Systems (SEAMS), pp. 167–178. IEEE (2021)
21. Rodrigues-Filho, R., Sene, I., Jr., Porter, B., Bittencourt, L.F., Kon, F., Costa, F.M.: Exploring emergent microservice evolution in elastic deployment environments. J. Syst. Softw. **219**, 112252 (2025)

22. Rossi, F., Cardellini, V., Presti, F.L., Nardelli, M.: Dynamic multi-metric thresholds for scaling applications using reinforcement learning. IEEE Trans. Cloud Comput. **11**(2), 1807–1821 (2022)
23. Sampaio, A.R., Rubin, J., Beschastnikh, I., Rosa, N.S.: Improving microservice-based applications with runtime placement adaptation. J. Internet Ser. Appl. **10**(1), 1–30 (2019)
24. Sat4j: A satisfiability library. https://www.sat4j.org/. Accessed 24 Sept 2025
25. Siegmund, N., et al.: Predicting performance via automated feature-interaction detection. In: 34th International Conference on Software Engineering (ICSE), pp. 167–177. IEEE (2012)
26. Sutton, R.S., Barto, A.G.: Reinforcement Learning: An Introduction, 2nd edn. MIT Press, Cambridge, MA (2018)
27. Weyns, D., et al.: Self-adaptation in industry: a survey. ACM Trans. Auton. Adapt. Syst. (TAAS) **18**(3), 1–48 (2023). https://doi.org/10.1145/3589227
28. Xie, R., Ma, L., Zhang, S., Xia, F., Lin, L.: Reweighting clicks with dwell time in recommendation. In: Companion Proceedings of the ACM Web Conference 2023, pp. 341–345 (2023)
29. Zhang, S., Zhang, M., Ni, L., Liu, P.: A multi-level self-adaptation approach for microservice systems. In: 2019 IEEE 4th International Conference on Cloud Computing and Big Data Analysis (ICCCBDA), pp. 498–502. IEEE (2019)

Carbon-Aware Service Request Scheduling in Kubernetes

Ornela Danushi(✉), Giovanni Bellini, Stefano Forti, Jacopo Soldani, and Antonio Brogi

Department of Computer Science, University of Pisa, Pisa, Italy
ornela.danushi@phd.unipi.it

Abstract. Carbon-awareness in software services can help reducing the increasing environmental impact of ICT, e.g., by increasing the computational workload when the carbon intensity of the power grid is low and decreasing it when the carbon intensity is high. Following this intuition, this article introduces an architectural solution for the carbon-aware scheduling of requests sent to software services, based on Kubernetes, the *de-facto* standard for their deployment. The proposed solution enables reducing carbon emissions, e.g., by processing an incoming request with alternative implementations that provide akin functionality but feature lower energy consumption and/or deferring to the near future, if the carbon intensity is expected to decrease. To illustrate our proposal, we release an open-source prototype and report on controlled experiments showing that our prototype can significantly reduce services' carbon emissions, without compromising the overall output quality and with low overhead.

Keywords: Carbon Efficiency · Software Engineering · Sustainable Computing · Environmental Sustainability

1 Introduction

Information and Communication Technology (ICT) is currently contributing to an estimated 2–3% of global carbon emissions [1,19,21]. As software plays an increasingly active role, the need for environmentally-sustainable, *carbon-aware* computing is gaining more and more momentum in the software development lifecycle [7].

At the same time, container orchestration represents the *de-facto* standard for deploying and managing software services. With the growing interest in environmental sustainability, the request scheduling in containerised services should not only consider Quality of Service (QoS) metrics (e.g., average response time and throughput), but also incorporate carbon-emission reduction goals. More precisely, the scheduling of requests should consider the carbon emissions due to their processing, which depend on the energy mix of the power grid, otherwise called *carbon intensity*, which fluctuates in time [11,24].

Published by Springer Nature Switzerland AG 2027
D. Balouek et al. (Eds.): ESOCC 2026, LNCS 16834, pp. 36–51, 2027.
https://doi.org/10.1007/978-3-032-37831-6_3

Recent work [8,10] showed that services' carbon-awareness can be achieved by aligning the workload with periods characterised by lower carbon intensity, as well as by relying on different service *flavours*. Drawing on the principles of approximate computing [22], flavours enable software developers to design or refactor software services into multiple alternative implementations that provide akin functionality but feature different characteristics of execution time, hence resulting in different energy consumptions and carbon emission. For instance, a machine-learning task can be implemented using two different flavours, namely a *high* flavour employs a powerful model to ensure minimal error, but taking 20 s of execution time on average, and a *low* flavour that employs a lightweight model, which features an average execution time of 1 s at the price of a 6% error. With this in mind, we aim at (*i*) selecting a flavour for processing a certain request and (*ii*) possibly scheduling its execution during greener time periods (i.e. when carbon intensity is lower), while maintaining the average error under control.

In this article, we propose an *architectural solution* for the dynamic, carbon-aware scheduling of requests to software services deployed in Kubernetes (K8s), the de-facto standard for software service orchestration.

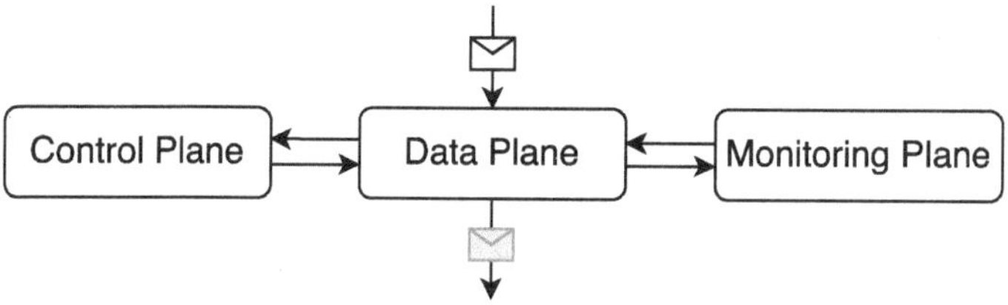

Fig. 1. Bird's-eye view of our proposed architectural solution.

The architectural components building our proposal are organised in three interacting planes (Fig. 1). The data plane receives requests and relies on the control plane which decides when to process a request, and with which flavour, among those running in the data plane itself. The control plane embeds a K8s operator, and enacts customisable request scheduling policies, based on current and forecast carbon intensities, as well as on the characteristics of the available flavoured service instances. This is the core of our proposal, as the K8s operator can decide to proactively defer the execution of a service request to greener time periods, as well as select more lightweight flavoured service instances, yet keeping the average error limited. Finally, the monitoring plane continuously observes the load of the available flavoured service instances, to suitably adapt the consumer replicas used for their processing.

To show the feasibility of our proposed architectural solution, we introduce an open-source *prototype*, called CarbonRouter, capable of installing and managing the data, control, and monitoring plane in a K8s deployment. We also illustrate how CarbonRouter was used to run *controlled experiments* aimed at assessing the effectiveness of our proposal in reducing carbon emissions of running services. Our experiments' results show that our approach can reduce a service's daily carbon emissions by more than 30%, as well as the autoscaling capabilities of our proposal can further reduce such carbon emissions by an additional 17%. The rest of this article is organised as follows. Section 2 provides an example motivating the need for our proposal. Section 3 introduces the full system architecture, which is then implemented by CarbonRouter, presented in Sect. 4. Section 5 presents the controlled experiment results. Finally, Sects. 6 and 7 discuss related work and draw some concluding remarks, respectively.

2 Motivating Scenario

Consider a service offering a machine-learning classification task, and suppose to have the service available in three different flavours, each using a different machine learning model. The *high* flavour achieves a 100% classification accuracy with an average execution time of 20 s. Conversely, the *low* flavour introduces a 6% error rate but reduces the average execution time to 1 s. Finally, the *medium* flavour is a compromise among the previous two, yielding 3% error rate and an average execution time of 10 s.

Suppose that the service receives three requests while running on a 50W server, and that – when receiving the requests – the carbon intensity of the grid powering the server is 100gCO_2-eq/kWh. To feature carbon-aware computing, we would like to suitably serve the requests by also reducing carbon emissions. Each request's emissions can be estimated as the product of the carbon intensity and the energy consumed to process such request, i.e., the energy consumed by the server multiplied by the execution time of the flavour used to process the request [10].

Without a dynamic and carbon-aware scheduling support, we should select a priori the flavour with which to serve *all* requests. For instance, if selecting the *high* flavour (Fig. 2a), the three requests would result in 83.33 mgCO_2, with 0% average error. Instead, fixing the flavour to *medium* or *low* would lower the emissions to 41.67 mgCO_2 and 4.17 mgCO_2, and we would obtain 3% or 6% average error, respectively.

A better trade-off between carbon-emission reduction and average error could be achieved if the flavour could be chosen dynamically. For instance, we could serve two requests with the flavour *medium* and one request with the flavour *high* (Fig. 2b), for total carbon emissions of 55.56 mgCO_2 and 2% average error. Compared to the scenario in which we processed all the requests with the *high* flavour (Fig. 2a), this scheduling achieves a reduction of ~33% in terms of carbon emissions.

Even better results could be achieved by possibly deferring the request processing, knowing the forecast carbon intensities for the near future. Suppose, for instance, that the near-next time slot is expected to exhibit 60 gCO_2-eqkWh of carbon intensities. The processing of the three requests could consist of scheduling one request with the *medium* flavour to be immediately processed and of deferring one request with flavour *medium* and one with flavour *high*, to be possibly processed in the next immediate slot, if it is greener than the current one (Fig. 2c). This choice enables that the carbon emission would be further lowered to 38.89mgCO_2, yet keeping the average error stable to 2%. Compared to the scenario in which we processed all the requests with the *high* flavour (Fig. 2a), this scheduling achieves ~53% in terms of carbon-emission reductions.

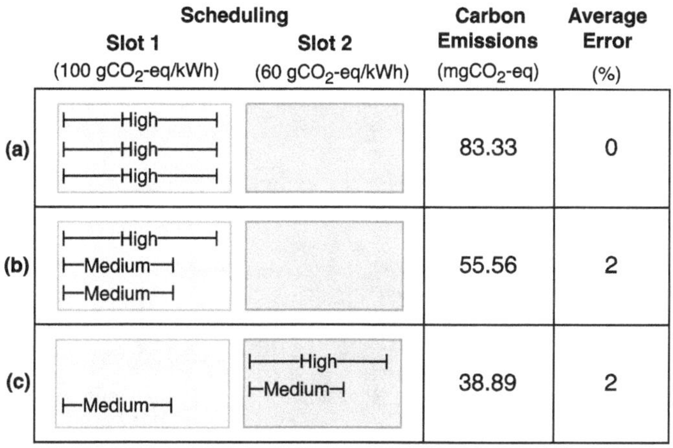

Fig. 2. Three examples of request scheduling, i.e., (a) a priori selection of the *high* flavour, (b) dynamic flavour selection, and (c) dynamic flavour selection with possibly deferred processing.

The above example showcases how dynamically choosing the flavour *and* deferring each incoming request can significantly reduce carbon emissions, incurring limited average error. To enable this, we show next an architectural solution supporting the carbon-aware orchestration of containerised services, by means of customisable policies for dynamically selecting which flavour to use for processing incoming requests and whether to defer such processing.

3 Architectural Solution

To enable request scheduling for software services, we propose the architectural solution in Fig. 3. Our proposal reuses existing components (i.e., K8s operator, RabbitMQ, Prometheus, KEDA, and Grafana), suitably configured to interact with ad-hoc components implemented to deliver the desired carbon-aware request scheduling, whose flow is represented by solid arrows in the figure. Particularly, when a client request enters the data plane, its carbon-aware scheduling begins. The request is forwarded to the control plane, which applies a customisable, carbon-aware scheduling policy to determine the service flavour to be used to serve such request. The scheduling information is passed back to the data plane, which then proceeds with the actual request processing.

Our proposed architectural solution also features telemetry and autoscaling, whose flow is denoted by dashed arrows in Fig. 3. Particularly, the above described request scheduling considers the carbon intensity of the power grid – assumed to be available from an external API – and the current processing status. The monitored information is also used to scale the replicas of available flavour instances, e.g., by scaling out flavour instances to ensure timely processing of requests, and made viewable to the application administrator via the monitoring plane.

We hereafter provide further details on the components in the data, control, and monitoring plane, by focussing on their use in request scheduling (Sect. 3.1) and autoscaling (Sect. 3.2).

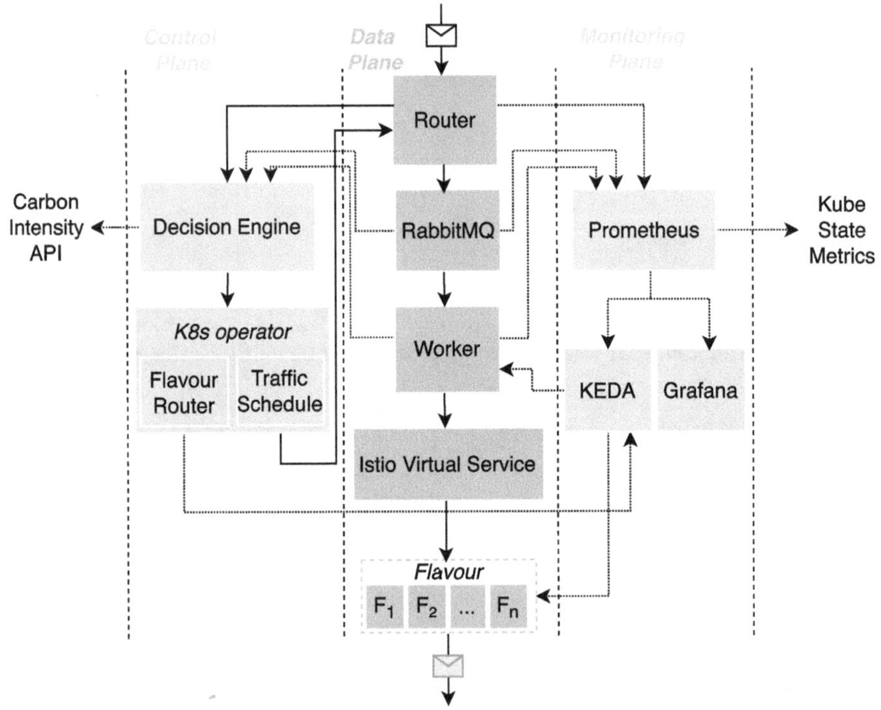

Fig. 3. Our proposed architectural solution. Solid and dashed arrows model the flow for scheduling an incoming request and autoscaling service flavours.

3.1 Request Scheduling

Client requests arrive at the data plane's Router component, which queries the control plane's Decision Engine component to determine which flavour to use to serve a request. The Decision Engine determines such flavour by applying a configurable carbon-aware request-scheduling policy, which employs a *credit-ledger* mechanism, aimed at modulating carbon emissions while adhering to given error constraints.

Particularly, the policy keeps track of the accumulated *credit* or *debit* over time, intended as the cumulative deviation of the average realised error from the target average error. A *credit* indicates that the processing enacted with the formerly selected flavour resulted in an average realised error *below* the target average error threshold. Conversely, a *debit* indicates that the average realised error is *above* the target average error threshold. Based on the actual credit or debit, the policy can be configured to take different decisions. By default, when the carbon intensity is low, it selects lower-error flavours to continue to accumulate credit or to pay off debit. Otherwise, when the carbon intensity is high, it selects higher-error flavours to reduce energy consumption – and thus carbon emissions. This is done when there is credit to spend or when the debit does not exceed a given debit threshold. Instead, if the debit threshold is reached, even in case of high carbon intensity, lower-error flavours are selected to start paying off the debit itself.

Once a flavour is scheduled to serve a request, the Decision Engine interacts with the K8s operator that – through the Traffic Schedule – notifies such scheduling to the Router. The latter enqueues the scheduled request into RabbitMQ [2], in the queue of requests that must be processed by the selected flavour. Scheduled requests are then dequeued by the Worker, which forwards each request to the Istio Virtual Service [16], which in turn passes such request to the instance of the flavour selected to process it. Flavour instances run in dedicated Docker containers, which can be independently spawned to facilitate their scalability.

3.2 Autoscaling Flavour Instances

Consumer resources, specifically Worker and Flavour Instances, are autoscaled to ensure the timely processing of requests (with selected flavours) while also reducing carbon emissions. The Decision Engine determines autoscaling decisions based on the carbon-intensity of the power grid (taken from an external Carbon Intensity API[1]), the number of to-be-processed requests (taken from the queues in RabbitMQ), and the number of active Worker instances, which together define the current operational state.

The autoscaling mechanism aims at gathering the most of computing efforts in periods when the carbon intensity is low. Specifically, to decrease carbon emissions, it *scales in* consumer replicas during high-intensity periods or when there are few-to-none requests to be processed. Alternatively, it *scales out* consumer replicas to increase throughput to gather the processing when in a low-intensity period, or when the queues of to-be-processed requests get overloaded. At the same time, the autoscaling mechanism ensures that consumer replicas cannot be reduced below a minimum level intended to prevent service starvation, as well as they cannot exceed the maximum degree of supported parallelism dictated by the underlying infrastructure. The actual number of consumer replicas is computed

[1] For instance, data can be retrieved from https://carbonintensity.org.uk.

by the Decision Engine following the above described intuition and based on a throttling factor, which can be configured to increase/decrease the adaptation speed.

Once an autoscaling decision is taken, the Decision Engine communicates such decision to the K8s operator. The latter, through its internal Flavour Router, determines the configuration needed to obtain the desired scaling of consumer resources, which is then forwarded to KEDA [18]. KEDA then autonomously triggers events to enforce the desired configuration (including scaling in/out consumer replicas), based on what it can observe through the telemetry collected by Prometheus and Kube State Metrics.

4 Prototype Implementation: CarbonRouter

To show the feasibility of our proposal, we implemented an open-source prototype, called CarbonRouter,[2] which realises the architectural solution presented in Sect. 3. CarbonRouter enables registering custom resource definitions to extend a K8s cluster, establishing a dedicated namespace for resource isolation, and managing a deployment through a Helm chart (i.e., carbonrouter-umbrella) to ensure adherence to cloud-native orchestration standards [5,15]. This can be done in practice with the steps shown in Table 1.

In its current release, CarbonRouter natively features three built-in scheduling policies, intended to also provide a template for developers to build upon:

- *Credit-Greedy*: Upon receiving a request, the *Credit-Greedy* policy reactively selects the flavour for processing such request only based on the credit-ledger and on the current carbon intensity. If the carbon intensity is low, the policy selects a lower-error flavour to continue to accumulate credit (or to pay off debit). Conversely, if the carbon intensity is high, it opts for a higher-error flavour to reduce energy consumption – and thus carbon emissions. Yet, in the worst-case of long periods with high emissions, the *Credit-Greedy* policy keeps error under control by selecting lower-error flavours to ensure that the set threshold of maximum average error is satisfied.
- *Forecast-Aware*: Upon receiving a request, the *Forecast-Aware* policy extends the *Credit-Greedy* policy by proactively selecting the flavour for processing such request also based on the forecast carbon intensity for the near-next time period. Particularly, the *Forecast-Aware* policy compares current carbon intensity with that forecast for the next time period. If the forecast carbon intensity is expected to be higher than the current one, the policy selects a lower-error flavour to continue to accumulate credits. Conversely, if the forecast carbon intensity is expected to decrease, the policy selects a higher-error flavour to reduce energy consumption and carbon emissions. In the latter case, the debit accumulate with the current processing is expected to be paid off in the next time period.

[2] https://github.com/di-unipi-socc/k8s-carbonrouter.git.

- *Forecast-Aware-Global*: This policy extends the *Forecast-Aware* policy by considering a longer forecast horizon (by default, 3 h) and by also considering the forecast workload (i.e., expected amount of requests). Similarly to the *Forecast-Aware* policy, if carbon intensity is expected to increase/decrease, the *Forecast-Aware-Global* policy selects a lower-/higher-error to accumulate credit/debit. This is done by also considering the expected amount of requests for the next time periods, which – together with the forecast carbon intensities – allow to estimate whether/how to amortise the debit/credit accumulated with a scheduling decision over the next time periods (by essentially estimating "how much" credit/debit can be accumulated in such time periods). The expected amount of requests is also used to drive the autoscaling, namely to avoid deferring too many requests to time periods where the expected workload is already high and might not be handled with the available resources.

CarbonRouter can be configured to run with any of the above listed policies, provided that the necessary data is available. For instance, if the forecast of incoming requests and carbon intensities for the next time periods is available, then the *Forecast-Aware-Global* policy could be selected to take the most informed scheduling decisions. Instead, if no data is available beside the current carbon intensity, then it makes more sense to go with the *Credit-Greedy* policy.

Table 1. Installation and lifecycle procedure steps.

Command	Step
`kubectl apply -f tests/keda-2.18.0-crds.yaml`	KEDA installation
`kubectl create namespace carbonrouter-system`	Namespace creation
`cd helm/carbonrouter-umbrella`	Initialization
`helm dependency update`	Dependency synchronisation
`helm install carbonrouter . -n carbonrouter-system --create-namespace`	CarbonRouter deployment
`kubectl apply -f demo/trafficschedule.yaml`	Policy injection
`helm uninstall carbonrouter -n carbonrouter-system`	CarbonRouter removal

5 Evaluation and Results

We hereby assess[3] the effectiveness of our proposed architectural solution in reducing carbon emissions. To this end, we report on a controlled experiment aimed at answering the following research questions:

[3] The source code of the controlled experiment is publicly on GitHub available at https://github.com/di-unipi-socc/k8s-carbonrouter/tree/main/experiments.

- RQ_1 To what extent can CarbonRouter reduce carbon emissions while keeping the average error under control?
- RQ_2 To what extent does the autoscaling mechanism in CarbonRouter contribute to further reducing carbon emissions?

In our controlled experiment, we also measured the carbon footprint induced by CarbonRouter itself. However, such overhead turned out to be neglibile with respect to that of the actual service request processing. For this reason, after presenting the experiment design (Sect. 5.1), we hereafter focus on answering to RQ_1 (Sect. 5.2) and RQ_2 (Sect. 5.3).

5.1 Experiment Design

Our experiment was designed to emulate the daily working of a service available in three different flavours (with 0%, 50%, and 70% error, respectively), with a target error threshold of 15%. To this end, we realised a scenario with fluctuating carbon intensity and realistic workload profiles. In particular, early morning hours are characterised by low carbon intensity (i.e., 80 gCO_2-eq/kWh). The morning proceeds with significant increases in carbon intensity (reaching a peak of 300 gCO_2-eq/kWh). Noon and the early afternoon are then characterised by a lower carbon intensity due to the production of solar energy (with a bottom value of 50 gCO_2-eq/kWh), which then starts increasing again as the sun starts setting down – generating a characteristic U-shaped profile. The peak of carbon intensity (i.e., 300 gCO_2-eq/kWh) is then reached during the evening, followed by a sudden drop to a very low carbon intensity (i.e., 40 gCO_2-eq/kWh) due to switching the powering of the server to geothermal energy.

The workload profile was instead set to simulate a service with a low workload (i.e., 50 end-users) in the early morning, which raise to the peak of 250 end-users during the morning. The workload keeps stable during noon and the early afternoon, to then start decreasing up to reaching 100 end-users right before the evening starts. The workload finally keeps stable at 100 end-users during the evening.

The above described scenario was condensed in a 10-minute experiment, where the first 2 min modelled the early morning, minutes 2–5 model noon and early afternoon, and the final 5 min modelled the period from late afternoon to the end of the evening. The resulting experiment was then run on a MacBook Pro 14" (2021) host machine, equipped with an Apple M1 Pro (10-core CPU) and 16 GB of unified memory. The software environment was orchestrated via Docker Desktop, leveraging a localised K8s cluster (8 vCPU, 12 GB RAM allocated).

5.2 Answering RQ_1

Given the lack of solutions for the carbon-aware scheduling of requests to multi-flavoured services (see Sect. 6), we compared our proposal to what can be currently done with K8s. In particular, we considered a *Baseline* where requests are processed by the least-error version as soon as they arrive, to essentially mirror the basic K8s request scheduling with no support to flavours nor carbon-awareness. We then considered other two possible configurations of K8s, in which the target service is deployed in three different flavours, and incoming requests are immediately scheduled to be processed by a flavour selected by applying a *Round-Robin* or *Random* policy. The latter two configurations thus introduce the support for flavours, yet disregarding carbon-awareness, and they were considered for direct comparison with the three built-in policies available in CarbonRouter (with no autoscaling).

Carbon emissions were estimated on a per-request basis, by essentially multiplying the time needed to process such request with the carbon intensity (at the time when the request was processed) and with a fixed value of power consumption for the server (i.e., 50W). Given that the obtained values are estimations, rather than providing the obtained absolute values, we hereby consider the relative reduction of carbon emissions achieved by the different policies as compared to the *Baseline*, which models the emissions we would have with K8s without flavours and carbon-awareness.

The results of our experiment are reported in Fig. 4, which reports the overall average error and carbon emissions reduction – with respect to the *Baseline* – of all considered policies.

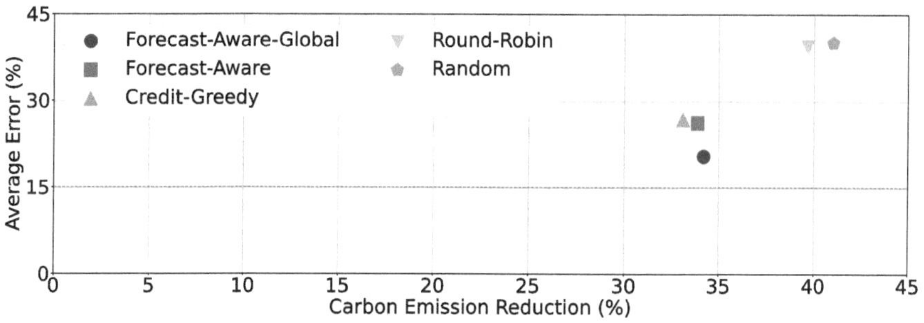

Fig. 4. Carbon-emission reductions with respect to the *Baseline* policy and average error, with average error threshold set to 15%.

The *Round-Robin* and *Random* policy achieve a higher reduction in carbon emissions (around 40%), mainly due to the fact that they schedule more requests to be processed with the higher-error flavours. This is because they do not consider the target 15% average error threshold, which also leads to a much higher overall average error, i.e., around 40%. The same does not hold for CarbonRouter's built-in policies, which end up selecting the least error flavour due to the *credit-ledger* mechanism trying to meet the average error threshold, yet achieving an overall reduction of carbon emissions of between 33–34%.

As we expected, the most informed policy (i.e., *Forecast-Aware-Global*) actually provides the best performances in the considered scenario, with the highest carbon emissions reduction and an overall average error close to the target 15% threshold. Yet, the threshold itself is not enforced by neither of the built-in policies, and this is mainly because of the heuristic way in which they exploit the *credit-ledger* mechanism. The development of a policy that enforces the target threshold is outside of the scope of this work and left for future work.

5.3 Answering RQ_2

To assess whether the autoscaling in CarbonRouter contributes to further reducing carbon emissions, we compared the results of the *Forecast-Aware-Global* policy without autoscaling (Sect. 5.2), with those we achieved by running the same policy with the autoscaling set.

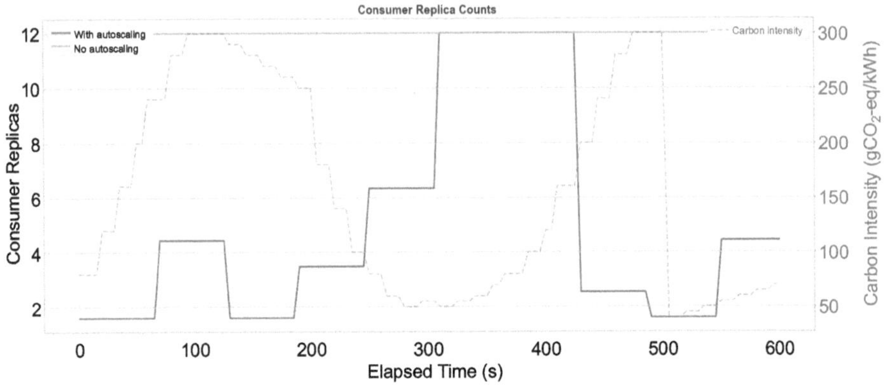

Fig. 5. Consumer replicas with and without autoscaling.

Figure 5 compares the numbers of consumer replicas resulting from the two different configurations of the *Forecast-Aware-Global* policy, with the no-autoscaling configuration keeping the number of replicas stable to 12. The autoscaling-enabled configuration instead reduces/increases the number of consumer replicas based on the carbon intensity (also displayed as a dashed grey line in Fig. 5). From the figure, one can readily observe that – besides fluctuations due to workload increases/decreases – when the carbon intensity increases, the autoscaling reduces the consumer replicas to reduce carbon emissions, and that the converse happens when carbon intensity lowers.

Figure 6 displays the cumulative carbon emissions resulting from the two different configurations of the *Forecast-Aware-Global* policy. The figure shows that, besides an initial period where the autoscaling is starting to adapt consumer replicas, then the cumulative emissions with autoscaling steadily stand below those of the no-autoscaling configuration. At the end of our experiment, this results in a further 17.08% of carbon emission reduction with respect to the *Forecast-Aware-Global* policy running without autoscaling. This results in a total

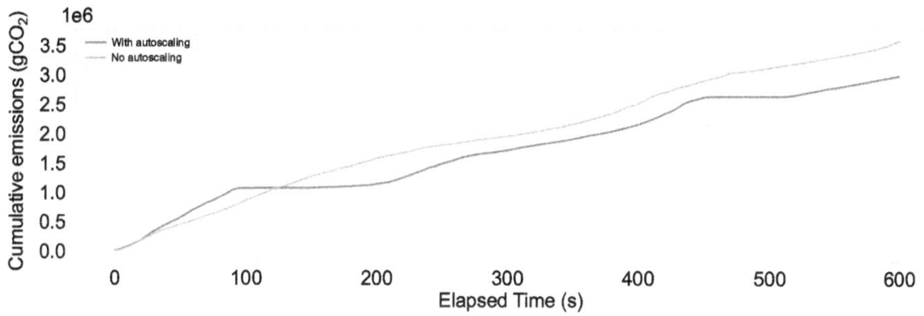

Fig. 6. Cumulative carbon emissions with and without autoscaling.

reduction of carbon emissions of around 40% with respect to the *Baseline*, thus reaching akin reductions as the nave policies, yet keeping the overall average error close to the threshold.

6 Related Work

Research on *energy-aware* software design and development is more extensive than for *carbon-aware* approaches [7], with the latter often balancing carbon emissions against QoS constraints. Regarding energy-aware design, Canino & Liu [6] introduce a proactive framework based on mixed type checking to embed energy information at the programming language level. Similarly, Sampson et al. [25] and Han & Orshansky [12] propose approximate type systems that trade data precision for reduced energy consumption. Shifting to component-based software, Bunse & Hpfner [3,4] leverage resource substitution – such as the Strategy pattern – to balance energy, performance, and hardware usage. Further extending this to service compositions, de Oliveira & Ledoux [23] employ an orchestration component to trigger reconfigurations for sustainable application deployment.

In the domain of energy-aware autoscaling, Hasan et al. [13,14] introduce an autonomic self-adaptive framework for Software-as-a-Service, which incorporates response times, availability, and energy source quality (e.g., green vs brown). Xu et al. [27] extend this adaptation to Cloud deployments by considering both workload types and the current energy mix. Furthermore, Kavanagh et al. [17] address runtime migration of high-performance computing tasks across heterogeneous accelerated infrastructures to optimise resource usage. However, while the proposed autoscaling is energy-aware, it does not explicitly account for the carbon intensity of the energy powering the service.

Regarding carbon-aware design, our recent studies [8,10] showed how to design carbon-aware software services that natively account for carbon intensity while serving incoming requests. Here, we complement our previous work by enabling to adapt existing services to account for carbon-awareness without necessarily needing to change their internal business logic.

Wiesner et al. [26] target location-constrained Cloud services through a Mixed Integer Linear Program problem designed to minimise emissions. Their approach manages response quality by strategically timing quality reductions during high-carbon periods. However, rather than relying on optimisation-based allocation, we introduce a *credit-ledger* mechanism to manage QoS-carbon trade-offs under bounded degradation. This credit-balance dynamic enables the system to prioritise lower-carbon variants while ensuring that long-term quality targets can be eventually met.

In the domain of carbon-aware autoscaling, Fairbanks [9] extends KEDA by adjusting maximum replica counts based on carbon-intensity data, enabling workloads to scale according to renewable energy availability. Similarly, Microsofts carbon-aware KEDA extension [20] modulates concurrency levels though regional carbon APIs, enabling the temporal shifting of non-critical workloads to periods of lower carbon footprint. Our approach builds upon this integration with KEDA, adopting the concept of a bounded consumer replicas from Fairbanks [9] but modifying the computation logic. We compute this replicas bound as a function of both carbon intensity and the current state of quality credits. This creates a feedback loop where quality credits act as a control parameter for carbon-aware scheduling: as credit levels fluctuate, they modulate the effective number of replicas. This mechanism is designed to prevent QoS degradation from exceeding defined thresholds during intervals of high-carbon intensity.

In this context, CarbonRouter extends the current state-of-the-art by leveraging on the implementation and integration of specific architectural components. While existing research focuses primarily on pod placement decisions, determining the spatial execution of workloads, our approach targets carbon-aware request scheduling. By controlling the flow of requests through deployed services, we shift the optimisation focus from infrastructure provisioning to traffic engineering.

In contrast to a framework requiring application-level modifications or external orchestration components for enabling deployments (e.g., Bunse & Hpfners EMC [3,4]), CarbonRouter operates at infrastructure level. It manages requests across independently deployed service flavours, enabling a black-box deployment model where service implementations remain unaltered. Furthermore, the architecture decouples request ingress from service invocation by introducing an asynchronous buffer. This decoupling enables carbon-aware autoscaling through queue-based backpressure, effectively applying some temporal shifting to interactive workloads.

7 Conclusions

In this article, we presented an architectural solution for dynamic, carbon-aware scheduling of requests to software services deployed in K8s. The architectural components building our proposal are organised in three interacting planes. The *data plane* receives requests and relies on the *control plane* which decides when to process a request, and with which flavour, among those running in the data plane itself. The control plane embeds a K8s operator, and enacts customisable request scheduling policies, based on current and forecasted carbon intensities, as well as on the characteristics of the available flavoured service instances. The core of our proposal is the K8s operator that can decide to proactively defer the execution of a service request to greener time periods, as well as select more lightweight flavoured service instances, yet keeping the average error limited. Finally, the *monitoring plane* continuously observes the load of the available flavoured service instances, to suitably adapt the consumer replicas used for their processing.

To show the feasibility of our proposed architectural solution, we introduced an open-source *prototype*, called CarbonRouter, capable of installing and managing the data, control, and monitoring plane in a K8s deployment. We also illustrated how CarbonRouter was used to run *controlled experiments* aimed at assessing the effectiveness of our proposal in reducing carbon emissions of running services. Our experiments' results showed that our approach can reduce a service's daily carbon emissions by more than 30%, increased by a further 17% with autoscaling capabilities, while keeping the average error limited. The current built-in policies of CarbonRouter rely on heuristics that approximate the target error, and the development of policies to enforce the target average error is left for future work.

Next, we discuss some observations and future work to enhance our proposal. Currently, system parameters are primarily static or operate at coarse temporal granularities. For instance, the autoscaling mechanism updates consumer replicas periodically rather than in response to real-time fluctuations. The per-request energy consumption is calculated by multiplying the runtime by a fixed baseline server power consumption, rather than accounting for fluctuating software-level consumptions. However, to better reflect realistic operational scenarios, future extensions of this work will incorporate more dynamic power models. Future enhancements will focus on extending observability to support both intrinsic scheduling of service requests and enable distributed end-to-end tracing, thereby facilitating both automated scheduling and anomaly debugging. The security within CarbonRouter needs to be enhanced: the architectural components do not use authentication mechanisms and communicate without encryption, beyond what the underlying network policies provide.

Furthermore, the scheduling policies are applied independently to each workload, without considering cross-service dependencies or global carbon budgets spanning multiple applications. A multi-tenancy-aware scheduling solution that coordinates carbon optimisation across an entire cluster (or namespace) could improve the global carbon efficiency, though at the cost of increased coordination complexity and potential resource contention.

Acknowledgments. This work was partly supported by the *FREEDA* research project (CUP: I53D23003550006), funded by PRIN (MUR, Italy) and Next Generation EU.

Disclosure of Interests. The authors have no competing interests to declare that are relevant to the content of this article.

References

1. Belkhir, L., Elmeligi, A.: Assessing ICT global emissions footprint: trends to 2040 & recommendations. J. Clean. Prod. **177**, 448–463 (2018). https://doi.org/10.1016/j.jclepro.2017.12.239
2. Broadcom: RabbitMQ. https://www.rabbitmq.com
3. Bunse, C., Höpfner, H.: Resource substitution with components - optimizing energy consumption. In: Proceedings of the 3rd International Conference on Software and Data Technologies, ICSOFT, vol. 2, pp. 28–35. INSTICC, SciTePress (2008). https://doi.org/10.5220/0001879000280035
4. Bunse, C., et al.: Choosing the "best" sorting algorithm for optimal energy consumption. In: Proceedings of the 4th International Conference on Software and Data Technologies, ICSOFT, vol. 2, pp. 199–206. INSTICC, SciTePress (2009). https://doi.org/10.5220/0002245401990206
5. Burns, B., et al.: Kubernetes: Up and Running: Dive into the Future of Infrastructure, 3rd edn. O'Reilly Media Inc, Sebastopol, CA (2022)
6. Canino, A., Liu, Y.D.: Proactive and adaptive energy-aware programming with mixed typechecking. In: Proceedings of the 38th ACM SIGPLAN Conference on Programming Language Design and Implementation, p. 217–232. PLDI 2017, ACM, New York, NY, USA (2017). https://doi.org/10.1145/3062341.3062356
7. Danushi, O., et al.: Carbon?efficient software design and development: a systematic literature review. ACM Comput. Surv. **57**(10), 267 (2025). https://doi.org/10.1145/3728638
8. Danushi, O.: Time to go green: carbon-aware request scheduling in software services. In: 16th International Conference on Cloud Computing and Services Science, CLOSER 2026, SciTePress (2026). Accepted for publication
9. Fairbanks, R.: Carbon aware temporal shifting of kubernetes workloads using KEDA. Ross Fairbanks' Blog. https://rossfairbanks.com/2023/06/05/carbon-aware-temporal-shifting-with-keda/
10. Forti, S., et al.: Carbon-aware software services. In: Papadopoulos, G.A., et al. (eds.) Service-Oriented and Cloud Computing. Lecture Notes in Computer Science. ESOCC 2025, vol. 15547, pp. 65–80. Springer Nature Switzerland (2025). https://doi.org/10.1007/978-3-031-84617-5_6
11. Gsteiger, V.U., et al.: Caribou: fine-grained geospatial shifting of serverless applications for sustainability. In: Proceedings of the ACM SIGOPS 30th Symposium on Operating Systems Principles, pp. 403–420. SOSP '24, ACM (2024).https://doi.org/10.1145/3694715.3695954
12. Han, J., Orshansky, M.: Approximate computing: an emerging paradigm for energy-efficient design. In: 18th IEEE European Test Symposium, pp. 1–6 (2013). https://doi.org/10.1109/ETS.2013.6569370
13. Hasan, M.S., et al.: Enabling green energy awareness in interactive cloud application. In: IEEE International Conference on Cloud Computing Technology and Science, pp. 414–422 (2016). https://doi.org/10.1109/CloudCom.2016.0071
14. Hasan, M.S., et al.: Investigating energy consumption and performance trade-off for interactive cloud application. IEEE Trans. Sustain. Comput. **2**(2), 113–126 (2017). https://doi.org/10.1109/TSUSC.2017.2714959

15. Helm Authors: Helm. https://helm.sh
16. Istio Authors: Istio service mesh. https://istio.io
17. Kavanagh, R., et al.: Energy-aware self-adaptation for application execution on heterogeneous parallel architectures. IEEE Trans. Sustain. Comput. **5**(1), 81–94 (2020). https://doi.org/10.1109/TSUSC.2019.2912000
18. KEDA: Kubernetes event-driven autoscaling. https://keda.sh
19. Malmodin, J., et al.: ICT sector electricity consumption and greenhouse gas emissions–2020 outcome. Telecommun. Policy **48**(3), 102701 (2024). https://doi.org/10.1016/j.telpol.2023.102701
20. Microsoft: Carbon-aware KEDA operator. https://github.com/Azure/carbon-aware-keda-operator
21. Mingay, S., Pamlin, D.: Assessment of global low-carbon and environmental leadership in the ICT sector, vol. ID G00161337 (2008)
22. Mittal, S.: A survey of techniques for approximate computing. ACM Comput. Surv. **48**(4) (2016). https://doi.org/10.1145/2893356
23. Alvares de Oliveira, F.G., Ledoux, T.: Self-optimisation of the energy footprint in service-oriented architectures. In: Proceedings of the 1st Workshop on Green Computing, p. 4–9. GCM '10, ACM, New York, NY, USA (2010). https://doi.org/10.1145/1925013.1925014
24. Piontek, T., et al.: Carbon emission-aware job scheduling for Kubernetes deployments. J. Supercomputing **80** (2024). https://doi.org/10.1007/s11227-023-05506-7
25. Sampson, A., et al.: EnerJ: approximate data types for safe and general low-power computation. In: Proceedings of the 32nd ACM SIGPLAN Conference on Programming Language Design and Implementation, pp. 164–174. PLDI '11, ACM, New York, NY, USA (2011). https://doi.org/10.1145/1993498.1993518
26. Wiesner, P., et al.: Carbon-aware quality adaptation for energy-intensive services. In: Proceedings of the 16th ACM International Conference on Future and Sustainable Energy Systems, p. 415–422. E-Energy '25, ACM (2025). https://doi.org/10.1145/3679240.3734614
27. Xu, M., et al.: A self-adaptive approach for managing applications and harnessing renewable energy for sustainable cloud computing. IEEE Trans. Sustain. Comput. **6**(4), 544–558 (2021). https://doi.org/10.1109/TSUSC.2020.3014943

How Much Model Is Enough? Model Sufficiency for Workflow Generation

Abubakari Alidu(✉), Michele Ciavotta, and Flavio De Paoli

Department of Informatics, Systems and Communication, University of Milano–Bicocca, Milan, Italy
a.alidu@unimib.it

Abstract. Large language models can generate plausible workflow code, but deployment decisions depend on a different question: which serving configuration is sufficient to produce executable workflows at acceptable cost and latency. We study this problem through two linked studies over ten workflow-generation tasks and three orchestrators under a fixed direct single-shot evaluation protocol. Study 1 shows that executability failures arise from distinct system-level causes, including non-compiling code, dependency and import issues, and orchestrator-level structural rejections, with failure patterns concentrated in a small subset of workflows. Study 2 evaluates model sufficiency across ten hosted deployment configurations and a paired self-hosted versus provider-hosted comparison for `Qwen3.5-9B`. We observe strong trade-offs between cost, latency, and executability: `gpt-5.4` reaches 0.911 executability, while `gpt-5.4-nano` achieves 0.700 at $0.005 per executable workflow. In the self-hosted setting, `Qwen3.5-9B` improves executability over the hosted variant (0.467 vs. 0.367) but incurs a 5.8× latency overhead. We show that workflow generation requires engine-aware evaluation beyond function-level correctness, and that serving configuration is a first-class factor in deployment performance.

Keywords: executable workflow generation · model sufficiency · cost-aware evaluation · open-weight models · self-hosted inference

1 Introduction

Large language models (LLMs) can now generate plausible workflow code, but deployment turns on a different question: how much model, in which deployment setting, is actually needed to produce workflow code that a target orchestrator will accept. Throughout the paper, we use *serving condition* for that deployment setting: the combination of model, provider or host, and execution setup under which generation is performed. By *workflow code*, we mean a Python artifact defining tasks, dependencies, and orchestration structure for a target engine such as Airflow, Prefect, or Dagster; *workflow* denotes the orchestrated computation represented by that artifact. This follows systems work that treats model

Published by Springer Nature Switzerland AG 2027
D. Balouek et al. (Eds.): ESOCC 2026, LNCS 16834, pp. 52–68, 2027.
https://doi.org/10.1007/978-3-032-37831-6_4

choice and serving configuration as deployment-time decisions rather than fixed background details [4]. In practice, the issue is whether smaller, cheaper, and faster serving conditions can still produce accepted workflows at an acceptable rate, close to the performance of stronger conditions. We call that deployment question *model sufficiency.*

Workflow generation is a stricter and more realistic setting than the function-level benchmarks that commonly dominate LLM-based code evaluation. Benchmarks such as HumanEval [5] and MBPP [3] consist of short, self-contained programming tasks where a model is asked to generate a single function that satisfies a set of unit tests, thus primarily assessing local functional correctness. In contrast, workflow generation requires assembling multiple interdependent components into a coherent executable structure. Beyond producing syntactically valid code, symbols must correctly import under pinned framework versions, dependencies across tasks must be consistently resolved, and the resulting task graph must satisfy the structural and semantic constraints imposed by the target orchestrator (e.g., acyclicity, valid data and control flow, and compatible interfaces between tasks). As a result, even a minor structural inconsistency can invalidate the entire workflow. A generated workflow may therefore appear as valid Python code and still be rejected at deployment or execution time by the orchestrator.

Execution-based evaluation is established for function synthesis and is beginning to reach workflow generation. Existing works include Prompt2DAG that evaluates Airflow DAG prompting strategies with executability-focused scores [2], and WorkflowLLM that introduces a benchmark and fine-tuned model for API-focused workflow tasks [7]. Neither of them examines deployment conditions across multiple orchestration engines under a fixed controller. On the systems side, scaling results and cascaded serving show how capability and cost trade off [4, 9, 11], while quantization methods such as GPTQ, QLoRA, and AWQ make local hosting cheaper [6, 8, 12]. Recent Qwen3/Qwen3.5 releases target code and agentic tasks [13]. Table 1 positions this paper relative to that prior work. What remains missing is a deployment study of how far smaller or cheaper serving conditions can go on workflow-generation tasks when success is normalised by accepted executable workflows rather than by raw request count.

We frame workflow code generation as a deployment problem that leads to these research questions:

RQ1 (Workflow code acceptance): What constitutes acceptable *LLM-generated workflow code* in executable workflow generation, and where do generated workflows fail: at code emission, import/load, or orchestrator-level structural validation?

RQ2 (Model sufficiency): How far can smaller, cheaper, and faster serving conditions go while still producing *LLM-generated workflow code* that an orchestrator will accept at acceptable cost and latency?

To answer these research questions, we define two studies. *Study 1* uses engine-aware executability, gate-level analysis, and workflow-level difficulty analysis across hosted serving conditions and three orchestrators to characterise what

Table 1. Positioning relative to adjacent work. Exec. = execution-based evaluation used as primary outcome; Multi = multiple orchestration engines; Cost = cost-normalised analysis; Open = open-weight models included; Self = self-hosted deployment analysis.

Study	Task	Exec.	Multi	Cost	Open	Self	Unit
Chen et al. [5]	Function synth.	✓	—	—	—	—	Model
Austin et al. [3]	Short programs	✓	—	—	—	—	Model
Prompt2DAG [2]	Workflow/DAG	✓	—	∼	—	—	Method
WorkflowLLM [7]	Workflow orch.	∼	—	—	∼	—	Model
FrugalGPT [4]	LLM serving	—	—	✓	—	—	Service
AWQ [12]	Local inference	—	—	—	✓	✓	System
This work	Workflow code	✓	✓	✓	✓	✓	Condition

constitutes accepted workflow code and to identify where failures arise. *Study 2* examines model sufficiency through the hosted quality–cost frontier and a paired provider-hosted (i.e., third-party managed API inference) versus self-hosted (i.e., a locally deployed model served on user-managed infrastructure) comparison, quantifying the executability, cost-accounting, and latency trade-offs of serving condition and serving mode. Together, these studies provide deployment guidance on when smaller conditions are sufficient and when stronger or differently served conditions justify the additional cost and latency.

The rest of the paper is structured as follows. Section 2 defines workflow code acceptance and model sufficiency. Section 3 describes the methodology and experimental setup. Section 4 reports the results of the studies. The paper then concludes in Sect. 5.

2 Problem Definition

2.1 Workflow Code Acceptance

The task is to translate a natural-language workflow description into a Python artifact that a target orchestrator will accept and execute. Correctness goes beyond Python syntax: each orchestrator imposes specific rules on tasks, dependencies, and graph composition, so code may be syntactically valid yet structurally invalid.

Listing 1.1 shows an example for Airflow. The code imports the appropriate TaskFlow decorators and defines two tasks, but Airflow requires these tasks to be *invoked* within the DAG body to register them and establish dependencies. As a result, the DAG imports successfully but contains no runnable tasks—a framework-contract violation that standard syntax checks do not detect.

We operationalise workflow code acceptance as two sequential validation checks over a generated artifact. *Gate 1* requires that the code is syntactically valid, imports successfully, and can be loaded by the target orchestrator. *Gate 2* requires that the resulting workflow graph satisfies the orchestrator's task, dependency, and composition rules. A workflow is accepted if and only if it passes both gates. We refer to this as *engine-aware executability* (v_{exec}), the primary outcome variable of this study.

Listing 1.1. An example of valid Python code that Airflow imports as an empty DAG.

```
from airflow.decorators import dag, task
from datetime import datetime

@dag(start_date=datetime(2024, 1, 1), schedule="@daily")
def pipeline():

    @task
    def extract():
        return fetch_data()

    @task
    def load(data):
        write_to_db(data)

    # tasks are never called, so Airflow registers an empty DAG

pipeline()
```

For generated workflow attempt i, let $g_{1,i}, g_{2,i} \in \{0,1\}$ denote the binary outcomes of *Gate 1* and *Gate 2* on the same generated artifact. The run-level executable outcome is defined as:

$$v_{\text{exec},i} = g_{1,i} \times g_{2,i}. \tag{1}$$

For a serving condition evaluated over N runs, we report the engine-aware executable rate as:

$$\bar{v}_{\text{exec}} = \frac{1}{N}\sum_{i=1}^{N} v_{\text{exec},i} = \frac{1}{N}\sum_{i=1}^{N} g_{1,i} \times g_{2,i}. \tag{2}$$

We also report the marginal gate rates:

$$\bar{g}_1 = \frac{1}{N}\sum_{i=1}^{N} g_{1,i}, \qquad \bar{g}_2 = \frac{1}{N}\sum_{i=1}^{N} g_{2,i}. \tag{3}$$

For diagnostic interpretation, we additionally use the conditional Gate 2 rate among loadable artifacts:

$$\Pr(g_2 = 1 \mid g_1 = 1) = \frac{\sum_{i=1}^{N} g_{1,i} \times g_{2,i}}{\sum_{i=1}^{N} g_{1,i}}, \quad \text{when } \sum_{i=1}^{N} g_{1,i} > 0. \tag{4}$$

This conditional quantity is a reporting diagnostic: it asks, among generated artifacts that load successfully, how often the orchestrator-structure gate also passes.

2.2 Model Sufficiency

Workflow generation is a *sufficiency* problem rather than a capability-maximisation exercise. For a given workflow task, the practical question is not which serving condition is globally strongest, but which one is good enough to achieve the target executable outcome at the lowest acceptable cost and wall-clock time. Paying for substantially more than that means paying for capability that may go unused.

To make this concrete, we evaluate each serving condition using four quantities:

$\bar{v}_{\text{exec}}$ engine-aware executable rate, that has been defined in the previous section.

c_{actual} actual monetary efficiency, expressed as the average cost in USD required to produce a workflow instance, thus capturing the real economic impact of a serving condition under the adopted generation strategy.

We define actual cost as cost per executable workflow:

$$c_{\text{actual}}(s) = \frac{\sum_{i=1}^{N} c_{\text{total},i}}{\sum_{i=1}^{N} v_{\text{exec},i}}, \quad \text{when } \sum_{i} v_{\text{exec},i} > 0. \tag{5}$$

where $c_{\text{total},i}$ is the API cost of run i, computed from input and output token counts using the provider's published per-million-token price.

$\bar{w}$ operational responsiveness, measured as the mean wall-clock time needed to generate a workflow, reflecting the latency experienced in practical usage scenarios.

We treat latency as an operational constraint rather than a quality signal. For a serving condition s, mean wall-clock time is:

$$\bar{w}(s) = \frac{1}{N}\sum_{i=1}^{N} w_i, \tag{6}$$

where w_i is the wall-clock generation time of run i.

$\bar{\iota}$ mean issue burden, i.e., the average number of issues or error signals produced during generation and validation, providing a proxy for the residual debugging effort required even when executability is achieved.

It is defined as:

$$\bar{\iota}(s) = \frac{1}{N}\sum_{i=1}^{N} \iota_i, \tag{7}$$

where ι_i is the total number of issues flagged by the Gate 1 and Gate 2 checks for run i.

We define a *sufficient condition* as the cheapest serving condition that is good enough to achieve near-best executable quality without incurring a significantly higher issue burden. Rather than selecting the globally strongest condition, we aim to identify the least expensive one whose performance is practically indistinguishable from the best observed outcome.

Operationally, let S be the set of serving conditions under comparison, and let

$$\bar{v}_{\text{exec}}^{\max} = \max_{s \in S} \bar{v}_{\text{exec}}(s)$$

denote the highest observed executable rate. Among the conditions that achieve this level of executability, we define

$$\bar{\iota}^* = \min_{s \in S:\, \bar{v}_{\text{exec}}(s) = \bar{v}_{\text{exec}}^{\max}} \bar{\iota}(s)$$

as the lowest mean issue burden.

We introduce two fixed tolerances: $\delta = 5\,\text{pp}$ (percentage points) on executable rate and $\varepsilon = 1$ issue on mean issue burden. These define practical equivalence with respect to the best-performing conditions. A serving condition $s \in S$ is therefore considered *admissible* if:

1. its executable rate is within δ percentage points of the best observed executable rate;
2. its mean issue burden does not exceed $\bar{\iota}^*$ by more than ε.

Let S_{adm} be the set of admissible conditions:

$$S_{\text{adm}} = \{s \in S : \bar{v}_{\text{exec}}^{\max} - \bar{v}_{\text{exec}}(s) \leq \delta \text{ and } \bar{\iota}(s) - \bar{\iota}^* \leq \varepsilon\}\,. \tag{8}$$

Among these, the *sufficient condition* is the one with minimum actual cost:

$$s^* = \arg\min_{s \in S_{\text{adm}}} c_{\text{actual}}(s), \tag{9}$$

This sufficiency framing identifies the cheapest deployable condition directly, enables fair comparison across serving configurations, and supports escalation when more complex workflows exceed the capabilities of lower-cost conditions. In the empirical study below, we instantiate this rule with fixed values of δ and ε.

3 Methodology and Experimental Setup

This section describes the methodology used to select workflow descriptions, orchestrators, and models, as well as the experimental execution protocol and decision rules.

To the best of our knowledge, there are no publicly available benchmarks that provide workflow or pipeline descriptions paired with their corresponding executable implementations. Based on a targeted literature search and manual inspection of public GitHub repositories and README-style workflow documentation, we did not find a benchmark that jointly offers natural-language workflow descriptions, executable implementations, and evaluation across multiple orchestration engines. We therefore mined public repositories and README files for natural-language pipeline descriptions, then added synthetic descriptions covering common topology patterns.

The collected pipelines were then partitioned based on the availability of executable artifacts. Pipelines for which only a textual description was available were used to construct the set of natural-language task descriptions, which serve as inputs to the models in our experiments. In contrast, pipelines for which an implementation was available (e.g., code defining the workflow or its orchestration) were used to build a curated benchmark, enabling validation and contextualization of the results and supporting a more grounded assessment of executability and structural correctness.

The final corpus consists of ten workflow-generation tasks, five adapted from public repository READMEs and five synthetically generated. In addition, for qualitative context only, we inspect a small auxiliary subset of 15 publicly available workflow implementations from GitHub. This subset is not part of the evaluated corpus and is used solely for descriptive analysis to contrast curated task specifications with real-world workflow structures. Table 2 summarises the corpus and reports structural features used later to interpret workflow acceptance difficulty.

Table 2. Workflow corpus ($N=10$) with structural complexity characteristics. Topology: Lin = linear; StETL = staged ETL; FoFi = fan-out/fan-in; BrMr = branch/merge; FoOnly = fan-out only; SG = sensor-gated.

Pipeline	Source	Topology	Domain	# tasks	Edges	Parallel tasks	Branches
Government Data Integration Pipeline	Real	StETL	Government	24	30	2	0
Triggered Sales ETL	Synthetic	SG	Sales	3	2	0	1
Healthcare Case Data Integration	Real	FoFi	Healthcare	24	39	3	0
Fraud Detection Triage	Synthetic	BrMr	Fraud	5	5	0	0
Multi-Region E-Commerce Analytics	Synthetic	FoFi	E-commerce	11	13	2	0
Multi-Channel Marketing Campaign	Synthetic	FoOnly	Marketing	4	3	1	0
E-Commerce Customer Sync	Real	Lin	E-commerce	3	2	0	0
Genomic Data Analysis	Real	Lin	Genomics	2	1	0	0
Healthcare Claims Processing	Synthetic	StETL	Healthcare	5	4	2	0
PM2.5 Air Quality Pipeline	Real	Lin	Air quality	3	2	0	0

All workflows are expressed in Python, as it is the primary language adopted by Apache Airflow, one of the most widely used workflow orchestrators. Its adoption in other orchestration frameworks such as Prefect and Dagster further enables comparative studies across execution environments. To reduce environment drift and ensure reproducibility, we use pinned software versions throughout the setup: Python 3.12.3, Apache Airflow 2.8.4, Prefect 3.6.7, and Dagster 1.12.7.

The cohort of LLMs evaluated in this study is designed to cover practical deployment configurations rather than to be exhaustive. We therefore sample practically relevant deployment tiers: frontier hosted models, lower-cost hosted tiers, open-weight hosted models, and one self-hosted open-weight configuration. This keeps the comparison deployment-oriented while preserving a manageable experimental matrix, with local hardware enabling controlled self-hosted evaluation without reliance on external APIs.

The resulting cohort includes frontier proprietary hosted tiers, lower-cost proprietary tiers, and open-weight models evaluated under a common experimental harness. Table 3 summarises the model cohort, serving endpoints, and pricing. For each provider-hosted model, we report the technical profile and published costs, while the self-hosted configuration incurs no provider-billed API cost.

Hosted Qwen models are accessed via DeepInfra's OpenAI-compatible endpoint. The hosted Qwen cohort includes `Qwen3.5-9B`, `Qwen3-14B`, `Qwen3-32B`, and `Qwen3-235B`, reflecting availability at benchmark time. Proprietary OpenAI and Claude models are accessed through their respective provider APIs. The self-hosted condition runs a `Qwen3.5-9B` GGUF checkpoint under `Q4_K_M` quantization via LM Studio on a Mac Mini M4 Pro with 48 GB of unified memory. Across all conditions, temperature is fixed at 0.0 and the maximum number of output tokens at 10 000.

For the paired provider-hosted versus self-hosted `Qwen3.5-9B` comparison, the self-hosted checkpoint is configured with `Q4_K_M` quantization, a context length of 100 000 tokens, and parallel generation set to 1. Qwen-family models are operated in non-thinking, direct-response mode wherever supported by the runtime. As provider-hosted and self-hosted environments rely on different mechanisms to enforce this setting, this analysis is interpreted as a comparison of deployment modalities rather than a strict checkpoint-level equivalence.

Each experimental condition is evaluated across 10 pipelines, 3 orchestrators, and 3 repetitions, yielding 90 runs per condition and 990 runs overall. Repetitions are retained even under temperature-zero decoding, as serving-stack and runtime effects may still introduce variability across nominally identical requests. Three repetitions are sufficient to expose gross failures and to distinguish conditions that differ by more than the practical 5 pp margin, as differences of this magnitude consistently manifest across repeated runs, although they are not intended to support fine-grained statistical claims on smaller differences.

For the aggregate hosted comparison, we instantiate the sufficiency rule with $\delta = 5$ pp and $\varepsilon = 1$ issue. The executable-rate margin is practical rather than statistical, and the $\varepsilon = 1$ issue tolerance treats one additional validation issue per run on average as an acceptable residual debugging burden difference.

At the per-pipeline level, each model–pipeline cell contains only nine runs. In this setting, the executable-rate margin $\delta = 5$ pp does not affect selection, as it does not change the set of models tied for the best executable rate on any pipeline. We therefore adopt a reduced pipeline-level rule: for each pipeline, we consider only the conditions achieving the best observed executable rate, retain those whose mean issue burden lies within $\varepsilon = 1$ of the lowest-issue condition in that set, and select the minimum-cost condition.

For proprietary models, we refer to vendor-assigned tier labels (e.g., *nano*, *mini*, *Haiku*, *Sonnet*, *Opus*), as parameter counts are not publicly disclosed. These labels denote relative service tiers within each provider and should not be interpreted as a uniform measure of model size across providers.

Table 3. Model cohort and provider pricing (April 1, 2026).

Model	Endpoint / checkpoint	Family	Scale	In $/M	Out $/M
Q3.5-9B (self)	GGUF Q4_K_M/LM Studio	Qwen3.5	9B	—	—
Q3.5-9B (provider)	Qwen/Qwen3.5-9B @ DeepInfra	Qwen3.5	9B	0.04	0.20
Q3-14B	Qwen/Qwen3-14B @ DeepInfra	Qwen3	14B	0.12	0.24
Q3-32B	Qwen/Qwen3-32B @ DeepInfra	Qwen3	32B	0.08	0.28
Q3-235B	Qwen/Qwen3-235B @ DeepInfra	Qwen3	235B	0.071	0.10
gpt-5.4-nano	gpt-5.4-nano @ OpenAI	OpenAI	Small	0.20	1.25
gpt-5.4-mini	gpt-5.4-mini @ OpenAI	OpenAI	Med.	0.75	4.50
gpt-5.4	gpt-5.4 @ OpenAI	OpenAI	Large	2.50	15.00
claude-haiku	claude-haiku-4-5-20251001 @ Anthropic	Claude	Small	1.00	5.00
claude-sonnet	claude-sonnet-4-5-20250929 @ Anthropic	Claude	Med.	3.00	15.00
claude-opus	claude-opus-4-5-20251101 @ Anthropic	Claude	Large	5.00	25.00

4 Results and Discussion

4.1 Study 1a: Where Accepted Workflow Code Fails

Table 4 shows that hosted models can fail in different ways even when their final executable rates look similar. The strongest proprietary models, `gpt-5.4`, `claude-opus`, and `claude-sonnet`, have nearly flat gate profiles: their marginal Gate 1 rates are almost identical to their final executable rates, and their conditional Gate 2 success rates are effectively perfect. In practice, this means that once these models generate loadable code, they almost always also satisfy the orchestrator's structural constraints. Their residual failures therefore arise primarily before or at loadability rather than at graph composition.

The hosted Qwen conditions are more heterogeneous. `Q3-235B` reaches the same Gate 1 and executable rate (0.689), with perfect conditional Gate 2 success, so its failures are concentrated entirely at Gate 1. `Q3-32B` is the main exception in the hosted cohort: it reaches a Gate 1 rate of 0.700 and an executable rate of 0.689, with a conditional Gate 2 success rate of 0.984. This indicates a small but non-zero residual class of Gate 2 failures after code becomes loadable. Mean issue burden provides a secondary discriminator among otherwise similar gate profiles: for example, `claude-opus` is cleaner than `gpt-5.4` among the strongest hosted models, while the hosted Qwen models that achieve non-zero executability carry the highest residual issue burden. The most striking case is `Q3-14B`, which produces no executable workflows at all. Its Gate 1 rate is 0.000, while its marginal Gate 2 rate is just 0.011. Inspection of the failure logs shows that these failures are dominated by `PyCompileError`, indicating an output-contract failure in which the model does not reliably produce valid Python code. Under the present serving and prompting configuration, this model is not viable as a direct workflow-code generator.

Taken together, the gate decomposition shows that, for most hosted models in this corpus, failures are concentrated at Gate 1 and rarely at Gate 2. The important exception is Q3-32B, which retains a small amount of post-load structural failure. This is why executable rate alone is not enough: it tells us which models fail, but not whether the problem lies in code emission/loadability or in orchestrator-level structure.

Table 4. Hosted gate-level results with mean issue burden. † Q3-14B produced no executable workflows.

Model	Family	$\bar{g}_1$	$\bar{g}_2$	$\Pr(g_2{=}1 \mid g_1{=}1)$	$\bar{v}_{\text{exec}}$	$\bar{\iota}$
gpt-5.4-nano	OpenAI	0.700	0.944	1.000	0.700	11.89
gpt-5.4-mini	OpenAI	0.656	0.944	1.000	0.656	13.14
gpt-5.4	OpenAI	0.911	1.000	1.000	0.911	13.54
claude-haiku	Claude	0.633	1.000	1.000	0.633	13.78
claude-sonnet	Claude	0.744	0.989	1.000	0.744	12.47
claude-opus	Claude	0.878	1.000	1.000	0.878	12.18
Q3.5-9B	Qwen3.5	0.367	0.667	1.000	0.367	13.12
Q3-14B	Qwen3	0.000	0.011	—	0.000	—†
Q3-32B	**Qwen3**	**0.700**	**0.900**	**0.984**	**0.689**	**14.67**
Q3-235B	Qwen3	0.689	1.000	1.000	0.689	14.56

4.2 Study 1b: Which Workflows Are Hard to Get Accepted

Workflow difficulty is far from uniform. Table 5 shows that three pipelines stand out as the hardest in the hosted evaluation: Government Data Integration Pipeline, Triggered Sales ETL, and Healthcare Case Data Integration. At the other end, PM2.5 Air Quality Pipeline is the easiest overall. The gap is substantial, and even the strongest hosted models do not fully saturate the hardest cases.

The gate profile helps explain why these workflows are difficult. For nine of the ten pipelines, $\bar{g}_1$ and $\bar{v}_{\text{exec}}$ are identical, indicating that difficulty is concentrated primarily at import/load rather than at residual post-load structural validation. Only Multi-Channel Marketing Campaign shows a small gap between Gate 1 and final executability, suggesting that workflow hardness in this corpus is usually driven by producing loadable orchestrator-conformant code in the first place.

Table 2 suggests that the three hardest workflows draw their difficulty from different structural sources. Government Data Integration Pipeline combines 24 tasks, 30 dependency edges, and multiple parallel regions, demanding long-range consistency across a large artifact. Triggered Sales ETL is small in task count but includes an explicit gating condition, making it brittle to semantic omissions. Healthcare Case Data Integration combines breadth, many dependency edges, and multi-system coordination, suggesting that join-heavy integration structure is an independent source of difficulty. Step count alone does not explain acceptance difficulty.

A simple descriptive rule summarises this pattern on the present corpus: a workflow is *structurally demanding* if either its combined task-and-edge count exceeds 30 or it contains at least one explicit gate condition. On this ten-workflow corpus, that rule isolates exactly the three lowest-executability workflows from the remaining seven. We do not present it as a universal classifier; rather, it provides a compact description of where acceptance difficulty concentrates.

Table 5. Hosted workflow difficulty (hardest workflows are shown in bold).

Pipeline	$\bar{g}_1$	$\bar{g}_2$	$\bar{v}_{\text{exec}}$
Government Data Integration Pipeline	**0.432**	**0.802**	**0.432**
Triggered Sales ETL	**0.457**	**0.864**	**0.457**
Healthcare Case Data Integration	**0.580**	**0.852**	**0.580**
Fraud Detection Triage	0.667	0.889	0.667
Multi-Region E-Commerce Analytics	0.679	0.852	0.679
Multi-Channel Marketing Campaign	**0.716**	**0.877**	**0.704**
E-Commerce Customer Sync	0.741	0.864	0.741
Genomic Data Analysis	0.753	0.889	0.753
Healthcare Claims Processing	0.753	0.877	0.753
PM2.5 Air Quality Pipeline	0.790	0.889	0.790

These workflow differences matter operationally because they help explain why the lowest-cost feasible choice varies by pipeline. At this granularity, each model–pipeline cell contains only nine runs, and in the present data the executable-rate margin $\delta = 5\,\text{pp}$ does not change any pipeline-level selection relative to the models tied for the best executable rate. Table 6 therefore reports a reduced pipeline-level rule: for each pipeline, we consider only the conditions attaining the best observed executable rate, retain those whose mean issue burden lies within $\varepsilon = 1$ of the lowest-issue condition in that best-performing set, and then select the minimum-cost condition.

The resulting sufficient conditions are heterogeneous. Some pipelines admit relatively inexpensive choices, including `gpt-5.4-nano`, `Q3-32B`, and `claude-haiku`, while the two hardest pipelines, Triggered Sales ETL and Healthcare Case Data Integration, select `gpt-5.4`. The issue-aware rule also matters: several pipelines do not retain the cheapest exact-best model once issue burden is taken into account. Mean wall time is reported alongside the selected condition as an operational diagnostic, which is especially important when a model looks attractive on cost but is slow enough to be operationally awkward.

Table 6. Pipeline-level sufficient conditions under the issue-aware exact-best rule.

Pipeline	$\bar{v}_{\text{exec}}^{\max}$	$\bar{\iota}^*$	$\bar{\iota}(s^*)$	$c_{\text{actual}}(s^*)$	$\bar{w}(s^*)$	s^*
Government Data Integration Pipeline	0.778	15.3	15.3	0.02404	16.2	claude-haiku
Triggered Sales ETL	0.889	13.0	13.0	0.02406	15.7	gpt-5.4
Healthcare Case Data Integration	1.000	12.7	12.7	0.04178	27.5	gpt-5.4
Fraud Detection Triage	1.000	13.1	13.1	0.06884	27.7	claude-opus
Multi-Region E-Commerce Analytics	1.000	13.8	13.8	0.00988	8.5	claude-haiku
Multi-Channel Marketing Campaign	1.000	10.6	10.6	0.00224	9.8	gpt-5.4-nano
E-Commerce Customer Sync	1.000	11.0	11.0	0.02880	19.8	claude-sonnet
Genomic Data Analysis	1.000	13.4	14.3	0.00053	21.8	Q3-32B
Healthcare Claims Processing	1.000	11.7	11.7	0.05266	38.9	claude-sonnet
PM2.5 Air Quality Pipeline	1.000	8.7	8.7	0.07252	28.3	claude-opus

4.3 Study 2a: Hosted Model Sufficiency

Figure 1 gives the hosted quality–cost frontier, while Table 7 applies the paper's sufficiency rule to the hosted cohort. The frontier view remains useful because several models occupy interesting tradeoff positions, but the sufficiency analysis is more selective.

Under the hosted sufficiency rule, only two conditions are admissible: `gpt-5.4` and `claude-opus`. `gpt-5.4` achieves the highest executable rate in the hosted cohort, and `claude-opus` remains within the executable-rate and issue-burden tolerance band. Among those admissible conditions, however, `gpt-5.4` has the lower actual cost per executable workflow, making it the sufficient hosted condition.

Table 7. Model sufficiency results.

Model	Fam.	$\bar{v}_{\text{exec}}$	Δ_{exec} (pp)	$\bar{\iota}$	Δ_{ι}	c_{actual}	$\bar{w}$ (s)	Status
gpt-5.4	OAI	0.911	0.0	13.54	0.00	0.03185	20.6	sufficient
claude-opus	Cla	0.878	3.3	12.18	1.37	0.09510	32.0	admissible
claude-sonnet	Cla	0.744	16.7	12.47	-1.08	0.06517	33.5	–
gpt-5.4-nano	OAI	0.700	21.1	11.89	-1.66	0.00503	15.4	–
Q3-235B	Q3	0.689	22.2	14.56	1.01	0.00025	597.3	–
Q3-32B	Q3	0.689	22.2	14.67	1.12	0.00132	38.8	–
gpt-5.4-mini	OAI	0.656	25.6	13.14	-0.40	0.01054	8.2	–
claude-haiku	Cla	0.633	27.8	13.78	0.23	0.01610	9.3	–
Q3.5-9B	Q3.5	0.367	54.4	13.12	-0.42	0.00119	12.4	–
Q3-14B[†]	Q3	0.000	91.1	—	—	—	12.6	–

The other hosted models remain informative as frontier points but do not meet the sufficiency bar. `gpt-5.4-nano` is the strongest proprietary cost-efficiency point, while `Q3-32B` offers a comparatively inexpensive open-weight alternative. `Q3-235B` is especially striking because its actual cost per executable workflow is extremely low, yet its mean wall time of 597 s makes it operationally unattractive for most settings. At the other extreme, `Q3-14B` is not viable under the present configuration, producing no executable workflows at all.

The main lesson is that being on the hosted quality–cost frontier does not necessarily make a model the sufficient hosted condition. The frontier includes attractive low-cost and open-weight options, but once executable quality and issue burden constraints are enforced, the sufficient hosted condition narrows to `gpt-5.4`.

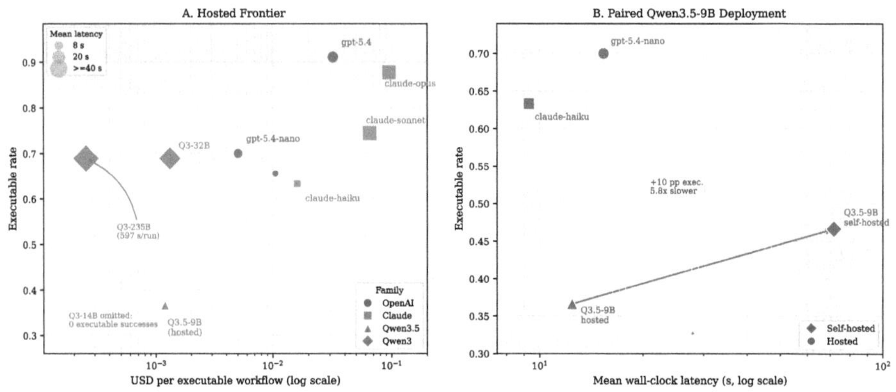

Fig. 1. (A) Hosted quality–cost frontier. The x-axis shows actual cost in USD per executable workflow on a log scale, the y-axis shows executable rate, and marker size indicates mean wall-clock time. Q3-14B is omitted because it produced no executable workflows; Q3-235B is annotated separately because its very high latency limits practical use despite low cost. (B) Paired provider-hosted versus self-hosted comparison for Qwen3.5-9B. The self-hosted condition is more executable but substantially slower than the provider-hosted condition.

4.4 Study 2b: Does Serving Mode Change the Result?

The hosted sufficiency analysis showed that open-weight conditions can be cost-attractive but uneven in executability. This subsection asks a narrower question: does serving mode change outcomes within the same nominal model class? For `Q3.5-9B`, the answer is yes. The self-hosted Mac Mini condition achieves a higher executable rate than the provider-hosted DeepInfra condition, but at a substantial wall-time penalty. Table 8 places that paired comparison alongside two entry-tier proprietary hosted baselines for context. The self-hosted result should be interpreted conservatively. Of the 90 planned runs, 84 completed and 6 did not produce a final artifact; those non-completions are counted as non-executable outcomes. Even under that conservative accounting, self-hosted `Q3.5-9B` improves on provider-hosted `Q3.5-9B` in executable rate, while remaining substantially slower. Both deployment modes nevertheless trail the entry-tier proprietary baselines on executable quality, and the self-hosted condition trails them heavily on wall time.

The self-hosted failures were concentrated and not diffuse. All six non-completions were generation-time failures in which the model response could not be parsed into valid Python, so no executable artifact was produced. They were confined to two pipeline–orchestrator combinations: *Healthcare Case Data Integration* under Airflow and *E-Commerce Customer Sync* under Dagster, with all three repetitions failing in each case. This concentration suggests a systematic workflow–orchestrator interaction effect and not ordinary run-to-run variance. By contrast, the provider-hosted `Q3.5-9B` condition completed all planned runs, and its failures were concentrated after generation at the import/load and executability stage.

Table 8. Paired provider-hosted versus self-hosted comparison for `Q3.5-9B`, with small-tier proprietary hosted baselines. Rates use planned-run denominators; the six self-hosted non-completions are counted as non-executable outcomes. The c_{actual} column is reported in USD per executable workflow. ⋆ Local cost is not yet instrumented.

Model	Planned	Completed	$\bar{g}_1$	$\bar{g}_2$	$\bar{v}_{\text{exec}}$	$\bar{w}$ (s)	c_{actual}
Q3.5-9B (self-hosted)	90	84	0.500	0.867	0.467	71.7	—⋆
Q3.5-9B (hosted)	90	90	0.367	0.667	0.367	12.4	0.00119
gpt-5.4-nano	90	90	0.700	0.944	0.700	15.4	0.00503
claude-haiku	90	90	0.633	1.000	0.633	9.3	0.01610

Table 9 shows that the deployment effect is pipeline-sensitive and not uniform. The largest self-hosted gains occur on Genomic Data Analysis and E-Commerce Customer Sync, while the largest losses occur on Multi-Channel Marketing Campaign and Triggered Sales ETL. Several pipelines show no difference at all, including two on which both deployment modes fail completely. The practical lesson is that serving mode should be treated as part of the system design: switching from hosted to self-hosted changes not only overall executability and wall time, but also which workflows are helped or hurt.

4.5 Pulling the Findings Together

A practical deployment rule emerges from the two studies: start with the smallest condition likely to work, validate the result with framework-aware gate checks, and escalate only when workflow structure or repeated failures justify it.

Study 1 shows that aggregate executable rate alone is an incomplete diagnostic. A workflow that looks like valid Python can still fail at import/load or at

Table 9. Per-pipeline paired provider-hosted versus self-hosted comparison for Q3.5-9B. Positive Δ_{exec} values favour self-hosted.

Pipeline	$\bar{v}^{\text{self}}_{\text{exec}}$	$\bar{v}^{\text{host}}_{\text{exec}}$	Δ_{exec} (pp)	$\bar{w}^{\text{self}}$ (s)
Government Data Integration Pipeline	0.000	0.000	±0	98.3
Triggered Sales ETL	0.333	0.667	−33.3	27.2
Healthcare Case Data Integration†	0.000	0.000	±0	164.4
Fraud Detection Triage	0.667	0.667	±0	74.4
Multi-Region E-Commerce Analytics	0.667	0.667	±0	110.1
Multi-Channel Marketing Campaign	0.333	0.667	−33.3	34.2
E-Commerce Customer Sync†	0.667	0.000	+66.7	52.9
Genomic Data Analysis	0.667	0.000	+66.7	35.0
Healthcare Claims Processing	0.667	0.667	±0	73.0
PM2.5 Air Quality Pipeline	0.667	0.333	+33.3	72.3

orchestrator-level structural validation. In this corpus, most hosted failures are concentrated at Gate 1, so the first question for an underperforming model is not simply whether it fails, but where it fails.

The hardest workflows in the corpus are not explained by task count alone. Difficulty concentrates in workflows with long-range dependencies, explicit gating semantics, or broad coordination requirements. By contrast, the small auxiliary GitHub subset is dominated by linear DAGs (10/15, 66.7%), suggesting that some sampled public workflows may be structurally simpler than the hardest cases in this corpus. This helps explain why the lowest-cost feasible condition varies by pipeline rather than collapsing to a single universal choice.

The most decision-relevant cost metric is not cost per request but cost per executable workflow. Under the hosted sufficiency rule, `gpt-5.4` is the sufficient hosted condition: it achieves the best executable rate and remains cheaper per executable workflow than the only other admissible condition, `claude-opus`. At the same time, the broader provider-hosted frontier still contains useful tradeoff points, including `gpt-5.4-nano` as the strongest proprietary cost-efficiency point and `Q3-32B` as a comparatively inexpensive open-weight alternative. Extremely cheap options such as `Q3-235B` are only attractive when their latency is acceptable.

Study 2 shows that serving mode changes outcomes even within the same nominal model class. Self-hosted `Qwen3.5-9B` improves executable rate over its provider-hosted counterpart, but at a substantial wall-time penalty, and the effect is pipeline-sensitive rather than uniform. The practical lesson is not that self-hosting is always better; it is that deployment modality is itself a design choice that should be evaluated alongside model family, cost, and latency.

5 Conclusion

We evaluated eleven serving conditions through two linked studies on ten workflow-generation tasks across three orchestrators under a fixed direct single-shot controller. The main findings are that `gpt-5.4` is the sufficient hosted condition, `gpt-5.4-nano` is the strongest proprietary cost-efficiency point, `Q3-32B` is the most attractive low-cost open-weight option when latency is acceptable, workflow difficulty concentrates in structurally demanding pipelines, gate-level analysis distinguishes compilation failures such as `Q3-14B` from narrower capability gaps, and self-hosted Qwen3.5-9B improves executable rate over the provider-hosted condition (0.467 vs. 0.367) at a 5.8x latency penalty.

The practical lesson is to start with the smallest condition likely to work, validate outputs with framework-aware gate checks, choose by cost per executable workflow rather than cost per request, and escalate only when workflow structure or repeated failures justify it. These findings should nevertheless be read as deployment evidence rather than as a universal ranking of LLMs for workflow generation, given the small corpus, the use of engine-aware executability as a deployment-boundary proxy, the coarse three-repetition comparison design, and the modality-sensitive self-hosted versus provider-hosted Qwen3.5-9B comparison. Natural next steps are direct energy instrumentation, a larger corpus, and a lightweight classifier based on the structural features in Table 2 to operationalise the routing pattern in Table 6.

Acknowledgment.. This work has been partially funded by the European innovation actions *DataPACT* (HE 101189771).

Data and Artifact Availability.. Workflow task descriptions are archived on Zenodo [1]; prompts, evaluation scripts, and aggregate result tables are provided as companion GitHub material [10].

References

1. Alidu, A., Ciavotta, M., De Paoli, F.: Structured ETL and data-preparation pipeline descriptions for LLM workflow generation studies (2026)
2. Alidu, A., Ciavotta, M., DePaoli, F.: Prompt2dag: a modular methodology for llm-based data enrichment pipeline generation. arXiv preprint arXiv:2509.13487 (2025). https://doi.org/10.48550/arXiv.2509.13487
3. Austin, J., et al.: Program synthesis with large language models. arXiv preprint arXiv:2108.07732 (2021). https://doi.org/10.48550/arXiv.2108.07732
4. Chen, L., Zaharia, M., Zou, J.Y.: Frugalgpt: how to use large language models while reducing cost and improving performance. arXiv preprint arXiv:2305.05176 (2023)
5. Chen, M.: Evaluating large language models trained on code, arXiv preprint arXiv:2107.03374 (2021)
6. Dettmers, T., Pagnoni, A., Holtzman, A., Zettlemoyer, L.: Qlora: efficient fine-tuning of quantized llms. In: Advances in Neural Information Processing Systems, vol. 36 (2023). https://arxiv.org/abs/2305.14314

7. Fan, S., et al.: Workflowllm: enhancing workflow orchestration capability of large language models. arXiv preprint arXiv:2411.05451 (2024)
8. Frantar, E., Ashkboos, S., Hoefler, T., Alistarh, D.: Gptq: accurate post-training quantization for generative pre-trained transformers. arXiv preprint arXiv:2210.17323 (2022). https://doi.org/10.48550/arXiv.2210.17323
9. Hoffmann, J., et al.: Training compute-optimal large language models. In: Advances in Neural Information Processing Systems, vol. 35, pp. 30016–30030 (2022). https://arxiv.org/abs/2203.15556
10. I2Tunimib: Prompt2DAG companion repository (2026). https://github.com/I2Tunimib/prompt2dag.git, gitHub repository
11. Kaplan, J., et al.: Scaling laws for neural language models. arXiv preprint arXiv:2001.08361 (2020). https://doi.org/10.48550/arXiv.2001.08361
12. Lin, J., et al.: Awq: activation-aware weight quantization for llm compression and acceleration. arXiv preprint arXiv:2306.00978 (2023). https://doi.org/10.48550/arXiv.2306.00978
13. Yang, A., et al.: Qwen3 technical report. arXiv preprint arXiv:2505.09388 (2025). https://doi.org/10.48550/arXiv.2505.09388

Bandwidth-Aware Execution Time and Energy Predictor for Secure Inference Services

Tanjina Islam[1(✉)], Ana Oprescu[1], Zoltán Ádám Mann[2], and Sander Klous[1]

[1] University of Amsterdam, Amsterdam, The Netherlands
t.islam@uva.nl
[2] University of Münster, Münster, Germany

Abstract. In Machine-Learning-as-a-Service, secure neural network inference (SNNI) enables privacy-preserving inference by protecting the client's input, output, and model parameters. The cryptographic techniques used in SNNI introduce significant computation and communication overhead, resulting in high energy consumption. Prior work on energy-efficient SNNI selection ignores network bandwidth, which affects both execution time and energy consumption due to the large volume of client-server data transfer. Existing ML energy prediction approaches focus on non-secure inference and overlook the overhead of cryptographic operations and communication in SNNI. We address this gap with GreenSIP, a bandwidth-aware approach for estimating SNNI energy consumption and execution time for a given neural network (NN). By considering both computation and communication overheads, GreenSIP guides the bandwidth-aware selection of energy-efficient SNNI–NN combinations that satisfy client-specific constraints. To our knowledge, it is the first method to incorporate network bandwidth into SNNI energy prediction. Experimental results confirm its effectiveness and practicality for adaptive, energy-efficient secure inference services.

Keywords: Machine Learning as a Service · Network bandwidth · Secure neural network inference · Energy consumption · Privacy-preserving machine learning

1 Introduction

Artificial intelligence (AI), particularly machine learning (ML), has been widely adopted in the past few years [18]. Neural networks (NNs) have achieved particularly good performance and are frequently used. ML service deployments have also raised strong awareness of privacy concerns. As a result, the field of privacy-preserving machine learning has gained significant attention [1]. The adoption of distributed ML services in privacy-sensitive applications has particularly driven interest in secure neural network inference (SNNI), which enables inference with NNs without revealing sensitive inputs and NN parameters.

Published by Springer Nature Switzerland AG 2027
D. Balouek et al. (Eds.): ESOCC 2026, LNCS 16834, pp. 69–86, 2027.
https://doi.org/10.1007/978-3-032-37831-6_5

SNNI refers to performing ML model inference in a client-server setup, where the server possesses a trained NN and the client provides an input for the NN [14]. This is particularly relevant in Machine Learning as a Service (MLaaS), where a cloud service provider offers inference as a service to clients, applying pre-trained models to clients' private input data. The aim of SNNI is that the client obtains the inference output while protecting sensitive data and model parameters. Input and output are not revealed to the service provider, and the NN parameters are not revealed to the client. As Fig. 1 shows, the client obtains $f(x)$ on their private input x, ensuring that both x and f remain secret.

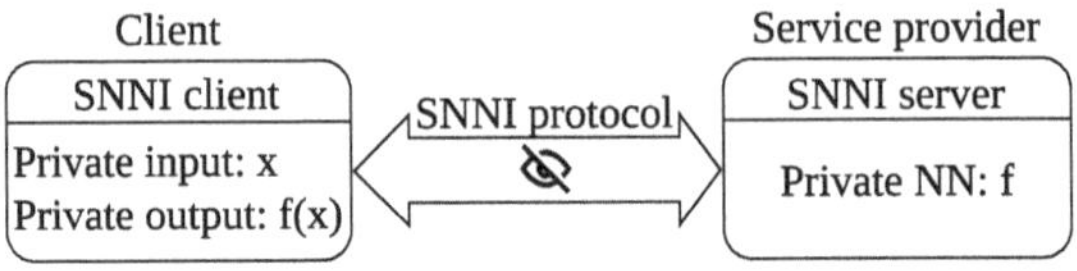

Fig. 1. Overview of SNNI in the MLaaS setting.

Several approaches have been proposed for SNNI based on cryptographic techniques, like homomorphic encryption (HE) and secure multiparty computation (MPC) [14]. These techniques guarantee privacy, but incur significant computation and communication overhead compared to non-secure inference, thus leading to high energy consumption [11,12]. The energy efficiency of SNNI has received little attention, despite its importance [16]. With the growing carbon footprint of ICT (Information and Communication Technology), reducing energy consumption is crucial. Thus, selecting an energy-efficient SNNI approach is important to balance privacy, performance, and energy efficiency in MLaaS.

In earlier work, we proposed a framework for selecting energy-efficient SNNI approaches [11]. Clients can specify the minimum required accuracy and the maximum allowed execution time in their inference requests. The framework selects the combination of NN and SNNI approach with the lowest energy consumption that satisfies the given constraints. However, that framework disregards the impact of the client's network capabilities. This is problematic because SNNI protocols transfer large amounts of data between client and server; thus, bandwidth limitations can lead to significantly higher execution time and energy consumption [16]. Different clients may have very different network connections to the server, with different bandwidths. The bandwidth may influence (i) which combinations of NN and SNNI approaches satisfy the given constraint on execution time and (ii) which of them have the lowest energy consumption. To solve this problem, a prediction mechanism is needed to estimate the execution time and energy consumption of SNNI for a given network bandwidth.

Recent work on energy prediction in ML focused on non-secure inference [3,6]. These works demonstrate the efficacy of energy consumption prediction, but disregard the compute and communication overheads of cryptographic mechanisms in SNNI. Unlike non-secure inference, the energy consumption of SNNI is influenced not only by the NN architecture and local hardware but also by cryptographic operations, interactions between client and server, and their network connection. Thus, energy prediction for SNNI fundamentally differs from that for standard inference, as it depends on bandwidth and communication behavior.

We address this gap by proposing GreenSIP (Green Secure Inference Predictor), a bandwidth-aware prediction approach for estimating the energy consumption and execution time of SNNI. GreenSIP profiles SNNI protocols and NNs across varying network bandwidth levels and trains analytical prediction models using the measured values. By explicitly accounting for both computation and communication costs, our approach enables energy-efficient and bandwidth-aware selection of an SNNI–NN pair for client devices operating under different network bandwidths. We make the following contributions:

- Design a prediction approach, GreenSIP, that estimates energy consumption and execution time of SNNI for a given NN under varying network bandwidth levels. To our knowledge, GreenSIP is the first solution to this problem.
- Develop analytical models using linear regression, linking network bandwidth to computation and communication-related energy and execution time.
- Experimentally substantiate the efficacy of GreenSIP in accurately predicting the energy consumption and execution time of SNNI across varied bandwidths.
- Show the practical applicability of GreenSIP in guiding the selection of energy-efficient SNNI–NN combinations tailored to client constraints in MLaaS.

2 Problem Statement

We aim to accurately estimate the energy consumption and execution time of an SNNI approach for a given NN under varying network bandwidths. For this, we need bandwidth-aware prediction models that account for both computation and communication costs of the SNNI protocol, enabling energy-efficient and bandwidth-aware selection of SNNI–NN for different clients.

Formally, we assume that the service provider supports a finite set S of SNNI approaches and a finite set N of NNs. (In practice, we expect both S and N to contain a handful of elements.) A client submits an inference request to the server. The network bandwidth between client and server is $b \in \mathbb{R}^+$. The inputs of the prediction problem are an SNNI approach $s \in S$, a NN $n \in N$, and the bandwidth $b \in \mathbb{R}^+$. The outputs are $E(s, n, b)$ and $T(s, n, b)$, estimates of the energy consumption and the execution time, respectively, of running SNNI approach s with NN n on a client-server network connection with bandwidth b.

The prediction should be fast, *i.e.*, it should be significantly faster than performing the inference and measuring its energy consumption and execution time. The prediction should yield estimates close to actual energy consumption and execution time. Such a predictor is useful for the service provider: for a client with bandwidth b, it enables computing and comparing predictions for all $s \in S$ and $n \in N$. Thus, the service provider can identify the most energy-efficient (s, n) pair that satisfies the client's execution time constraint.

3 Proposed Approach

GreenSIP uses analytical models to capture the dependence of energy consumption and execution time of SNNI on network bandwidth. We use profiling to train the analytical models to reflect the behavior of specific SNNI approaches on specific NNs. Figure 2 illustrates the three phases of GreenSIP: instrumentation, data collection, and model construction, each explained next in detail.

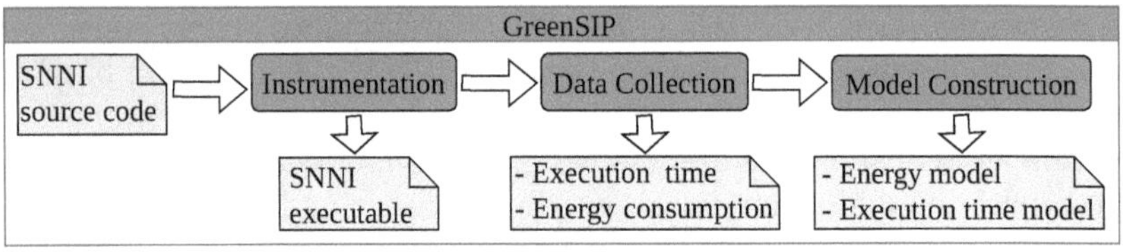

Fig. 2. Overview of our proposed approach – GreenSIP.

3.1 Instrumentation for Profiling

To generate data required for training the proposed prediction models, we first profile the execution time and power consumption of SNNI. For this purpose, we instrument the source code of the selected SNNI protocols: we identify the start and end points of SNNI protocol execution in the source code of the used SNNI library and inject calls to measurement hooks to record execution time and power consumption. We then build the instrumented SNNI executable.

We profile execution time and power consumption of the client machine during the secure inference process. We execute the instrumented code on our test infrastructure (see Sect. 4), and log the start and end time of the SNNI execution on the client side. Execution time is then calculated as the difference between these two system timestamps and is measured in milliseconds (ms). In parallel, we record the client's system power usage by periodically querying the Linux Hardware Monitoring (hwmon)[1] interface.. To avoid missing samples, we query the power meter every 10 ms. Power readings, logged with corresponding timestamps, are measured in microwatts and milliseconds, respectively. After profiling, the client's total energy consumption (Joules) is computed as the integral of system power usage over time, approximated using trapezoidal integration of the

[1] https://www.kernel.org/doc/Documentation/hwmon/sysfs-interface.

collected readings. Profiled execution time and energy consumption include both computation and network communication in the SNNI protocol.

GreenSIP could be used with any open-source SNNI approach. Our proof-of-concept implementation of GreenSIP uses two SNNI approaches: Cheetah and CryptFlow2 (SCI_HE), both available in the OpenCheetah SNNI library[2].

3.2 Data Collection

Using the instrumented SNNI code, we collect execution time and energy measurements for different SNNI–NN pairs with varying network bandwidths. For each SNNI approach $s \in S$ and NN $n \in N$, we define a set $B_{s,n}$ of representative bandwidths, containing at least three values ranging from low to high bandwidths observed in practice. We fix a number $k_{s,n} \in \mathbb{Z}^+$, specifying the number of repeated profiling runs. Both $B_{s,n}$ and $k_{s,n}$ may vary across SNNI–NN pairs.

For each SNNI approach $s \in S$ and NN $n \in N$, we iterate through $B_{s,n}$. For each $b \in B_{s,n}$, we set the bandwidth between client and server in our test infrastructure to b, and then run the instrumented code of s on n $k_{s,n}$ times. In run i $(1 \leq i \leq k_{s,n})$, let $\widehat{E}$ and $\widehat{T}$ be the measured energy consumption and execution time, respectively. We record the tuples $(s, n, b, i, \widehat{E})$ and $(s, n, b, i, \widehat{T})$ in our dataset of energy and execution time measurements, respectively.

Most SNNI approaches are tailored to specific types of NNs. Prior work mainly focused on image classification tasks, with standard open-source convolutional neural networks (CNNs) commonly used to evaluate SNNI solutions [14]. In line with this practice, we use three popular ImageNet-scale NNs: ResNet50, SqueezeNet, and DenseNet121. SqueezeNet achieves good accuracy with a significantly reduced number of parameters [10], ResNet50 is based on deep residual networks [7], and DenseNet121 features dense connectivity between layers [8]. These models are selected for their architectural diversity and widespread adoption in the SNNI field. As secure inference achieves the same accuracy as fixed-point accuracy [17], the top-1 fixed-point accuracy is used as the accuracy benchmark for each SNNI–NN pair. We evaluate Cheetah on eleven bandwidths and SCI_HE on only four per NN due to its slow execution at low bandwidths, which makes its data collection very time consuming.

3.3 Model Construction

This phase consists of formulating the energy and execution time prediction models and training them using data from the data collection phase.

Energy and Execution Time Modeling. For each SNNI approach $s \in S$ and NN $n \in N$, we construct two prediction models: one for energy consumption and one for execution time. The energy consumption and execution time of an

[2] https://github.com/Alibaba-Gemini-Lab/OpenCheetah.

SNNI–NN pair are modeled as functions of network bandwidth, including both computation- and communication-related factors:

$$E_{s,n}(b) = \alpha^{\mathrm{E}}_{s,n} + \frac{\beta^{\mathrm{E}}_{s,n}}{b}, \qquad T_{s,n}(b) = \alpha^{\mathrm{T}}_{s,n} + \frac{\beta^{\mathrm{T}}_{s,n}}{b}. \tag{1}$$

$\alpha^{\mathrm{E}}_{s,n}$ denotes the computation-related energy cost of SNNI, capturing the baseline energy consumed by the CPU during SNNI compute operations, and is independent of the bandwidth. $\beta^{\mathrm{E}}_{s,n}$ is the communication energy scaling factor associated with data transfer between client and server. Similarly, $\alpha^{\mathrm{T}}_{s,n}$ is the computation-related part of the SNNI execution time, while $\beta^{\mathrm{T}}_{s,n}$ is the scaling factor of the part of SNNI execution time associated with data transfer between client and server. b is the network bandwidth between client and server.

This model assumes that computation energy is bandwidth independent, whereas communication energy is influenced by bandwidth. The inverse bandwidth form is motivated by the well-established observation that both communication time and communication energy are inversely proportional to the available bandwidth. Network (*i.e.*, communication) energy consumption refers to the energy consumption per bit of transferred data. At lower bandwidths, the energy per bit is dominated by the fixed energy consumption of the network. As bandwidth increases, this fixed overhead is amortized over a larger data rate, resulting in a decrease in per-bit energy consumption [2]. Despite the technological differences, our work is inspired by Baliga *et al.*.

Model Training. Training sets the coefficients $\alpha^{\mathrm{E}}_{s,n}$, $\beta^{\mathrm{E}}_{s,n}$, $\alpha^{\mathrm{T}}_{s,n}$, $\beta^{\mathrm{T}}_{s,n}$ so that Eq. (1) gives good estimates. We use the data points from the data collection phase as training data, and for each SNNI–NN combination, the corresponding bandwidth-specific data points are used to fit the analytical models.

Since the models of Eq. (1) include a reciprocal form of the bandwidth, we introduce $x = \frac{1}{b}$ to transform the model into a linear form suitable for standard linear regression, enabling the parameters to be fitted using:

$$E_{s,n}(x) = \alpha^{\mathrm{E}}_{s,n} + \beta^{\mathrm{E}}_{s,n} \cdot x, \quad T_{s,n}(x) = \alpha^{\mathrm{T}}_{s,n} + \beta^{\mathrm{T}}_{s,n} \cdot x. \tag{2}$$

4 Empirical Evaluation

We evaluate the accuracy and generalizability of the proposed energy and execution time models by comparing predicted and measured values across all SNNI–NN combinations and bandwidths. Given the limited data points per combination, leave-one-out cross-validation (LOOCV) is used to maximize training data by iteratively leaving one sample for testing, while preserving an unbiased estimate of prediction error. Model accuracy is assessed using standard error metrics: mean absolute error (MAE), mean absolute percentage error (MAPE), root mean squared error (RMSE), root mean square percentage error (RMSPE), and the coefficient of determination (R^2). Goodness of the fit is further evaluated using error metrics computed on models trained on all available data.

Experimental Setup. Data collection, model training, and evaluation are performed on two identical machines with Intel(R) Xeon(R) E–2378 CPU (2.60 GHz, 8 cores), 64 GB RAM, running Ubuntu 22.04.2 LTS with kernel 5.15.0–83-generic (x86_64). The SNNI client and server run on separate machines, connected via LAN with a maximum bandwidth of 1000 Mbps and a latency of 0.3 ms. Our experimental setup ensures a controlled and comparable evaluation in line with prior work [4,16,19]. Although GPU-based acceleration is commonly used in standard ML training and inference, SNNI approaches rarely support GPU acceleration and run almost exclusively on CPUs [14]. We conduct our experiments with the Cheetah and SCI_HE SNNI approaches, which are CPU-based . Thus, evaluation on GPUs is out of scope.

We simulate client-server bandwidth variability by throttling with Traffic Control (tc) across 11 bandwidth levels (50–1000 Mbps). Actual bandwidth is measured with `iperf`[3] and is slightly below the set limit (see column 2 in Tables 3 and 4). Due to high execution time of SCI_HE at lower bandwidths, its evaluation is limited to 4 bandwidths (cf. Table 3). Three popular ImageNet-scale NNs: SqueezeNet, ResNet50, and DenseNet121 are used for evaluation. Execution time and energy consumption are measured for one secure inference on the client machine. For each SNNI–NN pair and bandwidth, measurements are repeated 30 times. The data and scripts of our experiments are publicly available[4].

Experimental Results and Insights. Tables 1 and 2 present LOOCV results for energy and execution time predictions, respectively, across different SNNI–NN pairs. Predictions achieve consistently high R^2 values (≥ 0.96, often > 0.99) and low relative errors (MAPE: 1–7%, RMSPE: 1–8%), demonstrating their high accuracy and practical usefulness. Since the evaluation of SCI_HE is limited to four bandwidths, this may limit the expressiveness of the prediction.

Table 3 reports actual and predicted energy and execution times for SCI_HE with SqueezeNet, ResNet50, and DenseNet121 across four bandwidths, including the computation and communication components of the predictions. As expected, at the lowest bandwidth, communication dominates both execution time and energy consumption. At higher bandwidths (*e.g.,* 478 and 941 Mbps), both energy consumption and execution time decrease due to faster data transmission and reduced communication overhead. Table 4 presents results for Cheetah for 11 bandwidths, using the same NNs; Table 5 shows results trained on 4 bandwidths to align with SCI_HE, ensuring a fair comparison of model generalization across SNNI protocols. For both Cheetah and SCI_HE, energy consumption and execution time increase as bandwidth decreases, with a significantly greater increase for SCI_HE than for Cheetah. This aligns with prior findings [9], as SCI_HE transfers substantially more data between client and server.

We compute MAPE and RMSPE for energy consumption and execution time for each NN and all bandwidths associated with each SNNI. Figure 3 shows MAPE values for energy (left) and execution time (right) models; Fig. 4 shows

[3] https://iperf2.sourceforge.io/iperf-manpage.html (version 2.1.5).
[4] https://github.com/tanjina12/GreenSIP-Green-Secure-Inference-Predictor.

Table 1. LOOCV results for energy prediction, for different SNNI approaches and NNs. SNet: SqueezeNet, RNet: ResNet50, DNet: DenseNet121. For Cheetah, model 1 is trained using 11 datapoints, model 2 using only 4 datapoints, corresponding to the bandwidth levels used for SCI_HE.

SNNI/model	NN	MAE (kJ)	MAPE (%)	RMSE (kJ)	RMSPE (%)	R2
Cheetah-model 1	SNet	0.06	3.04	0.10	3.75	0.9649
Cheetah-model 2	SNet	0.12	4.89	0.15	5.42	0.9601
SCI_HE	SNet	0.19	1.57	0.24	1.67	0.9994
Cheetah-model 1	RNet	0.19	1.91	0.31	2.40	0.9916
Cheetah-model 2	RNet	0.36	3.20	0.45	3.59	0.9905
SCI_HE	RNet	1.31	2.29	1.66	2.74	0.9987
Cheetah-model 1	DNet	0.22	2.26	0.33	2.56	0.9919
Cheetah-model 2	DNet	0.35	2.81	0.45	3.26	0.9920
SCI_HE	DNet	1.55	2.95	1.83	3.45	0.9989

Table 2. LOOCV results for execution time prediction. Notation as in Table 1.

SNNI/model	NN	MAE (s)	MAPE (%)	RMSE (s)	RMSPE (%)	R2
Cheetah-model 1	SNet	1.93	4.43	3.08	5.23	0.9710
Cheetah-model 2	SNet	3.46	6.49	4.45	7.52	0.9690
SCI_HE	SNet	5.78	2.63	6.76	3.57	0.9996
Cheetah-model 1	RNet	7.38	3.56	11.17	4.10	0.9898
Cheetah-model 2	RNet	12.91	5.04	15.82	5.77	0.9894
SCI_HE	RNet	24.29	2.84	26.47	3.80	0.9997
Cheetah-model 1	DNet	7.83	3.62	11.99	4.12	0.9903
Cheetah-model 2	DNet	14.12	5.42	17.17	6.23	0.9897
SCI_HE	DNet	29.02	3.44	30.73	4.69	0.9997

the corresponding RMSPE values for different SNNI–NN pairs. In both figures, error metrics are computed using models trained on all available data. These errors are lower than those reported in Tables 1 and 2, where LOOCV is used with one sample left out for testing. From the evaluated models, SCI_HE–SqueezeNet yields the smallest prediction errors for both energy and execution time, with MAPE of 0.79% (energy) and 1.34% (execution time), and RMSPE of 0.92% (energy) and 1.87% (execution time), respectively. Overall, the results show that the prediction models generalize well across different bandwidths, evaluated SNNI protocols, and NNs, with consistently low errors (MAPE $< 3\%$; RMSPE $< 4\%$).

Limitations. We have evaluated GreenSIP using two SNNI protocols, three NNs, two identical machines as client and server, and 11 and 4 bandwidth values

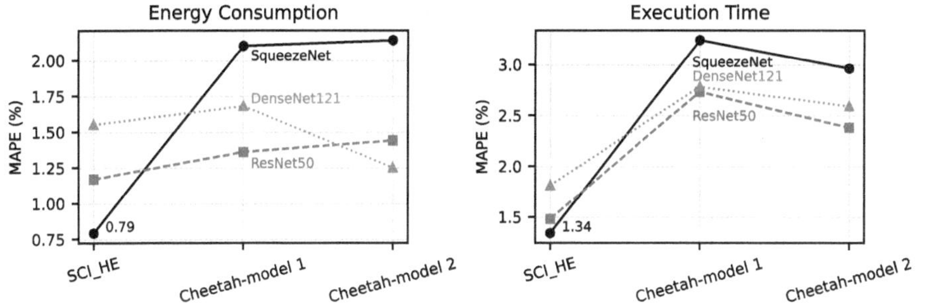

Fig. 3. Prediction error (MAPE) for energy and execution time models across SNNI protocols (x-axis) and NNs (annotated inline). SCI_HE and Cheetah-model 2 are trained on 4 bandwidths, Cheetah-model 1 on 11 bandwidths.

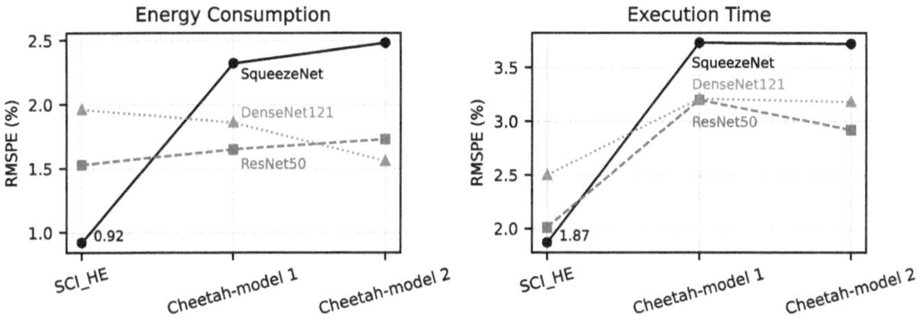

Fig. 4. RMSPE values related to the MAPE values of Fig. 3.

for Cheetah and SCI_HE, respectively. The evaluation is performed on a single hardware configuration with fixed network latency. Applying GreenSIP to other hardware platforms, SNNI approaches, NN models, or variable latency may yield different results.

5 Application of the Prediction Mechanism

GreenSIP enhances our previous framework [11] that recommends the most energy-efficient SNNI–NN tailored to client constraints, by estimating energy and execution time for bandwidths previously not appearing in the KB.

5.1 Proposed Extension

In prior work [11], we introduced a framework that relies on a knowledge base (KB) containing energy consumption and execution time for predefined client resource profiles, including network bandwidth. The framework assumes that future client inference requests match one of the existing KB entries (cf. [11] Fig. 2). To relax this unrealistic assumption and support inference requests from

Table 3. Actual and predicted energy and execution time for SCI_HE. For each bandwidth value, the throttling limit that was used to achieve that bandwidth is given in brackets. SNet: SqueezeNet, RNet: ResNet50, DNet: DenseNet121

NN	Bandwidth (Mbps)	Actual measurement		Pred. energy (kJ)			Pred. time (s)		
		Energy (kJ)	Time (s)	Total	$\alpha^{E}_{s,n}$	Comm.	Total	Comp.	Comm.
SNet	47.9 (50)	28.39 ± 0.51	877.7 ± 10.0	28.46	1.76	26.70	876.0	32.17	843.8
	95.7 (100)	15.27 ± 0.27	450.9 ± 4.4	15.13	1.76	13.36	454.5	32.17	422.3
	478 (500)	4.37 ± 0.15	115.8 ± 1.3	4.44	1.76	2.67	116.7	32.17	84.55
	941 (1000)	3.11 ± 0.11	77.91 ± 0.82	3.12	1.76	1.36	75.1	32.17	42.95
RNet	47.9 (50)	129.2 ± 1.7	3968.5 ± 19.0	129.7	8.35	121.3	3962.1	166.9	3795.2
	95.7 (100)	70.09 ± 1.29	2053.9 ± 14.1	69.08	8.35	60.73	2066.5	166.9	1899.6
	478 (500)	19.98 ± 0.56	539.6 ± 2.8	20.51	8.35	12.16	547.2	166.9	380.3
	941 (1000)	14.50 ± 0.35	374.0 ± 3.7	14.53	8.35	6.17	360.1	166.9	193.2
DNet	47.9 (50)	153.9 ± 1.8	4743.4 ± 20.8	154.4	8.50	145.9	4736.8	159.6	4577.2
	95.7 (100)	82.62 ± 1.01	2438.0 ± 15.5	81.52	8.50	73.01	2450.6	159.6	2291.0
	478 (500)	22.34 ± 0.44	605.7 ± 2.2	23.12	8.50	14.62	618.3	159.6	458.7
	941 (1000)	16.09 ± 0.46	411.2 ± 4.7	15.93	8.50	7.42	392.6	159.6	233.0

clients with bandwidths previously not present in the KB, we propose the following extension:

- The framework first filters out KB entries that are not compatible with the client's input size, ML task type, or accuracy requirements. The satisfaction of these requirements is independent of the bandwidth. This step identifies valid SNNI–NN configurations compatible with the client's request.
- If any valid configuration matches the client's bandwidth, the framework selects the SNNI–NN pair from the KB with the lowest energy consumption, which satisfies also the execution time requirement.
- If no entry in the filtered KB matches the client's bandwidth, the framework invokes GreenSIP to estimate execution time and energy consumption for all valid SNNI–NN configurations supported by the service provider.
- Specifically, for a given client with bandwidth b, the framework compares the predictions for all valid $s \in S$ and $n \in N$, where S and N are the sets of available SNNI protocols and pre-trained NN models, respectively.
- Using the bandwidth-aware predictions, the framework selects the (s, n) pair that minimises energy consumption while satisfying the client's constraints.

Figure 5 illustrates how GreenSIP is integrated into the framework. This extension preserves the filtering logic of the framework and augments it with bandwidth-aware predictions when no KB entry matches the client's bandwidth.

Table 4. Results for Cheetah. Notation as in Table 3.

NN	Bandwidth (Mbps)	Actual measurement		Pred. energy (kJ)			Pred. time (s)		
		Energy (kJ)	Time (s)	Total	Comp.	Comm.	Total	Comp.	Comm.
SNet	47.9 (50)	3.32 ± 0.09	87.8 ± 1.1	3.26	1.31	1.95	86.1	20.55	65.57
	95.7 (100)	2.20 ± 0.09	51.0 ± 0.3	2.29	1.31	0.98	53.4	20.55	32.82
	191.0 (200)	1.73 ± 0.07	34.8 ± 0.3	1.80	1.31	0.49	37.0	20.55	16.44
	287.0 (300)	1.62 ± 0.09	30.3 ± 0.3	1.64	1.31	0.32	31.5	20.55	10.94
	382.0 (400)	1.52 ± 0.07	28.4 ± 0.2	1.55	1.31	0.24	28.8	20.55	8.22
	478.0 (500)	1.52 ± 0.09	27.2 ± 0.2	1.51	1.31	0.19	27.1	20.55	6.57
	574.0 (600)	1.50 ± 0.07	26.4 ± 0.3	1.47	1.31	0.16	26.0	20.55	5.47
	669.0 (700)	1.47 ± 0.09	25.8 ± 0.4	1.45	1.31	0.14	25.2	20.55	4.69
	765.0 (800)	1.46 ± 0.08	25.6 ± 0.4	1.43	1.31	0.12	24.7	20.55	4.10
	861.0 (900)	1.44 ± 0.08	25.4 ± 0.3	1.42	1.31	0.11	24.2	20.55	3.65
	941 (1000)	1.44 ± 0.06	25.2 ± 0.3	1.41	1.31	0.10	23.9	20.55	3.34
RNet	47.9 (50)	17.76 ± 0.17	497.6 ± 2.4	17.59	5.46	12.13	491.5	89.72	401.8
	95.7 (100)	11.31 ± 0.11	283.5 ± 1.1	11.53	5.46	6.07	290.8	89.72	201.1
	191.0 (200)	8.27 ± 0.17	181.5 ± 0.4	8.50	5.46	3.04	190.5	89.72	100.8
	287.0 (300)	7.34 ± 0.14	151.2 ± 0.5	7.48	5.46	2.02	156.8	89.72	67.05
	382.0 (400)	6.96 ± 0.14	137.4 ± 0.5	6.98	5.46	1.52	140.1	89.72	50.38
	478.0 (500)	6.68 ± 0.14	130.4 ± 0.7	6.67	5.46	1.21	130.0	89.72	40.26
	574.0 (600)	6.49 ± 0.13	124.4 ± 0.6	6.47	5.46	1.01	123.3	89.72	33.53
	669.0 (700)	6.37 ± 0.13	120.4 ± 0.9	6.33	5.46	0.87	118.5	89.72	28.76
	765.0 (800)	6.31 ± 0.13	118.3 ± 0.5	6.22	5.46	0.76	114.9	89.72	25.16
	861.0 (900)	6.24 ± 0.14	116.6 ± 0.8	6.13	5.46	0.67	112.1	89.72	22.35
	941 (1000)	6.26 ± 0.13	117.2 ± 0.5	6.08	5.46	0.62	110.2	89.72	20.45
DNet	47.9 (50)	18.97 ± 0.14	535.5 ± 1.4	18.79	5.57	13.22	528.9	87.78	441.1
	95.7 (100)	11.97 ± 0.16	300.2 ± 0.9	12.19	5.57	6.62	308.6	87.78	220.8
	191.0 (200)	8.65 ± 0.19	189.3 ± 0.3	8.89	5.57	3.31	198.4	87.78	110.6
	287.0 (300)	7.59 ± 0.15	156.3 ± 0.4	7.78	5.57	2.27	161.4	87.78	73.62
	382.0 (400)	7.11 ± 0.15	140.6 ± 0.4	7.23	5.57	1.66	143.1	87.78	55.31
	478.0 (500)	6.93 ± 0.14	131.3 ± 0.4	6.90	5.57	1.32	132.0	87.78	44.20
	574.0 (600)	6.74 ± 0.16	125.8 ± 0.3	6.67	5.57	1.10	124.6	87.78	36.81
	669.0 (700)	6.57 ± 0.18	121.7 ± 0.4	6.52	5.57	0.95	119.4	87.78	31.58
	765.0 (800)	6.57 ± 0.16	119.3 ± 0.4	6.40	5.57	0.83	115.4	87.78	27.62
	861.0 (900)	6.40 ± 0.13	117.3 ± 0.6	6.31	5.57	0.73	112.3	87.78	24.54
	941 (1000)	6.42 ± 0.22	117.0 ± 0.5	6.24	5.57	0.67	110.2	87.78	22.45

Table 5. Results for Cheetah for 4 different bandwidths. Notation as in Table 3.

NN	Bandwidth (Mbps)	Actual measurement		Pred. energy (kJ)			Pred. time (s)		
		Energy (kJ)	Time (s)	Total	Comp.	Comm.	Total	Comp.	Comm.
SNet	47.9 (50)	3.32 ± 0.09	87.8 ± 1.1	3.28	1.31	1.97	86.6	20.49	66.11
	95.7 (100)	2.20 ± 0.09	51.0 ± 0.3	2.29	1.31	0.98	53.6	20.49	33.09
	478 (500)	1.52 ± 0.09	27.2 ± 0.2	1.51	1.31	0.20	27.1	20.49	6.62
	941 (1000)	1.44 ± 0.06	25.2 ± 0.3	1.41	1.31	0.10	23.9	20.49	3.36
RNet	47.9 (50)	17.76 ± 0.17	497.6 ± 2.4	17.63	5.48	12.15	493.3	91.11	402.2
	95.7 (100)	11.31 ± 0.11	283.5 ± 1.1	11.56	5.48	6.08	292.4	91.11	201.3
	478 (500)	6.68 ± 0.14	130.4 ± 0.7	6.70	5.48	1.22	131.4	91.11	40.30
	941 (1000)	6.26 ± 0.13	117.2 ± 0.5	6.10	5.48	0.62	111.6	91.11	20.47
DNet	47.9 (50)	18.97 ± 0.14	535.5 ± 1.4	18.85	5.61	13.24	530.9	88.22	442.6
	95.7 (100)	11.97 ± 0.16	300.2 ± 0.91	12.23	5.61	6.63	309.8	88.22	221.6
	478 (500)	6.93 ± 0.14	131.3 ± 0.4	6.93	5.61	1.33	132.6	88.22	44.36
	941 (1000)	6.42 ± 0.22	117.0 ± 0.5	6.28	5.61	0.67	110.8	88.22	22.53

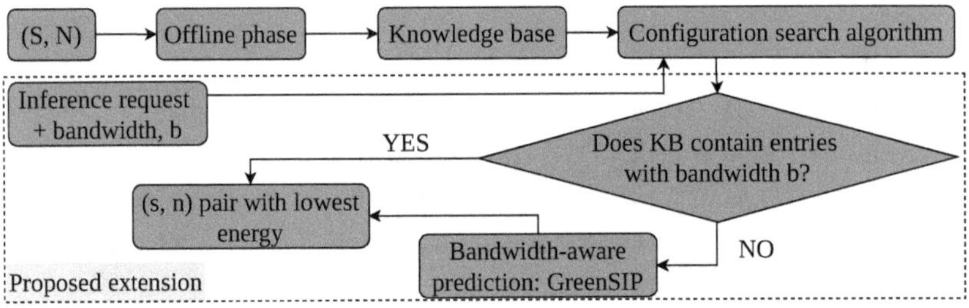

Fig. 5. Extension of an existing framework [11] with GreenSIP.

5.2 Example Client Scenarios

We illustrate the practicality of the extended framework through client scenarios with varying network bandwidth and execution time requirements. Table 6 presents these scenarios, including client request parameters and bandwidth.

Scenario 1: Medium-Bandwidth Client without Strict Execution Time Requirement. A new client requests secure inference for an image classification task on a 224x224 image with a network bandwidth of 478 Mbps, looking for an SNNI–NN combination that minimizes energy consumption while achieving at least 70 % accuracy, without any constraints on execution time.

The service provider forwards the request to the framework with integrated GreenSIP. Cheetah–SqueezeNet and SCI_HE–SqueezeNet are discarded due to low benchmark accuracy or incompatible input dimensions (cf. [11] Table II). The

Table 6. Example scenarios. IM: Image classification.

Scenario	Client's inference request				Bandwidth (Mbps)
	Input size	Type	Min. accuracy (%)	Max. exec. time (s)	
1.	224x224	IM	70	N/A	478
2.	224x224	IM	75	150	478
3.	227x227	IM	N/A	N/A	95.7

framework then evaluates the remaining KB entries. As no entry matches the client's 478 Mbps bandwidth, GreenSIP is invoked to estimate energy consumption and execution time of SNNI–NN combinations for this bandwidth (cf. Table 7). Among the valid options (Cheetah–DenseNet121, Cheetah–ResNet50, SCI_HE–DenseNet121, and SCI_HE–ResNet50) that meet all client requirements, the framework selects Cheetah–ResNet50, which provides the lowest energy consumption (6.67 kJ) with an estimated execution time of 130.0 s. Comparing predicted values against actual measurements for Cheetah–ResNet50 (cf. Table 4) validates GreenSIP's accuracy, with measured energy of 6.68 ± 0.14 kJ and execution time of 130.4 ± 0.7 s, confirming that the selected SNNI–NN pair is indeed optimal.

Table 7. Evaluation results for **Scenario 1** at 478 Mbps. SP: Service provider.

SP's options		Acc. (%)	Prediction results		Appropriate for request
SNNI	NN		Energy (kJ)	Time (s)	
Cheetah	SNet	55.90	1.51	27.1	NO: low accuracy
SCI_HE	SNet	55.90	4.44	116.7	NO: low accuracy
Cheetah	**RNet**	**76.45**	**6.67**	**130.0**	**YES: most energy-efficient**
SCI_HE	RNet	76.45	20.51	547.2	YES
Cheetah	DNet	74.35	6.90	132.0	YES
SCI_HE	DNet	74.35	23.12	618.3	YES

Scenario 2: Medium-Bandwidth Client with Strict Execution Time Constraint. The client requests secure inference with the same input size and network bandwidth as Scenario 1, with the requirements that it completes within 150 s, achieves at least 75 % accuracy, and minimizes energy consumption.

As no suitable entry exists in the KB for the specified bandwidth, GreenSIP estimates energy consumption and execution time for all valid SNNI–NN combinations (cf. Table 8) at 478 Mbps. Cheetah–SqueezeNet and SCI_HE–SqueezeNet are excluded for the same reasons as in Scenario 1. SCI_HE–ResNet50 and SCI_HE–DenseNet121 are eliminated as their predicted execution time exceeds

150 s. Both Cheetah–ResNet50 and Cheetah–DenseNet121 satisfy all requirements, but the framework selects Cheetah–ResNet50 for lower predicted energy (6.67 kJ vs. 6.90 kJ), 76.45 % accuracy, and a predicted execution time of 130.0 s. Validation against actual measurements (cf. Table 4) confirms the choice, with measured energy of 6.68 ± 0.14 kJ, and the execution time of 130.4 ± 0.7 s, verifying the optimality of the selected SNNI–NN pair.

Table 8. Evaluation results for **Scenario 2** at 478 Mbps.

SP's options		Acc. (%)	Prediction results		Appropriate for request
SNNI	NN		Energy (kJ)	Time (s)	
Cheetah	SNet	55.90	1.51	27.1	NO: low accuracy
SCI_HE	SNet	55.90	4.44	116.7	NO: low accuracy
Cheetah	**RNet**	**76.45**	**6.67**	**130.0**	**YES: most energy-efficient**
SCI_HE	RNet	76.45	20.51	547.2	NO: exceeds 150 s
Cheetah	DNet	74.35	6.90	132.0	YES
SCI_HE	DNet	74.35	23.12	618.3	NO: exceeds 150 s

Scenario 3: Low-Bandwidth Client with Energy Saving Focus. The client has a low network bandwidth of 95.7 Mbps and prioritizes the most energy-efficient SNNI–NN pair, as energy efficiency becomes critical under reduced data rates. The secure inference request concerns a 227x227 input image for an image classification task, with no accuracy or execution time constraints.

The only valid options are Cheetah–SqueezeNet and SCI_HE–SqueezeNet, as the other options do not match the requested input size. With no matching entry in the KB for the specified bandwidth, the framework invokes GreenSIP to estimate energy consumption and execution time for all valid SNNI–NN combinations (cf. Table 9). Based on the predicted energy consumption, the framework selects Cheetah–SqueezeNet (2.29 kJ) over SCI_HE–SqueezeNet (15.13 kJ), achieving 55.90 % accuracy and an estimated execution time of 53.4 s. Validation of the predictions against actual measurements (cf. Table 4) supports the selection, with measured energy of 2.20 ± 0.09 kJ and execution time of 51.0 ± 0.3 s, confirming the effectiveness of the selected SNNI–NN pair.

Table 9. Evaluation results for **Scenario 3** at 95.7 Mbps.

SP's options		Acc. (%)	Prediction results		Appropriate for request
SNNI	NN		Energy (kJ)	Time (s)	
Cheetah	**SNet**	**55.90**	**2.29**	**53.4**	**YES: most energy-efficient**
SCI_HE	SNet	55.90	15.13	454.5	YES
Cheetah	RNet	76.45	11.53	290.8	NO: input size mismatch
SCI_HE	RNet	76.45	69.08	2066.5	NO: input size mismatch
Cheetah	DNet	74.35	12.19	308.6	NO: input size mismatch
SCI_HE	DNet	74.35	81.52	2450.6	NO: input size mismatch

6 Related Work

In recent years, the SNNI problem has gained significant interest due to the growing demand for privacy-preserving ML services. Different cryptographic techniques are used in SNNI, including homomorphic encryption (HE), secure multi-party computation (MPC), oblivious transfer (OT), and garbled circuits. A survey by Mann *et al.* [14] provides a detailed overview of the characteristics and internals of different SNNI approaches. Several SNNI approaches, such as Gazelle [13] and Delphi [15], combine different cryptographic primitives tailored to specific NN layers. CryptFlow2 [17] uses HE or OT for linear layers and optimized MPC protocols for non-linear layers, achieving improvements over prior work in both execution time and scalability. More recent work, like Cheeath [9], adopts a similar hybrid protocol design but applies optimizations to reduce computation and communication overheads. Panther [5] introduces novel secure two-party protocols for further improvements. While prior work offered performance optimization in terms of execution time and accuracy, the energy consumption of SNNI approaches received little attention. Moreover, the impact of the network bandwidth between client and server on SNNI energy remains largely unexplored.

Work on energy prediction in ML has mainly focused on standard, non-secure inference. NeuralPower [3] proposed a predictive framework for estimating the runtime, power consumption, and energy consumption of CNNs during inference. SDEnergy [6] predicts the energy consumption of NN inference across various devices. While these works demonstrate the efficacy of energy consumption prediction, they do not account for the additional computational and communication overhead introduced by cryptographic mechanisms in secure NN inference. Unlike non-secure inference, the energy consumption of SNNI is influenced not only by the NN architecture and local hardware but also by the cryptographic operations, interactions between client and server, and network connections between them. As a result, energy prediction for SNNI fundamentally differs from that of standard inference, as accurate estimation of SNNI energy consumption strongly depends on network bandwidth and communication behavior.

While recent work proposed models for predicting the execution time of SNNI on a given NN [20], execution time alone is not sufficient to precisely capture the energy consumption. Although execution time and energy consumption are often correlated, energy consumption is also influenced by other factors, such as the underlying hardware platforms on which the computation is performed, and therefore cannot be accurately inferred from execution time-based estimation [4]. To the best of our knowledge, no prior work has addressed the problem of predicting the energy consumption for SNNI. Moreover, prior work on execution time prediction [20] did not consider network bandwidth.

Recent work by Damie *et al.* [4] investigates the energy consumption of various privacy-enhancing technologies (PETs), including encrypted ML inference. They present a methodology, based on existing open-source software, to measure the energy consumption and carbon footprint of PETs. Their experimental results highlight the significant overheads introduced by cryptographic operations compared to their non-private equivalents. However, their work focuses only on general PETs and does not address SNNI specifically. They do not consider how network bandwidth influences execution time and energy consumption in SNNI protocols. In our work, we fill this gap by proposing a bandwidth-aware prediction approach for estimating energy consumption and execution time of SNNI.

7 Conclusion

We propose GreenSIP, a lightweight bandwidth-aware prediction approach that estimates SNNI energy consumption and execution time across various network bandwidths. By modeling both computation and communication costs, it enables bandwidth-aware selection of energy-efficient SNNI–NN combinations tailored to client constraints. To our knowledge, GreenSIP is the first method to explicitly incorporate network bandwidth into SNNI energy prediction, bridging a key gap at the intersection of secure ML inference and energy-aware services. Future work includes extending GreenSIP to heterogeneous hardware platforms and a broader set of SNNI protocols, enabling more adaptive and energy-efficient privacy-preserving inference in MLaaS.

Acknowledgments. This research was supported by GreenDIGIT, an European Union project funded under the grant agreement 101131207.

References

1. Al-Rubaie, M., Chang, J.M.: Privacy-preserving machine learning: threats and solutions. IEEE Secur. Priv. **17**(2), 49–58 (2019)
2. Baliga, J., Ayre, R., Hinton, K., Sorin, W.V., Tucker, R.S.: Energy consumption in optical IP networks. J. Lightwave Technol. **27**(13), 2391–2403 (2009)
3. Cai, E., Juan, D.C., Stamoulis, D., Marculescu, D.: NeuralPower: predict and deploy energy-efficient convolutional neural networks. In: 9th Asian Conference on Machine Learning. PMLR, vol. 77, pp. 622–637 (2017)
4. Damie, M., Pop, M., Posthuma, M.: Energy consumption of TLS, searchable encryption and fully homomorphic encryption. In: 18th International Symposium on Foundations & Practice of Security (FPS) (2025)
5. Feng, J., Wu, Y., Sun, H., Zhang, S., Liu, D.: Panther: practical secure two-party neural network inference. IEEE Trans. Inf. Forensics Secur. **20**, 1149–1162 (2025)
6. Guo, C., Wang, S., Xie, R., Song, J.: Estimating energy consumption of neural networks with joint structure–device encoding. Sustain. Comput.: Inform. Syst. **45**, 101062 (2025)
7. He, K., Zhang, X., Ren, S., Sun, J.: Deep residual learning for image recognition. In: IEEE Conference on Computer Vision and Pattern Recognition (CVPR) (2016)
8. Huang, G., Liu, Z., van der Maaten, L., Weinberger, K.Q.: Densely connected convolutional networks. In: CVPR (2017)
9. Huang, Z., Lu, W.j., Hong, C., Ding, J.: Cheetah: lean and fast secure two-party deep neural network inference. In: 31st USENIX Security Symposium, pp. 809–826 (2022)
10. Iandola, F.N., Han, S., Moskewicz, M.W., Ashraf, K., Dally, W.J., Keutzer, K.: SqueezeNet: alexNet-level accuracy with 50x fewer parameters and <0.5 MB model size. arXiv preprint arXiv:1602.07360 (2016)
11. Islam, T., Oprescu, A., Mann, Z.Á., Klous, S.: A framework to optimize the energy cost of securing neural network inference. In: IEEE Green Computing & Communications (GreenCom), pp. 339–346 (2024)
12. Islam, T., Oprescu, A., Mann, Z.Á., Klous, S.: Profiling the energy consumption of secure neural network inference. In: 33rd International Symposium on Modeling, Analysis and Simulation of Computer and Telecommunication Systems (MASCOTS). IEEE (2025)
13. Juvekar, C., Vaikuntanathan, V., Chandrakasan, A.: GAZELLE: a low latency framework for secure neural network inference. In: 27th USENIX Security Symposium, pp. 1651–1669 (2018)
14. Mann, Z.Á., Weinert, C., Chabal, D., Bos, J.W.: Towards practical secure neural network inference: the journey so far and the road ahead. ACM Comput. Surv. **56**(5) (2023)
15. Mishra, P., Lehmkuhl, R., Srinivasan, A., Zheng, W., Popa, R.A.: Delphi: a cryptographic inference service for neural networks. In: 29th USENIX Security Symposium, pp. 2505–2522 (2020)
16. Prins, J., Mann, Z.Á.: Secure neural network inference for edge intelligence: Implications of bandwidth and energy constraints. In: Pal, S., Savaglio, C., Minerva, R., Delicato, F.C. (eds.) IoT Edge Intelligence. Internet of Things, pp. 265–288. Springer, Cham (2024). https://doi.org/10.1007/978-3-031-58388-9_9
17. Rathee, D., et al.: CrypTFlow2: practical 2-party secure inference. In: ACM SIGSAC Conference on Computer and Communications Security (CCS), pp. 325–342 (2020)

18. Shinde, P.P., Shah, S.: A review of machine learning and deep learning applications. In: 4th International Conference on Computing, Communication, Control, and Automation (ICCUBEA). IEEE (2018)
19. de Vries, R., Mann, Z.Á.: Secure neural network inference as a service with resource-constrained clients. In: 16th IEEE/ACM International Conference on Utility and Cloud Computing (UCC) (2024)
20. Zhang, E., Mann, Z.Á.: Predicting the execution time of secure neural network inference. In: ICT Systems Security and Privacy Protection, pp. 481–494 (2024)

SCI-Aware Application Placement in the Cloud-Edge Continuum

Jacopo Massa(✉), Stefano Forti, Sara Bruschi, Jacopo Soldani, and Antonio Brogi

Department of Computer Science, University of Pisa, Pisa, Italy
jacopo.massa@di.unipi.it

Abstract. The increasing environmental impact of ICT systems calls for carbon-aware management strategies for distributed multi-service applications. In cloud–edge environments, service placement decisions can significantly affect carbon emissions, yet existing approaches rarely rely on standardised carbon metrics.

In this article, we address the carbon-aware placement problem by leveraging the Software Carbon Intensity (SCI) metric, recently recognised as an ISO standard. We propose a declarative model for microservice-based application placement that accounts for application topology, request patterns, internal workflows, and both operational and embodied emissions. Building on this model, we introduce an optimal exhaustive strategy and a configurable greedy heuristic solution to determine eligible and SCI-aware placements, differently balancing among carbon emissions and decision-making time. Our experimental assessment shows that the heuristic achieves optimal or near-optimal placements with significantly lower execution times than the optimal exhaustive search.

Keywords: Software Carbon Intensity · carbon-aware application placement · microservice-based architectures · cloud-edge continuum

1 Introduction

Information and Communication Technologies (ICT) contribute significantly to global carbon emissions, accounting for approximately 2 % of total emissions and up to 6-9 % of worldwide energy consumption, with projections indicating further growth in the coming years [1,2]. This trend has intensified the need for sustainable computing practices, further reinforced by international commitments such as the Paris Agreement.[1] Consequently, recent research has increasingly focused on incorporating sustainability considerations across the software lifecycle, from design to deployment [3,4].

Microservice-based applications have become the main paradigm for modern distributed systems, particularly in cloud-edge environments [5]. However, their deployment poses significant challenges, as the number of candidate placements grows exponentially with the number of services and infrastructure nodes,

[1] https://unfccc.int/process-and-meetings/the-paris-agreement.

Published by Springer Nature Switzerland AG 2027
D. Balouek et al. (Eds.): ESOCC 2026, LNCS 16834, pp. 87–101, 2027.
https://doi.org/10.1007/978-3-032-37831-6_6

making the identification of eligible and optimal configurations computationally intensive. Indeed, the problem of multi-service application placement in cloud-edge settings has been proven NP-hard [6].

Although assigning services to nodes significantly affects not only performance and resource utilisation, but also carbon emissions, existing approaches to application placement rarely consider carbon emissions among the target objectives [5,7]. In these regards, the recent introduction of the Software Carbon Intensity (SCI) specification, proposed by the Green Software Foundation[2] and recently formalised as an ISO standard,[3] provides a principled way to quantify software carbon emissions. Yet, applying SCI to distributed microservice-based architectures is non-trivial, as it requires accounting for application topology and workflows, request patterns, and both operational and embodied emissions of deployment nodes. At the same time, to the best of our knowledge, SCI has not yet been integrated into placement strategies for cloud–edge resources.

In this article, we address this gap by proposing a SCI-aware placement approach for microservice-based applications deployed across heterogeneous cloud-edge nodes. We target deployment-time decisions in which an orchestrator has to place the services of a known application topology over nodes that differ in capacity, energy efficiency, carbon intensity, and embodied footprint. We extend the SCI model to capture the characteristics of distributed microservices and introduce both optimal and heuristic placement strategies based on declarative Prolog reasoning. Detailedly, we make the following contributions:

1. we define a declarative SCI model for microservice-based applications capturing their topology, request amounts and probabilities, and both operational and embodied emissions,
2. we develop an exhaustive placement strategy that guarantees optimality in terms of SCI, along with a configurable greedy heuristic supporting different trade-offs among carbon efficiency, resource utilisation, and execution time, and
3. we provide an experimental evaluation, in controlled settings, showing that heuristic strategies can achieve optimal or near-optimal placements with significantly lower execution times.

The rest of this article is organised as follows. Section 2 briefly introduces the SCI standard. Section 3 presents our declarative SCI-aware placement model and the proposed strategies. Section 4 describes the experimental setup and discusses experimental results. Finally, Sect. 6 outlines some directions for future work.

2 Background: Software Carbon Intensity

In this section, we briefly illustrate the methodology proposed by the specification of the SCI standard to quantify the carbon footprint of software. SCI

[2] https://greensoftware.foundation/.

[3] *ISO/IEC 21031:2024 Information technology—Software Carbon Intensity (SCI) specification.* Available at: https://sci.greensoftware.foundation/.

defines a normalised metric that relates carbon emissions to a specific functional unit, thus enabling consistent comparison across different deployments and execution environments. At its core, SCI expresses the carbon intensity of a software application as:

$$\texttt{SCI} = \texttt{C per R} \tag{1}$$

where C denotes the *total carbon emissions* generated by the application, and R represents its *functional unit* (e.g., number of requests served, number of processed tasks). This normalisation allows comparing systems with different workloads or scales. Carbon emissions C are further decomposed into two main components:

$$\texttt{C} = \texttt{O} + \texttt{M} \tag{2}$$

where O represents *operational* emissions and M denotes *embodied* emissions.

Operational emissions capture the carbon footprint associated with energy consumption during execution and are defined as:

$$\texttt{O} = \texttt{E} \cdot \texttt{I} \tag{3}$$

where E is the *energy* consumed and I is the *carbon intensity* of the energy source, expressed in $kgCO_2eq/kWh$. Embodied emissions account for the impact of manufacturing infrastructure hardware and are proportionally allocated to software based on usage:

$$\texttt{M} = \texttt{TE} \cdot \texttt{TS} \cdot \texttt{RS} \tag{4}$$

where TE is the *total embodied carbon* of the hardware, TS is the *time-share* (i.e., the fraction of the hardware lifetime used by the software), and RS is the *resource-share* (i.e., the fraction of hardware resources allocated to the application). In practice, this can be expressed as:

$$\texttt{TS} = \frac{\texttt{TiR}}{\texttt{EL}}, \quad \texttt{RS} = \frac{\texttt{RR}}{\texttt{ToR}} \tag{5}$$

where TiR is the *time reserved* for execution, EL is the *expected lifetime* of the hardware, RR denotes the *resources required* by the application, and ToR the *total available resources.*

While SCI provides a comprehensive and standardised framework for quantifying software carbon emissions, its application to distributed microservice-based systems is not straightforward. In the next section, we build on these foundations to define a formal SCI model tailored to microservice-based application placement in cloud–edge environments.

3 Methodology

Given an application composed of multiple microservices and a set of candidate nodes, the objective is to find an eligible placement that minimises the SCI. In this section, we first rely on declarative Prolog programming to define the SCI of alternative candidate placements, then we illustrate a declarative exhaustive strategy to determine optimal solution placement and a configurable greedy heuristic that tries to approximate the optimal solution while reducing decision-making times over large input instances.

3.1 System Model

We model both the application and the underlying infrastructure using a declarative representation based on Prolog facts.

An *application* is identified by a `Name` and consists of a set of `Microservices` and `Endpoints`:

```
application(Name, Microservices, Endpoints).
```

Each *microservice* is characterised by its `Name`, a tuple of resource requirements `rr` – including virtual `CPU`, `RAM`, `InboundBandwidth`, and `OutboundBandwidth` – and a reserved execution time `TimeReserved`:

```
microservice(Name, rr(CPU, RAM, InboundBandwidth, OutboundBandwidth), TimeReserved).
```

Each *endpoint* models a specific operation offered by the application to its users, corresponding to an internal workflow across the application topology. Each endpoint has a `Name` and specifies the list of `Microservices` it exploits to serve such operation:

```
endpoint(Name, Microservices).
```

To capture *workload* characteristics, each endpoint is associated with a `Probability` representing its relative frequency of invocation by end-users, so that different workflows can be weighted according to how often they are executed:

```
probability(EndpointName, Probability).
```

The *functional unit* is defined as the expected `NumberOfRequests` handled during the application lifetime:

```
functionalUnits(Application, NumberOfRequests).
```

The *infrastructure* is modelled as a set of heterogeneous nodes. Each infrastructure node is characterised by its `Name`, a tuple of its total available resources `tor`, `ExpectedLifetime` in years, its energy consumption per CPU unit `EnergyPerCPU`, its `EmbodiedCarbon` in kgCO_2-eq, and its `PUE`[4]:

```
node(Name, tor(CPU, RAM, InboundBandwidth, OutboundBandwidth),
    EnergyPerCPU, ExpectedLifetime, EmbodiedCarbon, PUE).
```

Here, `CPU`, `RAM`, `InboundBandwidth`, and `OutboundBandwidth` denote the total node capacities for computation, memory, and network resources. Each node is further associated with the `CarbonIntensity` of the energy mix that powers it up:

[4] PUE is a standard computing efficiency metric defined as the ratio of total energy consumption of an IT system to the energy used by computing equipment alone. A value of 1.0 indicates ideal efficiency.

```
carbonIntensity(Node, CarbonIntensity).
```

This representation provides all the information we need to estimate the SCI of a placement following the guidelines of the ISO standard (Sect. 2).

3.2 Declarative Specification of SCI for Microservice Placements

In this section, we define the SCI of a placement declaratively by specifying how carbon emissions are computed at the level of individual endpoints, which are then aggregated at the application level. Our declarative specification directly instantiates the SCI model introduced in Sect. 2 for our purposes. First, we compute the SCI contribution of an endpoint `EP` as per the rules in Fig. 1.

```
1  endpointSCI(EP, R, P, SCI) :-
2      endpoint(EP, EPMs),
3      findall(on(Ms,N), (member(Ms, EPMs), member(on(Ms, N), P)), FilteredP),
4      probability(EP, Prob),
5      carbonEmissions(FilteredP, C),
6      SCI is (C / R) * Prob.

7  carbonEmissions([on(Ms,N)|P], C) :-
8      carbonEmissions(P, AccC),
9      operationalCarbon(N, Ms, O),
10     embodiedCarbon(N, Ms, M),
11     C is AccC + O + M.
12 carbonEmissions([], 0).

13 operationalCarbon(N, Ms, O) :-
14     operationalEnergy(N, Ms, E), carbonIntensity(N, I),
15     O is E * I.

16 operationalEnergy(N, Ms, E) :-
17     node(N, _, PowerPerCPU, _, _, PUE),
18     microservice(Ms, _, TiR),
19     E is PUE * (TiR * 365 * 24) * PowerPerCPU.

20 embodiedCarbon(N, Ms, M) :-
21     node(N, tor(CPU,_,_,_), _, EL, TE, _),
22     microservice(Ms, rr(CPUReq,_,_,_), TiR),
23     TS is TiR / EL,
24     RS is CPUReq / CPU,
25     M is TE * TS * RS.
```

Fig. 1. Declarative specification of the SCI of an endpoint.

We first retrieve the list of microservices `Ms` ∈ `EPMs` involved in the endpoint operation (line 2), i.e., the workflow induced by the application topology for that endpoint, and their deployment nodes `N` as per the current placement `P`, represented as `on(Ms,N)` (line 3). We also retrieve the probability `Prob` that `EP` is invoked (line 4). Then, we compute the total carbon emissions `C` associated with the execution of such microservices (line 5) by invoking predicate `carbonEmissions/2`, which aggregates the operational `O` and embodied `M` carbon of each deployed microservice. Finally, the SCI contribution of `EP` is obtained by normalising `C` over the number `R` of functional units of the application, weighted by `Prob` (line 6).

The predicate `carbonEmissions/2` recursively scans the subset of the placement `FilteredP` involving the microservices of the endpoint. Hence, only the services belonging to the endpoint workflow contribute to its emissions, while other deployed services affect the SCI through the endpoints in which they participate. For each pair `on(Ms,N)`, it computes the operational carbon `O` and embodied carbon `E` of microservice `Ms` deployed on node `N` (lines 9–10), and accumulates their sum (line 11). The recursion terminates with the base case returning zero emissions (line 12).

The predicate `operationalCarbon/3` computes the operational emissions `O` associated with deploying a microservice `Ms` on a node `N` by combining the energy consumption `E` of the microservice with the carbon intensity `I` of the node (line 15). Such energy consumption is estimated by predicate `operationalEnergy/3`, which accounts for the node energy efficiency through its `PUE`, the energy consumption per CPU unit, and the reserved execution time `TiR` of the microservice over one year (lines 17–19).

The predicate `embodiedCarbon/3` computes the embodied emissions `M` associated with the deployment of a microservice by allocating a fraction of the total embodied carbon `TE` of the hosting node (line 21), proportional to both the time-share `TS` of the node usage (derived from the ratio between the reserved execution time `TiR` and the node lifetime `EL`) and the resource-share `RS` (computed as the ratio between the CPU demand of the microservice and the total CPU capacity of the node) (lines 23–25).

Finally, the SCI of an application is obtained by summing up the SCI contributions of all its endpoints, computed as per the predicates in Fig. 1. Overall, this set of predicates provides a fully declarative specification of SCI for microservice placements, explicitly capturing the interplay between application topology, infrastructure characteristics, and request patterns in determining carbon emissions per request.

3.3 SCI-Aware Application Placement

Let M be the set of microservices of an application and N the set of candidate cloud-edge nodes for their deployment. A placement is a mapping of each microservice in M to a node in N. A placement is *eligible* if, for every node in use, the aggregate resource requirements of the microservices assigned to that node do not exceed the node capacity. Given an eligible placement P, its quality can be evaluated through the SCI model introduced in Sect. 3.2. We hence focus on the following placement problem: given an application and an infrastructure, determine an eligible placement that minimises the application-level SCI.

In the following, we first introduce an exhaustive strategy, which captures SCI-optimality declaratively, and a configurable greedy heuristic, to determine near-optimal eligible placements while taming the exp-time complexity of the NP-hard problem at hand.

Exhaustive Strategy. The exhaustive strategy builds upon the predicates in Fig. 2, which capture feasibility, placement generation, and optimality, respectively.

The predicate `placementNode/3` checks whether a microservice can be assigned to a node without violating resource constraints. It retrieves the available resources of node `N` and the resources already allocated by the current partial placement `P`, and verifies that CPU, memory, and bandwidth capacities are not exceeded by the microservice being assigned (lines 26–30).

The predicate `placement/3` generates eligible placements for a microservice application `App`. It relies on `eligiblePlacement/2` (line 34) to recursively apply `placementNode/3` to all microservices of the application, thus constructing placements that satisfy all resource constraints. For each eligible placement `P`, it evaluates its SCI through predicate `sci/4` (line 35).

Finally, predicate `exhaustivePlacement/3` identifies SCI-optimal placements. A placement `POpt` is selected if no alternative placement `P` exists with strictly lower SCI (lines 36–38). This can be expressed declaratively through negation-as-failure (`\+`), which captures optimality without requiring explicit enumeration or ranking mechanisms.

```
26 placementNode(N, P, rr(CPUReq, RAMReq, BWinReq, BWoutReq)) :-
27     node(N, tor(CPU, RAM, BWin, BWout), _, _, _, _),
28     hardwareUsedAtNode(N, P, rr(UCPU, URAM, UBWin, UBWout)),
29     CPU >= UCPU + CPUReq, RAM >= URAM + RAMReq,
30     BWin >= UBWin + BWinReq,  BWout >= UBWout + BWoutReq.

31 placement(App, P, SCI) :-
32     application(App, Ms, EPs),
33     functionalUnits(App, R),
34     eligiblePlacement(Ms, P),
35     sci(EPs, R, P, SCI).

36 exhaustivePlacement(App, POpt, SCIOpt) :-
37     placement(App, POpt, SCIOpt),
38     \+ (placement(App, P, SCI), dif(POpt,P), SCI < SCIOpt).
```

Fig. 2. Exhaustive placement strategy.

This formulation guarantees placement optimality, at the cost of exploring the entire search space, which becomes impractical already for medium-scale problem instances (tens of services deployed over 100 s of nodes).

Greedy Strategy. To improve execution times, we introduce a configurable greedy heuristic that ranks nodes and microservices before constructing a placement. In general, lower scores denote more promising candidates.

For each node n, we compute a *resource score* $RS(n)$, a *carbon score* $CS(n)$, and a *weighted score* $WS(n)$. The *resource score* captures the relative amount of available resources (viz. CPU, RAM and bandwidth) of a node

$$RS(n) = \frac{1}{m}\sum_{i=1}^{m} \frac{MaxT(i) - t_{n,i}}{MaxT(i) - MinT(i)} \tag{6}$$

where $t_{n,i}$ is the amount of resource i available on node n, and $MaxT(i)$ and $MinT(i)$ are the maximum and minimum values of that resource across all nodes. Analogously, the *carbon score* combines normalised operational and embodied footprints

$$CS(n) = \frac{1}{2}\left(\frac{OF(n) - MinF(OF)}{MaxF(OF) - MinF(OF)} + \frac{MF(n) - MinF(MF)}{MaxF(MF) - MinF(MF)}\right) \tag{7}$$

where $OF(n)$ and $MF(n)$ denote the operational and embodied carbon footprints of node n.

The two dimensions – resources and carbon – are then combined into a linear (weighted) score, where equal weights are assumed by default ($\alpha = 0.5$), as follows

$$WS(n) = \alpha\, CS(n) + (1 - \alpha)\, RS(n). \tag{8}$$

Last, microservices are ranked according to their resource demands, so that more demanding services are placed first. Their score is computed as

$$RS(ms) = \frac{1}{m}\sum_{i=1}^{m} \frac{MaxR(i) - r_{i,ms}}{MaxR(i) - MinR(i)}, \tag{9}$$

where $r_{i,ms}$ is the requirement of microservice ms for resource i.

Using these rankings, we define three heuristic configurations:

- *Green-Only*, which orders nodes by the *carbon score* only (CS),
- *Capacity-Only*, which orders nodes by the *resource score* only (RS), and
- *Green&Capacity*, which orders nodes by the *weighted score* (WS).

All above configurations process microservices in decreasing order of resource demand (*fail-first*) and assign them to nodes explored in increasing order of score (*fail-last*). This reduces the search effort while still exploiting SCI-related information during placement since promising node–service assignments are prioritised early in the backtracking search.

4 Experimental Evaluation

This section evaluates the placement strategies introduced in Sect. 3. Our goal is to assess two complementary aspects: (i) *accuracy*, i.e., how closely the greedy strategies approximate the SCI-optimal placement, and (ii) *efficiency*, i.e., how their execution time scales with the size of the considered problem instance. More specifically, we address the following research questions:

- **RQ1**: *How accurately do the proposed greedy heuristics approximate the SCI-optimal placement?*
- **RQ2**: *How does the execution time of the heuristics evolve as the infrastructure size increases?*
- **RQ3**: *Which trade-off emerges between carbon optimality and execution time across the different heuristic configurations?*

Experimental Setup. We evaluate the proposed strategies across a set of experiments[5] on *Online Boutique*, a cloud-native microservice application released by Google and publicly available on GitHub.[6] The application is representative of realistic microservice-based systems and provides a non-trivial topology for assessing placement decisions.

The target cloud-edge infrastructure is generated synthetically for each experiment. We consider infrastructures whose size ranges from 2^5 to 2^{20} nodes. Larger infrastructures are constructed as supersets of smaller ones, so that each infrastructure includes all nodes of the previous one. This ensures that the SCI of the optimal placement cannot increase as the infrastructure grows. Last, input nodes are shuffled before writing them into the Prolog knowledge base, so as to avoid any biased ordering.

In preliminary experiments, the exhaustive strategy always reached the timeout threshold of 900 s even for the smallest infrastructures, i.e., 2^5 nodes. For this reason, we adopt a controlled environment specifically designed to make the optimal placement (and its associated SCI) known *a priori*, thus enabling a reliable evaluation of heuristic accuracy. The goal of this setup is not to reproduce a full production cloud-edge infrastructure, but to isolate the behaviour of the heuristic ranking policies and measure their distance from the optimum at scales where exhaustive search is not practical. In this environment, nodes are divided into three categories:

- *fit nodes*, each capable of hosting exactly one microservice of the *Online Boutique* application,
- *broken nodes*, which are infeasible because of insufficient resources, and
- *dirty nodes*, which are feasible but with higher carbon intensity than fit nodes.

By construction, the infrastructure admits a unique optimal solution, consisting of assigning each microservice of *Online Boutique* to its corresponding fit node.

[5] Experiments were run on a machine featuring Ubuntu 22.04.5 LTS (GNU/Linux 5.15.0-1065-nvidia x86_64) equipped with 1.5 TB of RAM and two 3.7 GHz AMD EPYC 9534 64-Core processors, Python 3.12.11, and SWI-Prolog 9.2.7. All code to run the experiments is publicly available at https://github.com/di-unipi-socc/sci-aware-msa-placement.

[6] https://github.com/GoogleCloudPlatform/microservices-demo.

Hence, the SCI-optimal placement is the one using all and only the fit nodes; other eligible placements – made of a mix of *fit* and *dirty* nodes – feature a higher SCI value. For each combination of infrastructure size and heuristic configuration, we run 10 independent experiments using different random seeds. We collect execution time and resulting SCI, together with the relative SCI distance from the optimal placement.

Results. In the following, we discuss the experimental results with respect to the research questions introduced before.

RQ1: *How accurately do the proposed greedy heuristics approximate the SCI-optimal placement?*
Figure 3a reports the SCI values (in g/request) obtained by the three heuristics. The *Green-Only* heuristic consistently achieves the lowest SCI, coinciding with the optimal placement in the considered experimental setting. The SCI values range approximately between ∼0.5 g/request and ∼3.5 g/ request across different infrastructure sizes. It is worth recalling that this means that each incoming request (i.e., functional unit) is estimated to emit such amount of carbon. The *Capacity-Only* heuristic yields the highest SCI values, indicating less carbon-efficient placements. In contrast, the *Green&Capacity* heuristic consistently produces SCI values between the optimal identified by *Green-Only* and the worse solution identified by *Capacity-Only*.

To better quantify this behaviour, Fig. 3b reports the relative SCI difference with respect to the SCI-optimal placement. The *Green-Only* heuristic exhibits 0 % deviation from optimal across all configurations, confirming that it identifies the optimal placement in this controlled scenario. The *Capacity-Only* heuristic shows the largest distance, reaching values up to approximately 500 %, while the *Green&Capacity* heuristic reduces this gap to around 200 %.

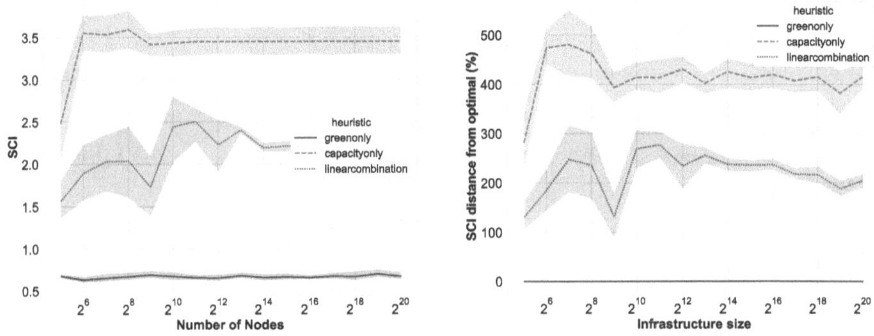

(a) SCI at increasing infrastructure sizes. (b) SCI distance from optimal.

Fig. 3. Comparison of heuristic strategies in terms of SCI.

RQ2: *How does the execution time of the heuristics evolve as the infrastructure size increases?*

Figure 4 reports the execution time of the three heuristic strategies as the infrastructure size increases from 2^5 to 2^{20} nodes. Overall, although the problem is inherently exponential, execution times remain within a few tens of seconds even for the largest infrastructure sizes.

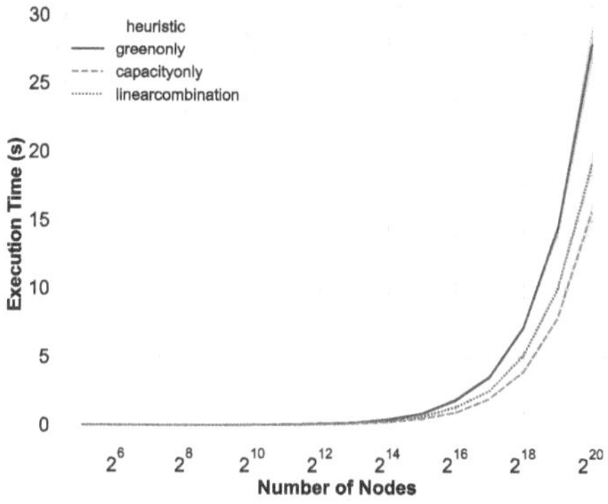

Fig. 4. Execution times of heuristic strategies at increasing infrastructure sizes.

More specifically, the *Capacity-Only* heuristic consistently achieves the lowest execution time, ranging from a few ms to 15 s. The *Green&Capacity* heuristic exhibits slightly higher execution times, up to approximately 20 s, while *Green-Only* is the slowest, reaching up to approximately 30 s for the largest infrastructures.

This behaviour can be explained by the node ordering strategy. Indeed, prioritising capacity leads to faster identification of eligible placements, whereas prioritising carbon efficiency may require exploring less suitable nodes before finding a solution.

RQ3: *Which trade-off emerges between carbon optimality and execution time across the different heuristic configurations?*
The results clearly highlight a trade-off between execution time and carbon optimality. The *Green-Only* heuristic achieves optimal SCI values but incurs the highest execution times. Conversely, the *Capacity Only* heuristic is the fastest but produces the least carbon-efficient placements. The *Green&Capacity* heuristic exhibits an intermediate behaviour, achieving near-optimal SCI values, while maintaining execution times closer to the fastest *Capacity-Only* approach.

Overall, the results do not reveal a universally "best" policy. In the considered controlled settings, *Green-Only* is preferable when SCI optimality is the primary objective, whereas *Capacity-Only* is preferable when decision time is critical. The *Green&Capacity* heuristic provides a compromise between these two extremes.

5 Related Work

In the last decade, the problem of determining multi-service application placements in cloud–edge environments has attracted growing interest. A range of strategies have been proposed to improve QoS and QoE in edge computing systems [8–11], alongside various methodologies for the placement and management of multiservice applications in cloud-edge environments [5,11].

Many existing approaches often attempt placing services closer to their users so as to optimise performance while reducing latency and, thus, response times [12–16]. Other proposals focussed on service placement from a data-aware perspective, aimed at reducing unnecessary data migration and containing access latency. Strategies such as moving data closer to computation units have been widely studied [17–19]. Data replication and placement models have also been proposed to improve system responsiveness [20,21]. Recent works address the interaction between service placement and data availability, as presented by [22], to jointly drive service placement and request scheduling for data-intensive applications, and [23], proposing a data placement and retrieval framework for cooperative edge clouds.

Mobility-aware approaches have also been studied, as reviewed in [10] for multi-access Edge computing. Security-aware placement mechanisms have also been explored to balance computation offloading with security risks. [24] propose a security-aware, time-efficient task scheduling model that optimises risk-aware service placement.

Overall, most works have explored MILP-based solutions for service placement in cloud-edge settings, focusing on different optimisation objectives. As an interesting example, [25] aim at determining energy-efficient service placement by minimising resource fragmentation in mobile Edge clouds. Similarly, [26] develop a MILP-based approach for service function chaining in Industrial IoT, incorporating heuristic approximations for large-scale networks. A cost-aware MILP formulation for Edge server deployment is introduced by [27], optimising the user experience while balancing deployment costs. Additionally, [28] present a hyper-heuristic MILP model that considers both service placement and QoE requirements in 5G Mobile Edge Computing. These works show that specialised optimisation formulations can be effective for medium-size instances, and represent a relevant trade-off between exhaustive declarative search and lightweight greedy heuristics. The BigMEC framework [29] leverages distributed reinforcement learning to improve scalability, at the expense of placement quality and migration efficiency.

Declarative Prolog programming has been used for the placement of services considering the constraints of QoS and cost [30]. Such technique also embedded continuous reasoning to improve runtime decision-making in cloud-edge placements. More recently, [31] proposed a MILP-based layered heuristic to continuously adapt deployments. Lastly, [32] applied logic programming to distribute base container images across cloud-edge networks, addressing a complementary challenge. To the best of our knowledge, some recent works have explored sustainability of cloud-edge application placements. The work by Aldossari et al. [33] is the first work including carbon emissions in the trade-off analyses to determine cloud-edge application placements, as per a MILP approach. Forti et al. [7] focus on a simple estimate of operational carbon emissions of application placements along with deployment costs, through a declarative approach. On a similar line, the FREEDA framework supports failure-resilient and energy-aware deployment across cloud-edge resources [34]. Very recently, [35] only considered reducing node carbon intensity when selecting placement nodes. While these approaches enable the generation of valid deployments under multiple constraints, carbon intensity included, they do not explicitly incorporate SCI estimation.

In summary, while service placement in cloud-edge settings has been widely studied under many different objectives, environmental sustainability has only recently entered the picture and is still often treated in a simplified way, for instance by neglecting application topology, number of service requests, and internal workflows. To the best of our knowledge, this work is among the first to explicitly adopt the SCI standard in this context, enabling carbon-aware placement decisions that account for application structure, requests workload, and both operational and embodied emissions in microservice-based applications.

6 Concluding Remarks

This article addressed the problem of carbon-aware placement of microservice-based applications in cloud-edge environments by leveraging the SCI standard. While the problem of deciding where to place application services across the cloud-edge continuum has been widely investigated [5], to the best of our knowledge, this work is the first proposing a declarative model to assess SCI at the level of microservice placements. The proposed model is integrated into both an exhaustive strategy that captures SCI-optimal placements and a configurable greedy heuristic that enables scalable carbon-aware placement decisions.

The experimental results show that the proposed heuristics effectively guide placement decisions. In our scenario, *Green-Only* consistently identifies optimal placements with execution times up to 30 s, whereas *Capacity-Only* achieves the lowest execution times (below 15 s) at the cost of substantially higher emissions (up to 400% above the optimum). The *Green&Capacity* strategy provides the best trade-off, achieving SCI values closer to optimal (within approximately 200% of the optimum) with execution times below 20 s.

The evaluation is conducted in a controlled setting, where the optimal placement is known *a priori*. While this enables a precise assessment of heuristic accuracy, it also represents a potential threat to validity, as real-world cloud-edge infrastructures may exhibit higher heterogeneity and dynamic behaviour, as well as different application topologies, request distributions, and stateful/stateless service mixes. Nevertheless, the observed trends provide clear insights into the behaviour of the proposed strategies within the considered setting.

Future work will focus on extending the SCI model to account for network-related emissions, evaluating the proposed strategies on larger and more heterogeneous infrastructures, including dynamic scenarios relying on the ECLYPSE simulator [36], and exploring additional heuristics and solver-based formulations to further investigate the trade-off between execution time and carbon optimality. Comparisons with latency-first and capacity-first placement baselines are also planned for future work, as well as integrating the approach into existing orchestration engines.

References

1. Belkhir, L., Elmeligi, A.: Assessing ICT global emissions footprint: trends to 2040 & recommendations. J. Clean. Prod. **177** (2018). issn: 0959-6526. https://doi.org/10.1016/j.jclepro.2017.12.239
2. Zulfiqar, M., et al.: Digitalized world and carbon footprints: does digitalization really matter for sustainable environment? Environ. Sci. Pollut. Res. **30**(38), 88789–88802 (2023)
3. Danushi, O., et al.: Carbon-efficient software design and development: a systematic literature review. ACM Comput. Surv. **57**(10), 1–35 (2025). https://doi.org/10.1145/3728638
4. Gaglianese, M., et al.: Green orchestration of cloud-edge applications: state of the art and open challenges. In: IEEE SOSE 2023. IEEE (2023). https://doi.org/10.1109/SOSE58276.2023.00036
5. Mahmud, R., et al.: Application management in fog computing environments: a taxonomy, review and future directions. ACM Comput. Surv. **53**(4), 1–43 (2020)
6. He, T., et al.: It's hard to share: joint service placement and request scheduling in edge clouds with sharable and non-sharable resources. IEEE ICDCS (2018). https://doi.org/10.1109/ICDCS.2018.00044
7. Forti, S., Brogi, A.: Green application placement in the cloud-IoT continuum. In: PADL, vol. 13165 (2022)
8. Salaht, F.A., et al.: An overview of service placement problem in fog and edge computing. ACM CSUR **53**(3), 1–35 (2020)
9. Santoso, G.Z., et al.: Dynamic resource selection in cloud service broker. In: HPCS. IEEE (2017)
10. Malazi, H.T., et al.: Dynamic service placement in multi-access edge computing: a systematic literature review. IEEE Access **10**, 32639–32688 (2022). https://doi.org/10.1109/ACCESS.2022.3160738
11. Taleb, I., et al.: A survey on services placement algorithms in integrated cloud-fog/edge computing. ACM Comput. Surv. **57**(11) (2025). ISSN: 0360-0300. https://doi.org/10.1145/3729214
12. Carrusca, A., et al.: Microservices management on cloud/edge environments. In: Yangui, S., et al. (eds.) ICSOC Workshops (2020)
13. Ullah, A., et al.: MiCADO-edge: towards an application-level orchestrator for the cloud-to-edge computing continuum. JDC **19**(4), 47 (2021)
14. Tang, J., et al.: Optimized Composition for Multiple User Service Requests Based on Edge-Cloud Collaboration. IEEE Access **9**, 94862–94878 (2021)
15. Maia, A.M., et al.: Optimized placement of scalable iot services in edge computing. In: IFIP/IEEE IM. IEEE (2019)
16. Guo, M., et al.: Energy-efficient and delay-guaranteed workload allocation in IoT-edge-cloud computing systems. IEEE Access **7**, 78685–78697 (2019)
17. Mordacchini, M., et al.: Human-centric data dissemination in the IoP: large-scale modeling and evaluation. ACM TAAS **14**(3) (2020). ISSN: 1556-4665
18. Patman, J., et al.: Data-driven edge computing resource scheduling for protest crowds incident management. In: IEEE NCA (2018)

19. Payberah, A.H., et al.: Lightweight gossip-based distribution estimation. In: IEEE ICC (2013)
20. Aral, A., Ovatman, T.: A decentralized replica placement algorithm for edge computing. IEEE TNSM **15**(2) (2018)
21. Li, C., et al.: Flexible replica placement for enhancing the availability in edge computing environment. Comput. Commun. **146** (2019)
22. Farhadi, V., et al.: Service placement and request scheduling for data-intensive applications in edge clouds. IEEE/ACM Tran. Net. **29** (2021). https://doi.org/10.1109/TNET.2020.3048613
23. Xie, J., et al.: A novel data placement and retrieval service for cooperative edge clouds. IEEE TSC **11** (2023). https://doi.org/10.1109/TCC.2021.3076229
24. Sun, H., et al.: Security-aware and time-guaranteed service placement in edge clouds. IEEE TNSM **20** (2023). https://doi.org/10.1109/TNSM.2022.3213761
25. Han, P., et al.: Energy-efficient service placement based on equivalent bandwidth in cell zooming enabled mobile edge cloud networks. IEEE TVT **71** (2022). https://doi.org/10.1109/TVT.2022.3194543
26. Asgarian, M., et al.: An efficient approximation algorithm for service function chaining placement in edge–cloud computing industrial internet of things. IEEE IoT-J **11** (2024). https://doi.org/10.1109/JIOT.2023.3338516
27. Shao, Y., et al.: Cost-aware placement optimization of edge servers for IoT services in wireless metropolitan area networks. Wirel. Commun. Mob. Comput. (2022) https://doi.org/10.1155/2022/8936576
28. Islam, S., et al.: A hyper-heuristic approach for quality of experience aware service placement scheme in 5G mobile edge computing. IEEE Access **12** (2024). https://doi.org/10.1109/ACCESS.2024.3403721
29. Brandherm, F., et al.: BigMEC: scalable service migration for mobile edge computing. IEEE/ACM SEC (2022). https://doi.org/10.1109/SEC54971.2022.00018
30. Massa, J. et al.: Combining declarative and linear programming for application management in the cloud-edge continuum. In: FGCS, vol. 176 (2026). ISSN: 0167-739X. https://doi.org/10.1016/j.future.2025.108224
31. Herrera, J.L., et al.: Multi-layered continuous reasoning for cloud-IoT application management. IEEE TSC **17**(6) (2024). https://doi.org/10.1109/TSC.2024.3451239
32. Azzolini, D., et al.: Continuous reasoning for adaptive container image distribution in the cloud-edge continuum. Clust. Comput. **28**(7) (2025). https://doi.org/10.1007/S10586-025-05253-9
33. Aldossary, M., Alharbi, H.A.: Towards a green approach for minimizing carbon emissions in fog-cloud architecture. IEEE Access **9** (2021). https://doi.org/10.1109/ACCESS.2021.3114514
34. Vitali, M.: FREEDA: Failure-Resilient, Energy-aware, and Explainable Deployment of Microservice-based Applications over Cloud-IoT Infrastructures (2024)
35. Azzolini, D., et al.: Application placement with constraint relaxation. Theory Pract. Log. Program. **25**(4) (2025). https://doi.org/10.1017/S1471068425100148
36. Massa, J., et al.: ECLYPSE: a python framework for simulation and emulation of the cloud-edge continuum. J. Softw. Evol. Process **38**(1) (2026)

Edge Computing Orchestration Overhead: Analysing Per-Container Decomposition of Kubernetes on Edge Using cgroup Telemetry

Diyaz Yakubov(✉), Sergio Moreschini, and David Hästbacka

Tampere Software Engineering Research Centre (TASE), Tampere University, Tampere 33014, Finland
{diyaz.yakubov,sergio.moreschini,david.hastbacka}@tuni.fi

Abstract. Edge computing in the cloud-edge continuum orchestrations is on the rise, driven by sensor analytics, real-time control, edge intelligence, and on-device AI inference. Kubernetes is increasingly deployed to resource-constrained edge nodes, yet comparative benchmarks report only system-level CPU and memory utilisation, which conflates orchestration overhead with workload consumption and cannot attribute costs to individual components. We present a per-container decomposition methodology that uses Linux cgroup telemetry, collected at per-second granularity (with Netdata), to isolate the resource footprint of each Kubernetes component. We study this for a Raspberry Pi 4 (ARM Cortex-A72) worker node running k0s. The decomposition reveals that a single Burstable system pod (likely konnectivity-agent, the k0s API server proxy) accounts for 66.7% of idle CPU overhead, while total containerised orchestration overhead consumes only 0.38% of node CPU capacity and 1.13% of RAM. Under control-plane stress (12 concurrent clients creating and deleting 120 pods), system CPU grows 9.2× but memory increases only 30%, indicating CPU-bound scaling. During data-plane workloads (Redis with memtier), the orchestration layer becomes CPU-invisible: workload containers consume 99.4% of all container CPU. The methodology is distribution-agnostic and applicable to other Kubernetes distributions and hardware platforms: idle-test enumeration for classification, multi-dimensional cgroup aggregation, and cross-run averaging.

Keywords: Orchestration · Edge Computing · Container Overhead · Linux cgroup · Per-Container Decomposition · Orchestration Tax

1 Introduction

Container orchestration platforms based on Kubernetes have become the standard for deploying workloads across cloud and edge environments [2]. At the edge, where nodes are resource-constrained (limited CPU, memory, and often

Published by Springer Nature Switzerland AG 2027
D. Balouek et al. (Eds.): ESOCC 2026, LNCS 16834, pp. 102–118, 2027.
https://doi.org/10.1007/978-3-032-37831-6_7

battery-powered), the overhead imposed by the orchestration layer itself becomes an important factor, e.g., when orchestrating deployments in the cloud-edge continuum, or ultimately in the cognitive cloud [17] that is capable of self-adaptation. Emerging use cases such as sensor analytics, real-time control, edge intelligence, and on-device AI inference amplify this concern: any compute-intensive container sharing a node with the orchestration layer competes for the same constrained CPU budget, making it essential to understand the per-component breakdown and how it shifts across workload conditions. Prior comparative studies, including our own benchmarks of five Kubernetes distributions [24,25], have measured this overhead at the system level: total CPU utilisation, total memory consumption, pod-startup latency, and throughput. These system-level metrics are valuable but have two limitations.

First, they cannot attribute resource consumption to specific Kubernetes components. When a Raspberry Pi worker node shows 4% idle CPU under k0s, it is unclear how much is kube-apiserver versus kube-proxy versus CoreDNS. This attribution matters for optimisation: if kube-apiserver dominates, reducing API polling frequency may help; if kube-proxy dominates, switching to a lighter networking mode may be more effective.

Second, system-level metrics cannot separate the *orchestration tax* (resources consumed by the platform itself) from workload resource use. Under a data-plane benchmark, is 90% of CPU consumed by the Redis workload or by the orchestration layer serving it? Answering this requires per-container decomposition.

We address both concerns through a cgroup-based decomposition methodology applied to k0s on a Raspberry Pi 4 cluster with two research questions:

- **RQ1 (Component Attribution):** Which Kubernetes system component dominates idle overhead, and how does the per-component breakdown change under control-plane versus data-plane load?
- **RQ2 (Orchestration Tax):** What fraction of edge node capacity is consumed by orchestration itself, and how does this tax scale with workload intensity?

The contributions are: (1) the first, to the best of our knowledge, per-container overhead decomposition of a Kubernetes distribution on real edge hardware; (2) quantification of the containerised orchestration tax under three workload conditions; (3) a reusable, distribution-agnostic methodology for cgroup-based overhead analysis; and (4) workload-type capacity planning rules and concrete architectural redesign levers derived directly from the decomposition results.

The remainder of this paper is organised as follows. Section 2 presents background and related work. Section 3 describes the methodology. Section 4 presents results. Section 5 discusses the implications. Section 6 addresses threats to validity, and Sect. 7 concludes.

2 Background and Related Work

This section provides the necessary background: prior measurements of Kubernetes overhead on edge hardware, the Linux cgroup telemetry interface on which the methodology depends, and the specific distribution under analysis.

2.1 Kubernetes Overhead on Edge Devices

On resource-constrained edge nodes, the orchestration layer itself competes with user workloads for CPU and memory, making its footprint a genuine design concern, not merely an implementation detail [1].

Several studies have quantified the resource footprint of Kubernetes on edge hardware [6,21]. Benchmarks of k3s, k0s, MicroK8s, and k8s on Raspberry Pi devices report idle memory of 300–500 MiB depending on the distribution [6]. Our own benchmarks [24,25] compared five distributions (k0s, k3s, k8s, KubeEdge, OpenYurt) across performance, security, resilience, and maintainability, finding that idle CPU ranges from 1.5% (k3s) to 6.8% (KubeEdge) and idle RAM from 348 MiB (k3s) to 440 MiB (KubeEdge). However, all such studies report aggregate node-level metrics. To the best of our knowledge, no prior work has decomposed the overhead into individual Kubernetes components using per-container cgroup telemetry on edge hardware.

Cgroup-derived metrics are well-established in cloud Kubernetes monitoring; cAdvisor and Prometheus expose them in every deployment, typically as inputs to auto-scaling and anomaly-detection pipelines [1]. However, the question those deployments ask is how much each container consumes, not how much the platform itself does. At cloud scale this is largely uninteresting, as the orchestration footprint is negligible against multi-hundred-GiB hosts. On a four-core node with 4 GB of RAM, the same footprint becomes a meaningful fraction of node capacity, and identifying which component is responsible directly informs both distribution selection and configuration tuning.

2.2 Linux Cgroup Metrics

Linux control groups (cgroups v2) [8] provide per-container resource accounting: CPU time (user + system), memory usage (RSS, swap, cache), network I/O, block I/O, CPU throttling events, and Pressure Stall Information (PSI) [13]. Kubernetes assigns each pod to a cgroup hierarchy under `/sys/fs/cgroup/kubepods/`, organised by QoS class (Guaranteed, Burstable, BestEffort) [12]. Monitoring agents such as Netdata [18] can collect per-second cgroup metrics and export them as chart contexts (e.g., `k8s.cgroup.cpu`, `k8s.cgroup.mem_usage`), enabling direct attribution of resource consumption to individual containers.

2.3 Distribution Under Test

We apply the decomposition to k0s[1] (v1.28.4) [4], a lightweight Kubernetes distribution that runs all control-plane components as containerised processes. This makes it well-suited for cgroup-based analysis: on the master node, kube-apiserver, kube-controller-manager, and kube-scheduler each run as separate containers (kube-scheduler is master-only and does not appear in the worker-node decomposition); on worker nodes, konnectivity-agent (the API server communication proxy) and kube-router (the default k0s CNI) appear alongside kube-proxy and CoreDNS as distinct cgroups. Distributions that embed components into a single binary (e.g., k3s [5]) may show a different decomposition profile, as multiple logical components share one cgroup.

Table 1. Experimental node configuration.

Feature	Master (NUC)	Workers (RPi4 ×3)
CPU	Intel i7-10710U (6C/12T @ 1.10 GHz)	ARM Cortex-A72 (4C @ 1.8 GHz)
RAM	64 GB DDR4	4 GB LPDDR4
Storage	1 TB NVMe	64 GB microSD
OS	Ubuntu 22.04.2	Ubuntu 22.04.2
Runtime	containerd v1.7.11	containerd v1.7.11

3 Methodology

The remainder of this section presents the experimental setup, the three workload types analysed, the procedure for classifying containers without process-level metadata, the cgroup metrics and aggregation rules, and the definition of the orchestration tax.

3.1 Experimental Setup

The experimental infrastructure is shared with [24,25], which permits direct cross-reference of the per-container overhead values reported here against the system-level metrics (idle CPU, RAM, throughput, latency) from those publications. Table 1 summarises the hardware configuration.

A sidecar NUC ran Netdata [18] v1.42, streaming per-second metrics to MongoDB 7.0 (~1.9 billion documents, 140 GB). The decomposition analyses data from worker node `node_2` (RPi4). Of the three worker nodes, only `node_2` had `k8s.cgroup.*` per-container collection active in the MongoDB stream during the k0s campaign; `node_1` and `node_3` operated with system-level aggregate collection only. Because all three workers run identical system pods (kube-proxy,

[1] https://k0sproject.io.

CoreDNS) under the same k0s configuration, `node_2`'s decomposition profile is representative of any worker node in this topology. It collected `k8s.cgroup.*` metrics across 27 chart context types.

3.2 Workload Types

Three workload types were analysed, each repeated 5 times with 30-minute stabilisation periods. They were chosen to cover three qualitatively different operating regimes encountered in edge deployments:

- **Idle:** No user workloads deployed. Measures the pure orchestration footprint; representative of edge gateways and sensor hubs in low-activity periods.
- **CP Heavy (12 clients):** k-bench [23] creating and deleting 120 pods across 12 concurrent clients (10 sequential create/delete cycles per client; pod image `gcr.io/google_containers/pause:3.1`; no resource limits; ~60-second active window; clients launched from the master node). Stresses the control plane (API server, scheduler, controller manager); representative of autoscaler-driven bursts and batch-job submission at the edge.
- **DP Redis Density:** Redis pod density test with memtier_benchmark [20] v2.0.0 (10 threads, 50 clients per thread, 1:10 set/get ratio, 32-byte values, 60-second duration; Redis image `redis:7.0-alpine`; no resource limits; all images pre-pulled to eliminate cold-start bias; memtier client co-located with Redis on `node_2`). Stresses the data plane while the control plane remains quiescent; representative of steady-state long-running edge workloads such as sensor ingestion and in-cluster caching.

3.3 Pod Classification

Since Netdata cgroup paths contain only opaque pod UUIDs and container hashes (not human-readable component names), we classify containers using *idle-test enumeration*:

1. All pods present during idle tests (when no user workloads are deployed) are classified as **system** pods.
2. Pods appearing only in loaded tests are classified as **workload** pods.

This identified 4 system pods (present across all test types) and 5 distinct workload pods across tests: 4 ephemeral k-bench pods during CP Heavy and 1 Redis pod during DP Redis, summarised in Table 2.

System component identities are inferred from resource profiles and QoS classes, cross-validated against known k0s architecture: the two Burstable pods with the highest and second-highest CPU match kube-apiserver (or its konnectivity-agent proxy, which tunnels API server communication on worker nodes) and kube-controller-manager (or kube-router, the default k0s CNI); the two BestEffort pods match kube-proxy and CoreDNS based on their network activity patterns. Process-level verification was not performed; see Sect. 6.

Table 2. Pod classification results (k0s, `node_2`).

Role	Count	QoS Class	Inferred Components
System	4	2 Burstable, 2 BestEffort	*kube-apiserver*†, *kube-controller-mgr*†, kube-proxy, CoreDNS
Workload (CP)	4	BestEffort	k-bench test pods (ephemeral)
Workload (DP)	1	BestEffort	Redis pod

† Inferred identity; on worker nodes, konnectivity-agent and kube-router likely serve these roles. See Sect. 3

3.4 Metric Computation

For each container, key metrics are computed from cgroup data (see Table 3).

Table 3. Cgroup metrics and aggregation rules.

Metric	Cgroup Context	Dimensions	Agg.
CPU usage	`k8s.cgroup.cpu`	user + system	Sum
Memory	`k8s.cgroup.mem_usage`	ram (excl. swap)	Max
Network	`k8s.cgroup.net_net`	received + sent	Sum
Disk I/O	`k8s.cgroup.io`	read + write	Sum
Page faults	`k8s.cgroup.pgfaults`	pgfault + pgmajfault	Sum
CPU throttle	`k8s.cgroup.throttled`	throttled	Sum
CPU pressure	`k8s.cgroup.cpu_some_pressure`	some (10 s)	Max
Mem pressure	`k8s.cgroup.memory_some_pressure`	some (10 s)	Max

Aggregation Procedure: (1) Filter to specified dimensions within each cgroup context; (2) aggregate dimensions at each one-second timestamp (sum for additive metrics, max for utilisation metrics); (3) time-average across ~250–300 active-window samples per run (the 30-minute stabilisation periods are excluded from analysis) to produce a per-pod, per-run scalar; (4) compute mean ± std across 5 runs for statistical robustness.

3.5 Containerised Orchestration Tax

The *containerised orchestration tax* measures the fraction of node capacity consumed by containerised Kubernetes system components (excluding non-containerised overhead from kubelet, containerd, and the OS kernel; see Sect. 6 for this scope limitation):

$$\text{CPU tax} = \frac{\sum_{i \in \text{system}} \overline{\text{CPU}_i}}{N_{\text{cores}} \times 100\%} \times 100\% \tag{1}$$

$$\text{Memory tax} = \frac{\sum_{i \in \text{system}} \overline{\text{RAM}_i}}{\text{Node RAM}} \times 100\% \tag{2}$$

where $N_{\text{cores}} = 4$ (Cortex-A72) and Node RAM = 4096 MiB.

CPU Normalisation. Per-cgroup CPU values are reported by Netdata as a percentage of one core; a value of 100% denotes one core fully utilised. The denominator $N_{\text{cores}} \times 100\% = 400\%$ therefore normalises the sum to total node CPU capacity. For example, the 1.52% sum across system containers at idle corresponds to a CPU tax of $1.52\%/(4 \times 100\%) = 0.38\%$ of node CPU capacity.

4 Results

4.1 Per-Container Idle Decomposition (RQ1)

Table 4 presents the per-container idle overhead. The dominant Burstable pod (*kube-apiserver*†, likely konnectivity-agent on the worker; see Table 2) dominates idle CPU at 1.014%, accounting for **66.7%** of total system CPU overhead (Fig. 1). Even in an idle cluster, the API server maintains watch connections [9], periodic health checks, and etcd interaction overhead, all of which generate per-worker proxy traffic on konnectivity-agent. The second Burstable pod (*kube-ctrl-mgr*†, likely kube-router) contributes 17.4% (reconciliation or routing-loop activity), while kube-proxy contributes 8.3% and CoreDNS 7.6%.

Table 4. k0s idle overhead per system container (`node_2`, RPi4, mean ± std over 5 runs). Pod names in italics are inferred identities; see Sect. 3 and Table 2.

System Pod	QoS	CPU (%)	Mem (MiB)	Net (kbit/s)	Pgfaults (/s)
kube-apiserver†	Burst.	1.014 ± 0.019	15.10 ± 0.23	0.047 ± 0.023	0.001 ± 0.001
kube-ctrl-mgr†	Burst.	0.265 ± 0.010	14.56 ± 0.26	–	0.041 ± 0.001
kube-proxy	BestEff.	0.127 ± 0.002	4.48 ± 0.12	0.459 ± 0.003	<0.001
CoreDNS	BestEff.	0.116 ± 0.008	12.19 ± 0.12	–	0.024 ± 0.002
Total		**1.522 ± 0.023**	**46.33 ± 0.39**	**0.506 ± 0.023**	**0.066 ± 0.002**

† Inferred identity; actual kube-apiserver and kube-controller-manager run on the master node. On the worker, the Burstable pods are likely konnectivity-agent and kube-router. Process-level verification not performed

Memory is more evenly distributed (Fig. 2): the dominant Burstable pod (*kube-apiserver*†) accounts for 32.6%, the second Burstable pod (*kube-ctrl-mgr*†) 31.4%, CoreDNS 26.3%, and kube-proxy 9.7%. This reflects Go runtime behaviour, where each binary pre-allocates a baseline heap at startup that grows with object allocations rather than with CPU scheduling activity [3]. Network traffic is captured for the dominant Burstable pod (0.047 kbit/s, reflecting

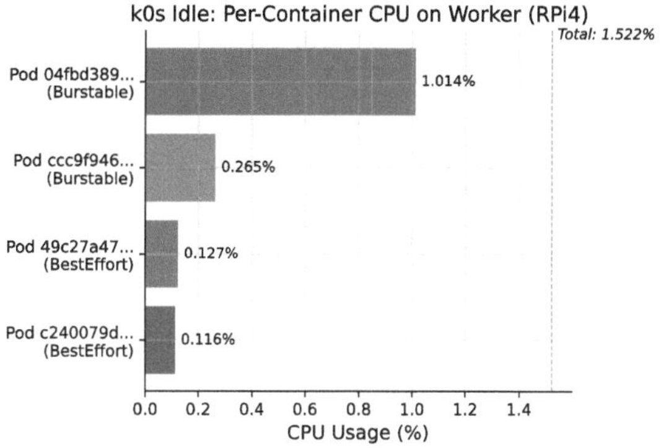

Fig. 1. Per-container idle CPU decomposition on RPi4 worker.

tunnel keepalive and health-probe traffic) and kube-proxy (0.459 kbit/s); the second Burstable pod and CoreDNS communicate over the pod overlay network via virtual interfaces not captured by the `k8s.cgroup.net_net` context in this Netdata version [18]. Page fault rates (Table 4) are highest for the second Burstable pod (0.041/s), consistent with periodic iteration over cached objects (network-policy state if it is kube-router, reconciliation cache if kube-controller-manager), while the dominant Burstable pod shows near-zero faults (0.001/s), reflecting steady-state I/O-bound operation with little new heap allocation [3].

CPU throttling, CPU pressure, and memory pressure are all **zero** across all system containers during idle (Table 7), confirming that the orchestration layer is not resource-constrained at rest on a 4 GB RPi4.

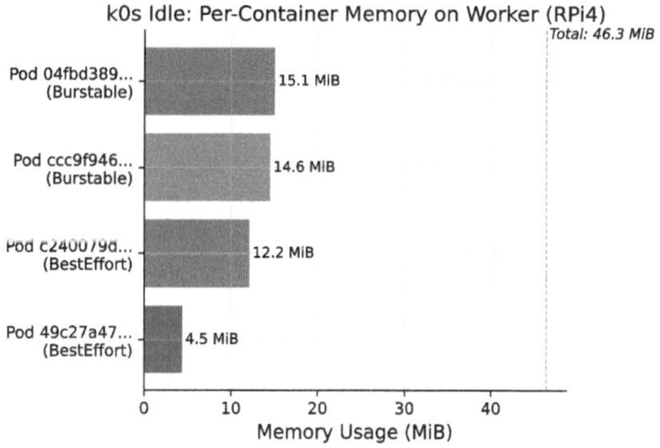

Fig. 2. Per-container idle memory decomposition on RPi4 worker.

Table 5. System overhead and containerised orchestration tax across workload types. CPU Tax and RAM Tax cover containerised system components only (see Sect. 6, Construct Validity).

Test Type	Sys CPU (%)	CPU Tax	Sys RAM (MiB)	RAM Tax
Idle	1.52 ± 0.02	0.38%	46.3 ± 0.7	1.13%
CP Heavy (12 cl.)	14.02 ± 0.59	3.50%	60.4 ± 0.4	1.47%
DP Redis Density	1.16 ± 0.12	0.29%	53.5 ± 0.3	1.31%

4.2 Overhead Under Load (RQ1, RQ2)

Table 5 summarises system overhead and the containerised orchestration tax (Eqs. (1)–(2)) across all three workload types. Three patterns are apparent:

1. Control-Plane Stress is CPU-Bound. Under CP Heavy, system CPU grows **9.2**× (from 1.52% to 14.02%), but memory increases only 30% (46.3 to 60.4 MiB). The API server and controller manager on the master node process a burst of pod creation/deletion requests that are computationally intensive but do not require proportionally more memory; the resulting API traffic and network-rule updates propagate to the worker-node system components, driving the observed CPU growth on `node_2`. CPU pressure rises from zero to 1.11% (detail in Sect. 4.3), indicating that system containers begin experiencing scheduling delays. Figure 4 visualises this growth.

2. Data-Plane Load is CPU-Invisible to the Orchestration Layer. Under DP Redis, system CPU drops to 1.16%, a statistically significant 24% decrease from idle (1.52%; 95% CIs non-overlapping: idle [1.50, 1.54]%, DP Redis [1.05, 1.27]%), as the quiescent control plane generates less API traffic and fewer network-rule updates than during idle background activity. System RAM, however, rises moderately to 53.5 MiB (+7.2 MiB versus idle), likely reflecting kube-proxy maintaining additional kernel NAT rules for the Redis Service endpoints. The single Redis workload pod scheduled on `node_2` consumes 206.1% CPU across multiple cores and 161.8 MiB RAM (Table 6), dominating the container-level resource budget (Fig. 3). The orchestration CPU tax drops to 0.29% as steady-state data-plane operations bypass most of the control plane.

3. Memory is Inelastic. Across all three conditions, system RAM varies only from 46.3 to 60.4 MiB, a 1.3× idle-to-peak range compared to CPU's 9.2× swing. This suggests that memory overhead is dominated by baseline allocations (Go runtime heaps, watch caches) rather than per-request processing.

Under DP Redis, the single workload pod consumes 99.4% of all container CPU (Table 6), meaning the orchestration layer consumes only 0.6% of the container-level CPU budget.

Table 6. System vs workload share under load.

Test Type	Sys CPU (%)	Wl CPU (%)	Wl RAM (MiB)	Wl Share
CP Heavy (12 cl.)	14.02	~0 (ephemeral)	– (ephemeral)	N/A
DP Redis Density	1.16	206.11	161.8	**99.4%**

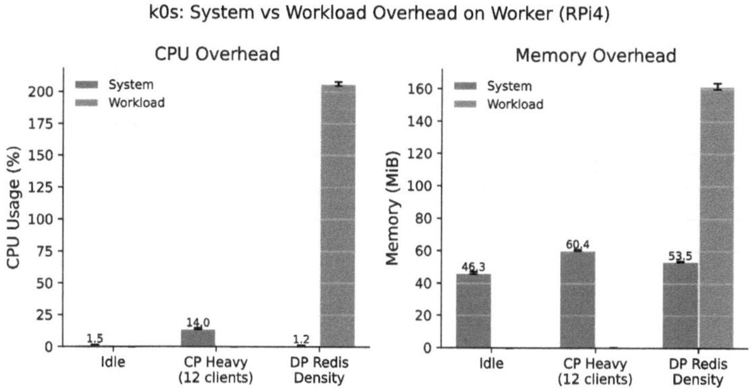

Fig. 3. System vs workload CPU and memory across test types.

4.3 Pressure Stall Information

PSI metrics [13] provide a complementary view of resource contention (Table 7).

Under CP Heavy, system containers experience modest CPU pressure (1.1%), confirming that the 9.2× CPU growth approaches but does not exceed available capacity. Under DP Redis, workload CPU pressure (5.9%) indicates that Redis + memtier are competing for CPU time across cores, while system containers remain minimally affected (0.2%). Memory pressure is 0.000% across all conditions for both system and workload containers (Table 7), confirming that the

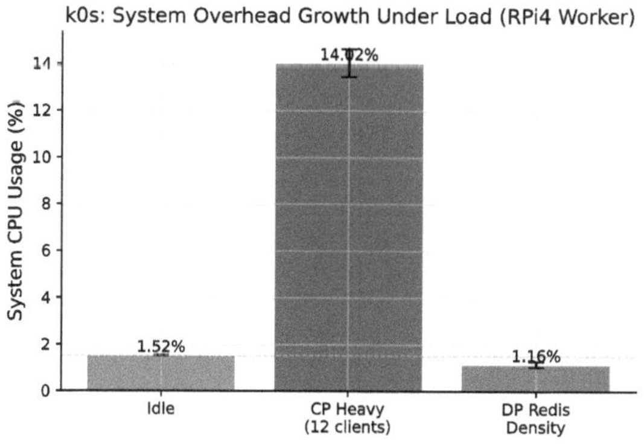

Fig. 4. System CPU growth from idle to loaded.

Table 7. PSI pressure (% of time stalled) across workload types.

Test Type	Sys CPU	Wl CPU	Sys Mem	Wl Mem
Idle	0.000%	–	0.000%	–
CP Heavy	1.113%	0.220%	0.000%	0.000%
DP Redis	0.192%	5.879%	0.000%	0.000%

4 GB RPi4 workers have sufficient memory headroom throughout all workloads; the ephemeral k-bench pods and single Redis container never approach memory limits at which the Linux kernel records stall time.

5 Discussion

5.1 API Server Communication as the Dominant Cost Centre

The finding that the inferred kube-apiserver communication overhead (likely konnectivity-agent on the worker) consumes 66.7% of idle CPU has actionable implications for edge deployments. For fleets of low-activity nodes, the API server's watch connections [9], health-check polling, and etcd interaction overhead represent a fixed per-node cost—incurred either directly by the API server or proxied through konnectivity-agent on the worker. Mitigations target the master-side API server in either case: reducing `--watch-cache-sizes`, increasing `--min-request-timeout`, or, for edge-specific distributions, caching API responses locally (as KubeEdge's EdgeHub does). However, each mitigation trades responsiveness for efficiency, creating a tension that operators must evaluate per deployment.

The memory distribution is notably more balanced than CPU: no single component dominates. Memory optimisation therefore cannot target a single component; it must address the collective baseline of all four system containers.

Comparison to Prior State of the Art. System-level benchmarks on the same hardware [24] report k0s idle CPU at 4.0%. Our decomposition accounts for 1.52% of this as containerised Kubernetes components; the remaining ~2.5% is attributable to non-containerised processes (kubelet, containerd, OS kernel threads), consistent with the construct validity bound in Sect. 6. Similarly, the 300–500 MiB idle RAM range reported in [6] dwarfs the 46.3 MiB of containerised components: between 85% and 91% of the system-reported memory footprint belongs to the distribution binary and runtime stack, not to the Kubernetes API components. This decomposition resolves a question that aggregate benchmarks leave open: which component is responsible, and quantifies the containerised orchestration tax independently of runtime costs.

5.2 Non-linear Scaling Under Control-Plane Stress

The 9.2× CPU growth under CP Heavy is disproportionate to a linear scaling baseline: the idle cluster sustains zero concurrent pod operations, so a proportional model would predict a moderate additive increase from introducing 120 pod lifecycles across 12 clients, not a near-order-of-magnitude amplification. This non-linear scaling arises from the control plane's coordination overhead. On the master, each pod creation triggers API server validation, etcd writes, scheduler decisions, controller reconciliation, and network rule updates [2, 11]; these operations are sequential per pod but concurrent across clients, creating contention on API server locks and etcd transactions [19]. The resulting traffic propagates to the worker through konnectivity-agent and the other worker-side system components, manifesting as the observed CPU growth on `node_2`.

This mechanism offers a consistent explanation for why distributions with higher baseline overhead (e.g., KubeEdge at 6.8% idle CPU [24]) exhibit disproportionate latency degradation under load. If the idle cost is already high, the multiplicative growth pushes system overhead into territory where the orchestration layer competes with workloads for CPU time.

5.3 Orchestration CPU Invisibility During Data-Plane Workloads

The 99.4% workload CPU share under DP Redis is a practically important result: once pods are running, k0s imposes negligible ongoing CPU overhead on data-plane operations. The orchestration layer's cost is concentrated in pod lifecycle management (creation, scheduling, deletion), not in steady-state workload execution.

The distinction has direct capacity planning implications. An edge node running long-lived data-plane workloads (sensors, inference, data aggregation) can treat the containerised orchestration tax as a small fixed cost (0.29% CPU, 1.31% RAM). A node running frequent short-lived jobs (batch processing, CI/CD) will experience the 3.5% CPU tax of control-plane operations.

5.4 Practical Implications and Redesign Guidance

Capacity Planning Rules. The decomposition yields workload-dependent rules for edge operators. For CP-intensive deployments (batch jobs, CI/CD, frequent pod churn), at least 3.5% node CPU and an additional 14 MiB RAM should be reserved for orchestration overhead, with PSI monitoring to detect when system containers begin competing with workloads. For long-lived data-plane deployments (sensor aggregation, inference, streaming), the orchestration layer is effectively CPU-invisible: operators can allocate nearly the full node capacity to workloads, budgeting only 0.29% CPU and 1.31% RAM as a fixed cost. In both cases, memory headroom of ~47–60 MiB per node should be subtracted from available capacity before workload scheduling decisions, as this cost is largely independent of workload intensity (this accounts for containerised system components only; non-containerised processes such as kubelet, containerd, and OS kernel threads contribute additional overhead beyond this figure, as discussed in Sect. 6).

Redesign Levers. The 66.7% idle CPU share borne by the API server communication path (the dominant Burstable pod on the worker, likely konnectivity-agent) is not fixed; it is a function of configuration choices. Replacing CoreDNS with NodeLocal DNSCache [14] eliminates the 12.2 MiB RAM and 0.116% CPU of the CoreDNS container (Table 4) while reducing DNS lookup latency. Reducing `--watch-cache-sizes` or increasing `--min-request-timeout` [10] lowers the API server's watch connection overhead at the cost of responsiveness. A single-binary architecture such as k3s [5] consolidates all control-plane components into one process and cgroup, which may reduce inter-component IPC overhead and watch connection duplication, though it forfeits per-component observability. KubeEdge's EdgeHub [7] directly addresses the API server dominance problem by caching API state locally on worker nodes, offloading watch connections from the central server, an architectural inversion of the pattern identified here. These options reflect a broader principle: the orchestration overhead profile is an architectural degree of freedom, not a hardware constraint [22].

5.5 Transferability of the Methodology

Beyond the k0s-specific results, the methodology itself is a contribution. The approach, which combines idle-test enumeration for pod classification, multi-dimensional cgroup aggregation with configurable dimension filtering, and cross-run statistical averaging, is applicable to any Kubernetes distribution that runs system components as containers with cgroup isolation. Distributions that embed components into a single binary (e.g., k3s) would show a single combined cgroup, producing a coarser decomposition but still enabling system-vs-workload separation and containerised orchestration tax computation.

The key requirement is enabling per-container cgroup collection in the monitoring agent. In our experimental setup, this was available only for k0s, a data availability limitation rather than a methodological one.

6 Threats to Validity

Internal Validity. Pod classification via idle-test enumeration is reliable for identifying system pods (anything running during idle = system) but assigns roles to opaque UUIDs. Component identities (kube-apiserver, etc.) are inferred from resource profiles and QoS classes, not verified at the process level. Additionally, the decomposition uses a single worker node (`node_2`); cross-worker validation was not performed. This reflects a data availability constraint: per-container cgroup metrics were active in the MongoDB stream only for `node_2` during the k0s campaign, not a hardware distinction between nodes. Five repeated runs were found sufficient given the low coefficient of variation observed (e.g., $\pm 1.5\%$ relative standard deviation on total idle system CPU).

External Validity. The results are specific to k0s v1.28.4 on RPi4 (Cortex-A72, 4 GB). Other distributions with different architectures (single-binary k3s, edge-extended KubeEdge) will show different decomposition profiles; extending to those distributions requires enabling per-container cgroup collection during benchmark campaigns [18]. The hardware platform is representative of low-power edge devices but does not generalise to x86 edge servers or other ARM SoCs. Importantly, the tested Kubernetes version (v1.28) predates several features that directly affect the overhead patterns we measured. Kubernetes v1.35 introduces *opportunistic scheduler batching* (KEP-5598) [16], which reuses scoring results across pods with identical scheduling signatures (likely reducing the 9.2× CPU growth observed under CP Heavy), and *in-place pod resize* [15], which modifies cgroup resource limits without pod restart and may alter the memory overhead profile. These features suggest that the absolute overhead values reported here represent an upper bound that newer Kubernetes versions may improve upon, though the decomposition methodology and relative patterns (e.g., API server dominance) are likely to persist.

Construct Validity. The containerised orchestration tax as defined does not account for non-containerised system processes (kubelet, containerd, OS kernel threads, host networking, file-system drivers). The true orchestration overhead is therefore higher than the cgroup-measured value; our metric captures only the *containerised* portion. As a sanity bound: system-level benchmarks on the same hardware [24] report k0s idle CPU at 4.0%, while the decomposition accounts for 1.52% as containerised components; the remaining ~2.5% is the non-containerised portion. Netdata exposes kubelet and containerd metrics via its systemd and process collectors; extending the metric to include them is left as future work. Additionally, the workload CPU share (99.4%) reflects container-level accounting; host-level kernel work (network stack, block I/O) on behalf of workloads is not attributed to workload cgroups.

7 Conclusion and Future Work

This paper presents, to the best of our knowledge, the first per-container overhead decomposition of a Kubernetes distribution on real edge hardware. Using Linux cgroup telemetry from k0s running on a Raspberry Pi 4 cluster, we establish three findings:

1. **A single proxy pod dominates idle overhead.** It accounts for 66.7% of system CPU—almost certainly konnectivity-agent on this worker (Sect. 3)—while the total containerised orchestration tax is only 0.38% of node CPU capacity.
2. **Control-plane stress scales non-linearly:** 9.2× CPU growth under 12-client pod creation, but memory grows only 30%.
3. **Data-plane workloads render orchestration CPU-invisible:** workload containers consume 99.4% of all container CPU, with the orchestration CPU tax dropping to 0.29%.

These findings collectively decompose what prior system-level benchmarks report as a single overhead figure [6,24] into component-level costs, enabling targeted optimisation: capacity planning rules that differ by workload type, identification of API server communication overhead as the primary redesign target, and a set of architectural levers (CoreDNS replacement, watch-cache tuning, single-binary consolidation, local API caching) that can alter the overhead profile without changing hardware. The methodology is distribution-agnostic and directly applicable to any Kubernetes distribution with cgroup-isolated system components. Four directions for future work present themselves:

- **Version-aware re-evaluation:** Repeating the decomposition on current Kubernetes (v1.35+) to quantify the impact of opportunistic scheduler batching (KEP-5598) on control-plane overhead.
- **Cross-distribution decomposition:** Repeating the analysis for k3s, k8s, KubeEdge, and OpenYurt by enabling per-container cgroup collection during benchmarks.
- **Process-level attribution:** Extending cgroup analysis with eBPF tracing to verify inferred component identities (Tables 2 and 4) and attribute overhead to specific API server endpoints, controller reconciliation loops, or networking functions within each container.
- **Energy integration:** Combining per-container CPU decomposition with DVFS power models to estimate per-component energy consumption on battery-powered edge devices.

Acknowledgement. This work is supported by Business Finland in projects Industry X and DAZE.

Data and Code Availability. The cgroup decomposition analysis pipeline is available at https://github.com/DiyazY/kd-edge-internals. The experimental infrastructure and raw benchmark data are available at https://github.com/DiyazY/iot-edge.

References

1. Aruna, K., Gurunathan, P.: Enhancing edge environment scalability: leveraging Kubernetes for container orchestration and optimization. Concurrency and Computation: Practice and Experience **36**(28) (2024)
2. Burns, B., Grant, B., Oppenheimer, D., Brewer, E., Wilkes, J.: Borg, omega, and Kubernetes. ACM Queue, **14**(1) (2016)
3. Go Authors: A guide to the Go garbage collector (2024). https://tip.golang.org/doc/gc-guide
4. k0s Project: Architecture (2024). https://docs.k0sproject.io/head/architecture/
5. k3s Project: Architecture (2024). https://docs.k3s.io/architecture
6. Koziolek, H., Eskandani, N.: Lightweight Kubernetes distributions: a performance comparison of MicroK8s, k3s, k0s, and MicroShift. In: Proceedings of the ACM/SPEC International Conference on Performance Engineering (ICPE '23), pp. 17–29. ACM, New York (2023)

7. KubeEdge Project: Architecture (2024). https://kubeedge.io/docs/architecture/
8. Kubernetes: About cgroup v2 (2024). https://kubernetes.io/docs/concepts/architecture/cgroups/
9. Kubernetes: Efficient detection of changes: API concepts (2024). https://kubernetes.io/docs/reference/using-api/api-concepts/#efficient-detection-of-changes
10. Kubernetes: kube-apiserver (2024). https://kubernetes.io/docs/reference/command-line-tools-reference/kube-apiserver/
11. Kubernetes: Pod lifecycle (2024). https://kubernetes.io/docs/concepts/workloads/pods/pod-lifecycle/
12. Kubernetes: Resource management for pods and containers (2024). https://kubernetes.io/docs/concepts/configuration/manage-resources-containers/
13. Kubernetes: Understand pressure stall information (PSI) metrics (2024). https://kubernetes.io/docs/reference/instrumentation/understand-psi-metrics/
14. Kubernetes: Using NodeLocal DNSCache in Kubernetes clusters (2024). https://kubernetes.io/docs/tasks/administer-cluster/nodelocaldns/
15. Kubernetes: In-place pod resize graduates to stable (v1.35) (2025). https://kubernetes.io/blog/2025/12/19/kubernetes-v1-35-in-place-pod-resize-ga/
16. Kubernetes Enhancement Proposals: KEP-5598: Opportunistic batching in kube-scheduler(2025). https://github.com/kubernetes/enhancements/tree/master/keps/sig-scheduling/5598-opportunistic-batching
17. Moreschini, S., et al.: Cognitive cloud: The definition. In: Omatu, S., Mehmood, R., Sitek, P., Cicerone, S., Rodríguez, S. (eds.) Distributed Computing and Artificial Intelligence, 19th International Conference, pp. 219–229. Springer International Publishing, Cham (2023)
18. Netdata Inc.: Kubernetes containers monitoring (2024). https://learn.netdata.cloud/docs/collecting-metrics/kubernetes/kubernetes-containers
19. Ongaro, D., Ousterhout, J.: In search of an understandable consensus algorithm. In: Proceedings of the 2014 USENIX Conference on USENIX Annual Technical Conference, pp. 305–320. USENIX ATC'14, USENIX Association, USA (2014)
20. Redis: memtier_benchmark: NoSQL redis and memcache traffic generation and benchmarking tool (2024). https://github.com/redis/memtier_benchmark
21. Sari, S.: Survey of container orchestration distributions in cloud-to-edge continuum. In: International Conference on Future Internet of Things and Cloud (FiCloud), pp. 39–45. IEEE (2025)
22. Shan, C., Wu, C., Xia, Y., Guo, Z., Liu, D., Zhang, J.: Adaptive resource allocation for workflow containerization on Kubernetes. J. Syst. Eng. Electron. **34**(3), 723–743 (2023)
23. VMware Tanzu: k-bench: Workload benchmark for Kubernetes (2023). https://github.com/vmware-tanzu/k-bench
24. Yakubov, D., Hästbacka, D.: Comparative analysis of lightweight Kubernetes distributions for edge computing: performance and resource efficiency. In: Pahl, C., Janes, A., Cerny, T., Lenarduzzi, V., Esposito, M. (eds.) Proceedings of the European Conference on Service-Oriented and Cloud Computing (ESOCC 2025). LNCS, vol. 15547, pp. 81–95. Springer, Cham (2025). https://doi.org/10.1007/978-3-031-84617-5_7

25. Yakubov, D., Hästbacka, D.: Comparative analysis of lightweight Kubernetes distributions for edge computing: Security, resilience and maintainability. In: Pahl, C., Janes, A., Cerny, T., Lenarduzzi, V., Esposito, M. (eds.) Proceedings European Conference on Service-Oriented and Cloud Computing (ESOCC 2025). LNCS, vol. 15547, pp. 96–104. Springer, Cham (2025). https://doi.org/10.1007/978-3-031-84617-5_8

A Framework for Telco and Service Hybrid Edge-Cloud Platform Cost Evaluation

Roberto Micali(✉), Marco Quagliotti, and Carlo Cavazzoni

TIM - Telecom Italia S.p.A, Via G. Reiss Romoli, 274 Turin, Italy
{roberto.micali,marco.quagliotti,
carlo.cavazzoni}@telecomitalia.it

Abstract. Building a cloud infrastructure for an operator offering both information technology and telecommunications services demands strategic decisions on implementation approaches, especially given the rapid technological evolution and intense market competition. This article introduces a model and methodology designed to support the technical and economic evaluation of cloud solutions that host both edge-cloud applications and telecommunications functions using either fully on-premises infrastructures or hybrid configurations that leverage public cloud resources. The model considers the degree of infrastructure centralization, encompassing the distribution of central, near edge, and far edge sites, while also incorporating the degree of utilization of public cloud resource pools versus proprietary on-premises resources to evaluate hybrid deployment scenarios under the constraint of sovereignty and proximity requirements. A case study showcases the model's applicability and the insights resulting from its techno-economic analysis methodology. Overall, the article presents a flexible evaluation framework that can be adapted to diverse edge-cloud platform deployment contexts. This work is developed within the IPCEI-CIS TIM Edge Cloud Continuum project and currently is in the research phase, without application in TIM's operational or commercial domains.

Keywords: hybrid cloud · telco cloud · cloud continuum · edge-cloud · cloud economics · cost model

1 Introduction

1.1 Cloud Computing Market, Technologies and Flavors

The cloud computing market, spanning private, public, and hybrid model, expands rapidly, especially among telecoms and enterprises. In 2025, private cloud achieves ~105–114 billion U.S. Dollar (USD), projected to reach 195 billion USD by 2030 (10–11% CAGR), fueled by secure, customizable needs in regulated sectors. Hybrid models will surge from 134–173 to over 578 billion USD by 2034 (17–18% CAGR), public cloud from ~370 to 2.700 billion USD by 2033 (15% CAGR), and telco network cloud, which TIM is focused on, from 17 to 25 billion USD by 2030 (7% CAGR) [1].

D. Balouek et al. (Eds.): ESOCC 2026, LNCS 16834, pp. 119–133, 2027.
https://doi.org/10.1007/978-3-032-37831-6_8

As far as technology is concerned, cloud computing is evolving toward cloud-native paradigms, where applications and network functions are designed as microservices running in containers and orchestrated dynamically, primarily through Kubernetes. Cloud-Native Applications (CNAs) represent a general architectural model, while Cloud-Native Functions (CNFs) are specific implementations for network functions, though both are treated under the broader CNA concept [2]. These technologies enable deployment across hybrid, multi-cloud [3], and federated environments [4], improving scalability, flexibility, and resilience while reducing vendor lock-in and supporting business expansion.

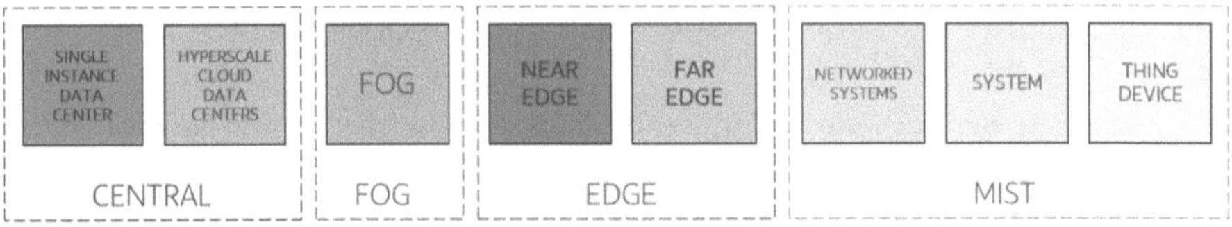

Fig. 1. The cloud continuum representation according to [5].

With the cloud continuum concept, a multi-tier architecture distributes computing, storage, and networking resources from centralized data centers to locations closer to users and devices, spanning mist, edge, fog, and central layers as depicted in Fig. 1 [5]. The figure illustrates a general model independent from resource ownership, whether on-premises (owned) or leased (e.g., from hyperscalers in central data center), encompassing private, public, or hybrid cloud scenarios.

The challenge is to manage such a distributed and heterogeneous environment, including orchestration, interoperability [6], governance [7, 8], security [9], and performance. Kubernetes plays a central role but faces limitations in edge scenarios, prompting the development of cost-aware scheduling and KPI-based monitoring to maintain quality of service [10]. In summary, governance frameworks and integrated architecture are needed to handle compliance and operational complexity. All these aspects collectively provide the context for evaluating cloud infrastructure cost.

1.2 Cloud Economics

The problem of the cost evaluation of cloud infrastructure is of fundamental importance for companies and operators who own and need to operate their own cloud. The cost evaluation of hybrid and distributed cloud infrastructure has been addressed in many works, some of them dating back more than ten years, considering specific aspects and following the evolution of technologies, services and market drivers. Without claiming to be exhaustive, below are some works that have addressed the cost modeling of a cloud infrastructure. The problem has been addressed from the point of view of the balance of resources (on-premises vs. on public cloud) in hybrid solutions by Weimann [11] highlighting that the hybrid solution is potentially the most convenient but that it depends on the type, and particularly on the degree of continuity in the resource needs of the applications. Weimann [12] also addresses the aspect of networking costs, often overlooked at first glance, highlighting how they play a determining role in the choice of an architecture from the point of view of cost. With decentralization and the role of the fog tier, new elements and new costs come into play and the model becomes more complicated as highlighted still by Weimann in [13], and also by other authors in works [14, 15].

More recently Weimann [5] proposes an interesting qualitative analysis of the trade-offs in the edge-cloud continuum highlighting pros and cons of potential placement in the different tiers of the continuum of applications having specific requirements (proximity, latency and sovereignty, among the others).

1.3 Cloud for Telco Operators and TIM's Path to Innovation

Telco operators like TIM must separate and securely interconnect core network operations from service delivery (e.g., consumer/enterprise services) for optimal performance, compliance, and efficiency. This requires synergistic integration to cut costs, improve security, and enable 5G/edge workloads in a context of growing complexity. Private cloud (on-premises, fully owned/managed) offers total control but risks inefficiencies; hybrid cloud allows sensitive data and critical functions in protected environments while leveraging hyperscalers' public cloud for non-sensitive workloads. The real challenge for a telco operator lies in optimizing costs while meeting performance (QoS) and security constraints.

TIM's platform, currently in transition from IaaS to CaaS with CNFs (e.g., 5G core network functions) and CNAs for business services, in 2024 launched the TIM Edge & Cloud Continuum (ECC) Project [16], within the EU-funded IPCEI-CIS initiative [17]. It tackles cloud-native transitions using Sylva [18], an open-source Kubernetes framework for bare-metal stack deployments tailored to telco-edge continuity. Sylva provides an open and free alternative to proprietary solutions: in this sense, it offers the opportunity to free operators from vendors and integrators lock-in enabling technological autonomy and economic savings.

1.4 Next Sections Topics

The article's content is organized as follows. Section 2 presents the architecture for the hybrid edge-cloud platform and an application classification scheme. Section 3 details the comprehensive platform cost model framework. Section 4 proposes an example of application of the cost model and related cost evaluation and comparison methodology through numerical examples. Section 5 concludes by summarizing the content and emphasizing the contribution's value in its generality and applicability.

2 Hybrid Edge-Cloud Architecture and Applications Classification

2.1 Hybrid Edge-Cloud Architecture

The telco and service hybrid edge-cloud platform representation used in this work is depicted in Fig. 2. It represents the high-level hybrid cloud structure used for the definition of the cost model presented in Sect. 3. It is divided horizontally into two levels, the centralized level (top part) and the distributed level (bottom part), the latter in turn being divided into the near edge and far edge sub-levels, not shown in the figure. Moreover, it divides the cloud platform vertically into physically separate telco and service sections, supporting telecommunications network functions (e.g., 5G core) and customer applications/services, respectively.

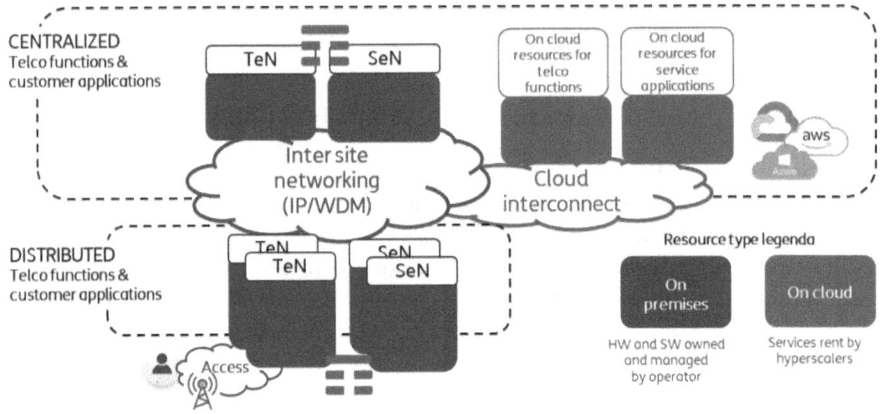

Fig. 2. Hybrid edge-cloud architecture

The cloud platform combines on-premises and public cloud resources across centralized and distributed levels. Centralized sites can use both operator-owned infrastructure and hyperscaler cloud resources, while distributed edge sites rely only on on-premises resources due to the limited geographical availability of public cloud infrastructure. Telco nodes (TeN) and service nodes (SeN) can be deployed at both levels, whereas public cloud resource pools are centralized only. The continuum characteristic of the platform is achieved through a balance of central, near-edge, and far-edge sites positioned progressively closer to end users.

As depicted in Fig. 2, TeN and SeN span centralized to distributed deployments and are connected via IP/WDM internetworking services and cloud interconnects (the blue cloud for inter-site networking and the red cloud for inter-cloud networking). The specific cloud platform instances differ in how the various blocks are configured, i.e. the on-premises parts (in blue), the parts on public cloud (in red) and the networking components.

2.2 Classification of Applications Based on their Requirements

The hybrid edge-cloud infrastructure described above hosts all applications required to operate the platform, telco networks (e.g., 5G Core), and services for internal and external users.

Applications have several requirements. The main ones include resource needs (vCPU, RAM, storage, networking, GPU), which determine infrastructure sizing or public cloud usage. Another key aspect is the usage time profile: it can be continuous or discontinuous (predictable or not), influencing resource pooling and cost efficiency.

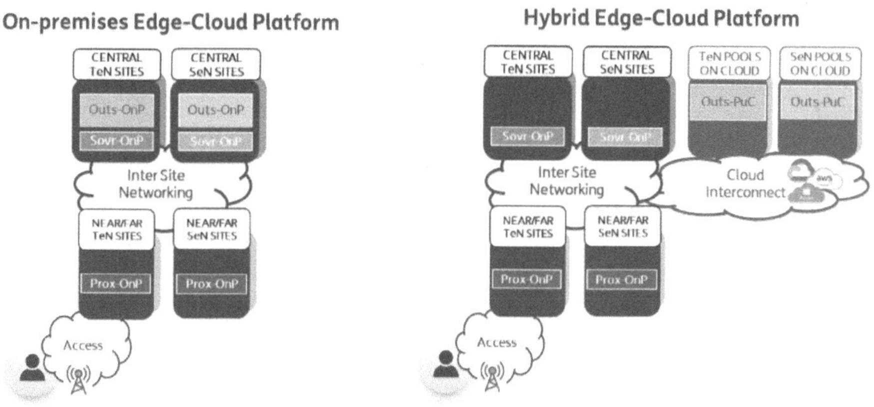

Fig. 3. Scenarios definition based on classification of applications

Two additional qualitative requirements are critical: not outsourceable and proximity. Not-outsourceable applications must remain on-premises for criticality or security reasons, while outsourceable ones may run on the public cloud. Proximity requires applications to be deployed close to users (wherever they are) and typically implies on-premises deployment due to unavailability of the public cloud at the edge.

Based on these requirements, four application categories are defined:

- Outs-PuC: outsourceable and deployed on public cloud,
- Outs-OnP: outsourceable but kept on-premises,
- Sovr-OnP: not-outsourceable, bound by sovereignty, always on-premises,
- Prox-OnP: proximity-constrained and on-premises near users.

Outsourceable applications (Outs-PuC + Outs-OnP) can be distributed between public cloud and on-premises, ranging from fully on-premises to fully on public cloud, including intermediate mix setups.

Figure 3 presents two extreme deployment models for an edge-cloud platform: a fully on-premises scenario, where all applications run on operator-owned infrastructure to ensure full control, and a hybrid scenario, where outsourceable applications are deployed on the public cloud via cloud interconnection, while sovereignty- or proximity constrained applications remain on-premises. Intermediate hybrid configurations are also possible, reflecting different trade-offs between infrastructure control and public cloud scalability.

The detailed sizing of the resources required by different applications and services (telco and non-telco), and their impact on edge-cloud infrastructure planning and design, is beyond the scope of this paper; nevertheless, application classification remains essential in motivating the need for an articulated edge-cloud hybrid platform.

3 Cost Evaluation Model Framework and Evaluation Methodology

As telecommunications operators like TIM transition toward a hybrid edge-cloud platform, the ability to homogeneously scale services from centralized clouds down to the network edge is becoming a fundamental enabler for high-performance, low-latency digital solutions. Implementing this edge-cloud continuum through a hybrid platform, which integrates proprietary on-premises resources at edge sites with public cloud resource pools from hyperscalers, introduces significant architectural and financial complexity. Consequently, a specialized cost evaluation model is essential for operators to precisely quantify both initial investments (CapEx) and recurring operational expenses (OpEx), facilitating a comprehensive Total Cost of Ownership (TCO) analysis. Such a model acts as a vital strategic planning tool, allowing operators to compare the long-term economic trade-offs of different deployment scenarios and determine the most efficient balance between owned infrastructure and external cloud capacity while adhering to strict sovereignty and proximity requirements.

In the following paragraphs, the cost evaluation model framework of the IPCEI-CIS TIM ECC project [16] is described. The multi-year hybrid edge-cloud platform is defined through a bottom-up hierarchical structure that integrates on-premises physical resources with elastic public cloud capacity in the same framework.

3.1 The Four-Level Data Model

The cost evaluation model of the IPCEI-CIS TIM ECC project is based on a four-level hierarchical data model designed to classify and quantify the costs of deploying and managing the hybrid edge-cloud continuum platform.

At the top of the hierarchy is the scope, which separate platform-wide common costs from those directly attributable to individual sites. These are followed by domain, which identifies technical areas, such as HW infrastructure or CaaS, which are further divided into specific operational functions (e.g. for HW infrastructure domain, compute, storage, networking, ...). The bottom level consists of elements, the atomic cost units (servers, SW licenses, workforce, etc.).

3.2 Element Catalog: The Core of the Cost Evaluation Model

The complete set of all elements with related cost information are defined in the element catalog, which is the core of the cost evaluation model. The Fig. 4 reports an example of element catalog definition. For each element a cost per year is specified, across each year of the multi-period evaluation horizon. When required, each element in the catalog is defined by specific numerical technical parameters (not shown in example of Fig. 4), such as the number of CPU cores or RAM capacity for a server, to accurately characterize its configuration.

3.3 Resource Template: Scalability and Flexibility

Together with the element catalog, described in the previous section, the resource template is another important part of the cost evaluation model framework. Definition of

SCOPE	DOMAIN	FUNCTION	ELEMENT	COST TYPE	COST Year1	COST Year2	COST Year3	COST Year4	COST Year5	COST Year6
INDIVIDUAL SITE	HW INFRASTRUCTURE	Compute	• Server Type 1 • Server Type 2	CapEx						
INDIVIDUAL SITE	HW INFRASTRUCTURE	Storage	• Storage Type 1 • Storage Type 2	CapEx						
INDIVIDUAL SITE	HW INFRASTRUCTURE	Management	• HW Configuration • HW Maintenance	CapEx						
INDIVIDUAL SITE	HW INFRASTRUCTURE	Hosting	• Power/Energy	OpEx						
INDIVIDUAL SITE	HW INFRASTRUCTURE	Hosting	• Space	OpEx						
INDIVIDUAL SITE	CAAS	Management	• Cluster Deployment • Cluster Engineering • Cluster Maintenance • Cluster Operations	CapEx	Cost per element per year					
PLATFORM	FEDERATION & MULTICLOUD	SW Development	• System Deployment & Management	CapEx						
PLATFORM	ORCHESTRATION	SW Development	• System Deployment & Management	CapEx						
PLATFORM	OBSERVABILITY & ANALYTICS	SW Development	• System Deployment & Management	CapEx						
PLATFORM	RESEARCH & DEVELOPMENT	Research	• Sylva Expert	CapEx						
INDIVIDUAL SITE	INTER SITE NETWORKING	Connectivity	• Backbone ports 100 Gb	CapEx						
INDIVIDUAL SITE	INTER SITE NETWORKING	Connectivity	• DWDM circuits	CapEx						
INDIVIDUAL SITE	PACKET CORE	SW Licence	• User Plane Licence • Control Plane Licence	CapEx						

Fig. 4. Example of element catalog

resources templates ensures scalability and flexibility of the model. Resources templates serve as standardized reference models that define the typical composition of components across the edge-cloud continuum platform. Each template is populated with specific units drawn from the element catalog, classified by the four-level hierarchy described in the previous chapter. Resource templates are designed with a multi-period structure that allows for the precise configuration of element quantities for each year of the planning horizon.

The resource templates define the standard composition and cost structure of platform resources. SeN/TeN templates describe the physical on-premises sites, including the elements, quantities, and associated one-shot and recurring costs over the asset lifecycle. Public cloud pool templates similarly define standardized sets of cloud resources, potentially from multiple hyperscalers and in different sizes. Additional templates are used for platform-wide capabilities (e.g., orchestration, observability, multicloud) and for lab environments, including hardware, software, and workforce resources. Figure 5 reports an example of SeN template with on-premises resources. The composition of each template is purely discretionary and may be tailored according to the needs of the analysis, by selecting the appropriate elements from the element catalog.

3.4 Definition of Multi-year Hybrid Edge-Cloud Platform

Given the definition of element catalog and resource templates, the last step to define the whole multi-year hybrid edge cloud platform is to determine the number of sites deployed for each type (SeN/TeN, central/near/far) and the number of public cloud pools required (SeN/TeN, large/medium/small) in the multi-year hybrid edge cloud platform for each year of the evaluation period, together with the platform development and lab site resources. Figure 6 reports the overall process of definition of multi-year hybrid edge-cloud platform, starting from element catalog and templates definition.

DOMAIN	FUNCTION	ELEMENT	UNIT	COST TYPE (O/R)	QTY Year 1	QTY Year 2	QTY Year 3	QTY Year 4	QTY Year 5	QTY Year 6
HW INFRASTRUCTURE	Compute	Server Type 1 Vendor X	N.	One Shot						
HW INFRASTRUCTURE	Networking	Networking Equipment Vendor Y	N.	One Shot						
HW INFRASTRUCTURE	Management	HW Configuration	Days	One Shot						
HW INFRASTRUCTURE	Management	HW Maintenance	Days	Recurrent						
HW INFRASTRUCTURE	Hosting	Space	SQM	Recurrent						
HW INFRASTRUCTURE	Hosting	Energy	KWH	Recurrent	Quantity per element per year					
INTER SITE NETWORKING	Connectivity	Backbone ports 100 Gb	N.	One Shot						
INTER SITE NETWORKING	Connectivity	DWDM Circuits	N.	One Shot						
CAAS	Management	Cluster Engineering and Deployment	Days	One Shot						
CAAS	Management	Cluster Maintenace and Operation	Days	Recurrent						

Fig. 5. Example of SeN template with on-premises resources

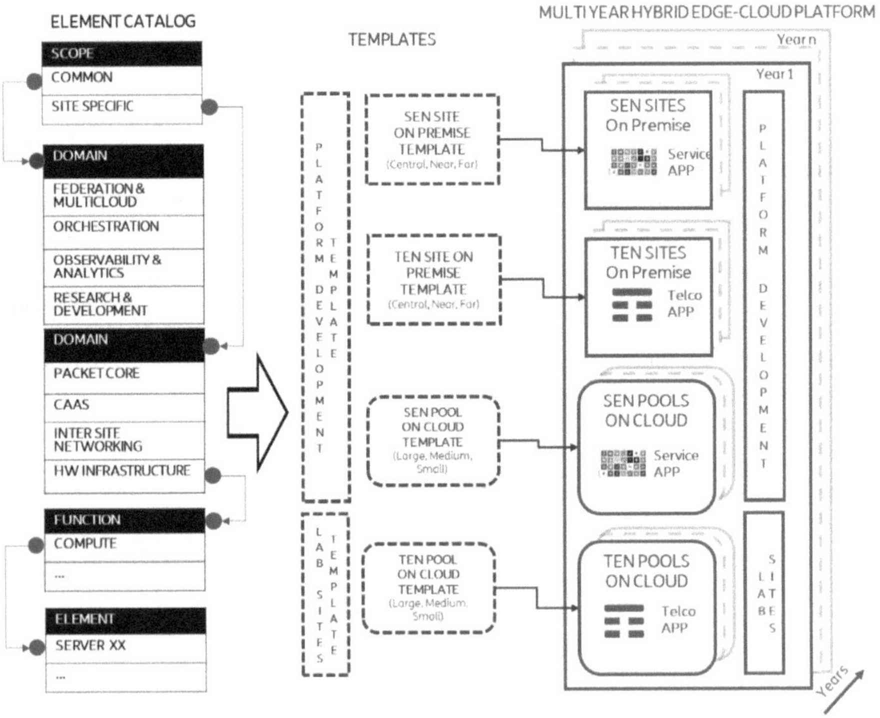

Fig. 6. Definition of multi-year hybrid edge-cloud platform

3.5 Calculation of CapEx/OpEx of the Edge-Cloud Continuum Platform per Year

The total CapEx and OpEx for a single resource template of any type (SeN/TeN, central/near/far, large/medium/small, platform development, lab site) in a specific year x is the sum of the unit costs of all elements included in the template.

The following formulas apply to resource template of type t:

$$TCT_{t,\ x} = \sum_{i=1}^{N} (PCE_{i,x} * QE_{i,x}) \tag{1}$$

$$TOT_{t,\ x} = \sum_{i=1}^{N} (RCE_{i,x} * QE_{i,x}) \tag{2}$$

where:

$TCT_{t,\ x}$ = Total CapEx per template of type t in year x,
$TOT_{t,\ x}$ = Total OpEx per template of type t in year x,
$PCE_{i,\ x}$ = Unit CapEx cost for element i in year x,
$RCE_{i,\ x}$ = Unit OpEx cost for element i in year x,
$QE_{i,\ x}$ = Quantity of element i in year x,
N = number of elements in template of type t.

Some of the CapEx costs for year x can be recurrent, which means that they are charged for year x and for following years in the evaluation period. The OpEx costs are always recurrent.

By combining the resources templates definition with the site/pool deployment plan, in terms of new sites/pools per type deployed per year, the model can define the whole hybrid edge-cloud continuum platform infrastructure and calculate the cumulative cost evolution of the platform, in terms of both CapEx and OpEx per year. This allows for strategic comparisons of long-term trends between different deployment scenarios, where resources can be on-premises, on public cloud or hybrid.

The following formulas apply:

$$TC_x = \sum_{t=1}^{M} (TCT_{t,x} * NSP_{t,x}) \tag{3}$$

$$TO_x = \sum_{t=1}^{M} (TOT_{t,x} * NSP_{t,x}) + TO_{x-1} \tag{4}$$

where:

$TCT_{t,\ x}$ = Total CapEx per template of type t in year x,
$TOT_{t,\ x}$ = Total OpEx per template of type t in year x,
$NSP_{t,\ x}$ = Number of sites/pools of type t deployed in year x,
TC_x = Total CapEx in year x,
TO_x = Total OpEx in year x,
TO_{x-1} = Total OpEx in year x-1,
M = number of types of resource templates.

4 Application Example and Main Results

In the first part of this section, we introduce a scenario-building methodology for evaluating hybrid edge-cloud platform options, accompanied by illustrative examples of the generated scenarios. We then apply the cost model to these scenarios and present a selection of the resulting numerical outcomes. Please note that neither these scenarios nor the parameters described herein reflect TIM's actual infrastructure; they are provided purely as didactic examples to demonstrate the analysis methodology and the practical application of the cost evaluation model presented in the previous section.

4.1 Scenario-Building Methodology

Figure 7 (a) exemplifies the scenario-building approach. The baseline is an on-premises scenario with a balanced resource distribution across central and edge sites (black dot, DD-OP, taken as a reference scenario). Within the pure on-premises context, scenarios shift toward more centralized (left, CC-OP and HC-OP) or distributed (right, HD-OP) configurations along the blue axis which tracks the increase in resources decentralization. From any all on-premises scenario, gradual migration to public cloud creates hybrid scenarios defined by percentages of public cloud resources. Figure. 7 (a) shows hybrid cloud scenarios starting from the full on-premises CC-OP case and applying three public cloud migration levels, i.e., dots CC-HY$_1$, CC-HY$_2$, CC-HY$_3$ on the red arrow tracking increasing percentages of public cloud resources.

Sensitivity analysis assesses cost parameter variations, such as public cloud resource costs, and constitutes a third direction along which the scenarios can be generated. Figure 7 (a) depicts this for CC-HY$_2$, with changes from nominal values via percentage variations of cost, i.e., dots CC-HY$_2$(−) and CC-HY$_2$(+) on the yellow arrow. In summary, this approach generates an N-dimensional lattice of cases (here, 3D; extensible to more dimensions), suitable for generalized "what-if" analyses.

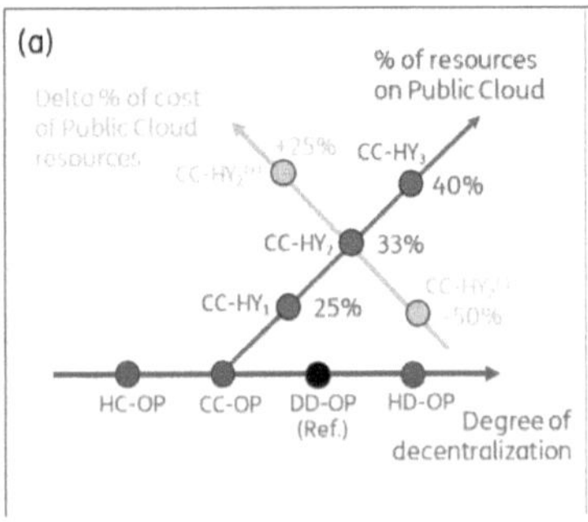

(b)

	Number of sites in the corresponding level		
Decentralization degree	Central	Near Edge	Far Edge
HC | Highly-Centralized	3	-	-
CC | Centralized	3	9	-
DD | Distributed (Ref.)	3	15	24
HD | Highly-Distributed	3	24	75

Fig. 7. Scenario-building scheme exemplified (a), and example of number of sites at different level corresponding to scenarios with different degrees of decentralization (b)

Figure 7 (b) tables reports an example of site counting per cloud hierarchy level for the four on-premises scenarios, from highly centralized (central sites only) to highly distributed (far edge count dominant). The rule adds peripheral sites with increasing decentralization, keeping number of central sites fixed. This is an example; absolute values of site counts and their relative proportions depend on the specific case study.

Assuming equal overall HW resources at platform level (CPU, RAM, Storage, GPU and networking), it is possible to define scenarios by splitting the overall resources across levels and between on-premises and public cloud. Figure 8 tables hypothetical shares for the four on-premises and the three hybrid scenarios shown in Fig. 7 (a). Let us remember that we assume that public cloud resources are centralized only, so tables for edge sites omit that column. Hybrid scenarios are classified based on the percentage of central site resources migrated from on-premises to the public cloud, i.e., low (25%), medium (33%), and high (40%). There is no need to include scenarios on yellow axis in Fig. 7 (a) as separated scenarios in the table of Fig. 8 as they match CC-HY_2's resource distribution (only cost parameters change).

	Site level			
	Central		Near Edge	Far Edge
Scenario / Type of resource	On-premises	Public Cloud	On-premises	On-premises
HC-OP | Highly-Centralized	100%	-	-	-
CC-OP | Centralized	50%	-	50%	-
DD-OP | Distributed (Reference)	33%	-	35%	32%
HD-OP | Highly-Distributed	26%	-	32%	42%
CC-HY_1 | Low % of Public Cloud	25%	25%	50%	-
CC-HY_2 | Medium % of Public Cloud	17%	33%	50%	-
CC-HY_3 | High % of Public Cloud	10%	40%	50%	-

Fig. 8. Share of resources across platform site levels for scenarios shown in Fig. 7 (a)

4.2 Results

Some numerical experiments were carried out by applying the model described in Sect. 3 to the scenarios derived in the previous subsection. A rather comprehensive catalog of elements has been used (HW, SW, hosting, workforce), which for confidentiality reasons cannot be disclosed. The numerical campaign concerned the cost calculation of the four all on-premises scenarios matching the number of sites shown in Fig. 7 (b).

The assumed edge-cloud platform deployment plan spans six years, with the first three years involving the installation of one third of the final infrastructure each (period predominated by CapEx) and the last three years running the platform maintenance (during which OpEx prevails). Over the three years of deployments, 600 servers per year are installed, half on the services sites (SeN) and half on the telco sites (TeN). In the services sites, one third of the servers are equipped with one GPU each. Number of total deployed sites in the six years of the plan range from 3 central sites of highly centralized scenario (which includes the central level only) to 102 sites of the highly decentralized scenario (3 central, 24 near edge and 75 far edge sites). Percentages of resources distribution across levels for each scenario are specified in Fig. 8.

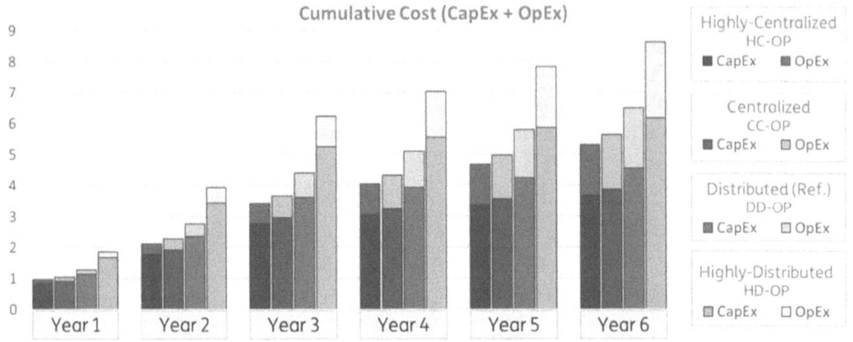

Fig. 9. Cumulative cost for a 6-year edge-cloud platform deployment plan for the four all on-premises scenarios (lighter color in bars means platforms more decentralized)

Figure 9 shows the cumulative cost (values are in normalized cost units) of the platform for the four on-premises scenarios corresponding to different levels of decentralization of resources. As expected, CapEx increases and dominates in the first three years and then flattens; while OpEx starts very low and grows continuously, becoming about 30% of the total in the last year. Decentralized structures entail significantly higher costs than centralized ones because each site requires fixed construction, hosting, networking, interconnection and other specific services and licenses that, contrary to what happens in centralized context, can be shared with a limited amount of HW resources. Difference is significant: increasing is of the order of 70% between the two extreme scenario configurations in the last year of the plan. As is known, cost isn't the only driver when one must develop an edge-cloud platform. If we take the reference configuration (DD-OP), the final cost is only about 20% higher than the highly centralized one (HC-OP); nevertheless, reference configuration maintains a physical presence across 42 sites (as opposed to 3), thereby enabling proximity services that centralized configurations cannot support.

Figure 10 shows the cumulative total cost trend of the centralized on-premises configuration (CC-OP) and some hybrid scenarios obtained varying the percentage of resources migrated to the public cloud. As can be seen, with the same cost catalog and 6-year development plan used to obtain the results of Fig. 9, the hybrid solutions initially appear slightly cheaper. However, this advantage disappears halfway through the plan; at Year 4 the on-premises solution turns out to be the cheapest with a net gap at the end of the plan. Note how the OpEx component increases markedly for the hybrid cases (yellow portions of the bars), at the end of the period being in order of or greater than 50% of the total cumulative cost, while for the on-premises case the OpEx share (in green) is around 30%.

Let's now move to consider an example of sensitivity analysis to cost parameters. Specifically, we considered variations in the price of public cloud resources and in the cost of HW. The results are reported in Fig. 11. The four continuous curves represent the

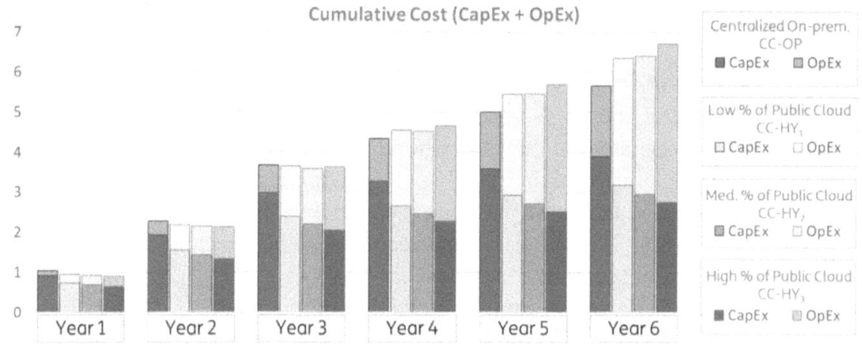

Fig. 10. Cumulative cost for a 6-year centralized (CC) platform deployment plan for different percentages of resources migrated to public cloud. (on-premises in blue-green and hybrid variants in red-yellow; darker red/yellow in bars means higher resources quota on public cloud)

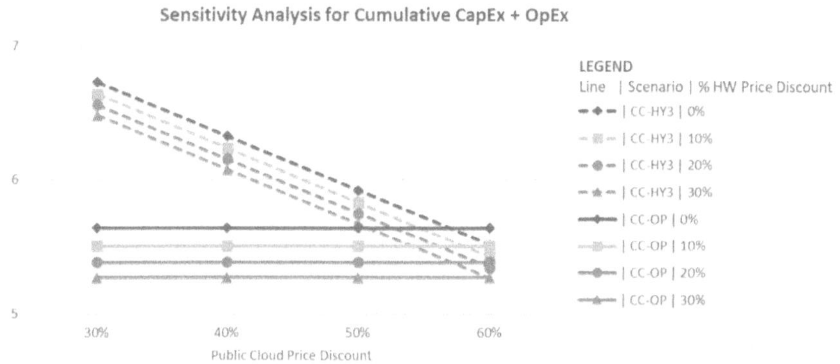

Fig. 11. Sensitivity analysis for scenarios CC-OP and CC-HY_3, based on public cloud price discount and yearly HW price discount (cumulative CapEx+OpEx in the last year of the plan)

value of the cumulative cost (CapEx+OpEx) in the last year of the plan for the CC-OP scenario with different percentage of HW price discount (assumed in the range 0%–30%). The other four curves (dotted) represent the cost for the CC-HY3 scenario, supposing the same percentages of HW price discount. The graph shows that an increase of the public cloud resources price discount (30% discount can be considered the minimum value for a big customer) significantly reduces total costs for the CC-HY3 scenario (steep downward lines), while CC-OP costs remain flat and only slightly decrease with higher HW discounts. At lower public cloud discount, CC-OP is clearly more cost-efficient across all HW discount levels. However, as the public cloud discount increases (particularly beyond ~50–60%), CC-HY3 becomes progressively more competitive and eventually the cheapest option, particularly when combined with higher HW discounts (20–30%).

5 Conclusions

The proposed framework provides a versatile and scalable methodology for the techno-economic evaluation of the edge-cloud continuum, specifically designed to support telecommunications operators in their transition toward cloud-native architectures. By utilizing a four-level hierarchical data catalog (scope, domain, function, element) combined with a multi-period templating system, the model enables a precise and granular Total Cost of Ownership (TCO) analysis that accounts for both technological evolution and physical deployment scales over a multi-year horizon.

A primary outcome derived from the application of this model is the possibility of performing multi-scenario sensitivity analyses, as the economic advantage of a hybrid cloud deployment over a traditional all on-premises setup is highly sensitive to external variables such as public cloud pricing discounts, HW procurement costs and decentralization degree of sites. Furthermore, the framework underscores that strategic infrastructure decisions must not be based solely on cost but must balance economic efficiency with rigorous sovereignty and proximity requirements to ensure that critical network functions remain under direct operator control. Ultimately, the techno-economic model presented in this paper serves as a robust strategic planning tool, allowing operators to determine the optimal distribution of resources across the continuum while managing the financial complexities inherent in hybrid environments.

The proposed methodology can also be extended to calculate unit costs for individual infrastructure resources (SKU elements): such unit costs can then be used as input for defining the pricing of services consuming those resources. Work on this important aspect is ongoing and will be the subject of future publications.

Acknowledgments. This research was supported by the IPCEI - Cloud Infrastructure and Services project, Funded by European Union, NextGenerationEU. However, the completion of this study, qualifying it as a spillover, required an essential self-funded investment by TIM beyond the original IPCEI financial scope.

References

1. Hybrid Cloud Market Size, Share and Trends 2025 to 2034, Precedence Research, https://www.precedenceresearch.com/hybrid-cloud-market (Accessed 23 Mar 2026)
2. CNCF Telco Microsurvey: Cloud-native Network Functions with Kubernetes are coming – but interoperability and portability are priorities, posted August 22th, 2022, online https://www.cncf.io/blog/2022/ (Accessed 23 Mar 2026)
3. H. A. Imran et al.: Multi-cloud: a comprehensive review. In: 2020 IEEE 23rd International Multitopic Conference (INMIC), Bahawalpur, Pakistan, pp. 1–5 (2020)
4. D. Kafka, P. Segec, M. Moravcik: Cloud federation: a comparative study and exploration of multi-cloud solutions in the digital era. In: 2025 International Conference on Emerging eLearning Technologies and Applications (ICETA), Stary Smokovec, Slovakia, pp. 315–320 (2025)
5. J. Weinman: Trade-Offs Along the Cloud-Edge Continuum," 2022 Cloud Continuum, Los Alamitos, CA, USA, pp. 1–7 (2022)

6. United States National Institute of Standard Technology (NIST), online https://www.nist.gov/ (Accessed 23 Mar 2026)
7. Pourmajidi, W., Zhang, L., Steinbacher, J., Erwin, T., Miranskyy, A.: A reference Archi-tecture for governance of cloud native applications. IEEE Trans. Cloud Comput. **13**(3), 935–952 (2025)
8. S. Rac and M. Brorsson: Cost-Effective Scheduling for Kubernetes in the Edge-to-Cloud Continuum. In: 2023 IEEE International Conference on Cloud Engineering (IC2E), Boston, MA, USA (2023)
9. P. Soumplis, G. Kontos, A. Kretsis, P. Kokkinos, A. Nanos, E. Varvarigos: Security-Aware Resource Allocation in the Edge-Cloud Continuum," 2023 IEEE 12th International Conference on Cloud Networking (CloudNet), Hoboken, NJ, USA, pp. 161–169 (2023)
10. Taghinezhad-Niar, A., Taheri, J.: Security, reliability, cost, and energy-aware scheduling of real-time workflows in compute-continuum environments. IEEE Trans. Cloud Comput. **12**(3), 954–965 (2024)
11. Weinman, J.: Hybrid cloud economics. IEEE Cloud Comput. **3**(1), 18–22 (2016)
12. Weinman, J.: The economics of networking and the cloud. IEEE Cloud Comput. **3**(3), 12–15 (2016)
13. Weinman, J.: The economics of the hybrid multicloud fog. IEEE Cloud Comput. **4**(1), 16–21 (2017)
14. Kim, D., Lee, H., Song, H., Choi, N., Yi, Y.: Economics of fog computing: interplay among infrastructure and service providers, users, and edge resource owners. IEEE Trans. Mob. Comput. **19**(11), 2609–2622 (2020)
15. E. J. Sacoto-Cabrera and E. Moreno-Cardenas: Shaping the Future of Fog Computing Economics: A Systematic Review of the Most Important Business Models. 2024 IEEE ANDESCON, Cusco, Peru, pp. 1–6 (2024)
16. TIM Edge & Cloud Continuum IPCEI project, online (Accessed 23 Mar 2026) https://www.8ra.com/projects/timecc/
17. IPCEI-CIS Reference Architecture, Version 2.0, January 2026, online https://www.8ra.com/wp-content/uploads/IPCEI-CIS_Reference-Architecture_2-0.pdf (Accessed 23 Mar 2026)
18. Sylva Project of The Linux Foundation, online https://sylvaproject.org/ (Accessed 23 Mar 2026)

Nocher, Application Lifecycle Management Across Computing Continuum

Christophe Dion[1,2(✉)], Adrien Lèbre[2,3], and Philippe Raipin Parvedy[1,2]

[1] Orange Innovation, Cesson-Sévigné 35510, France
christophe.dion@imt-atlantique.fr
[2] IMT Atlantique, INRIA, LS2N, Nantes, France
[3] Nantes University, École Centrale Nantes, UMR 6004, Nantes 44000, CNRS, France

Abstract. The Computing Continuum paradigm abstracts the increasing complexity of systems, marked by geo-distribution, extreme heterogeneity, and environmental volatility, into a perceived unified environment. However, current state-of-the-art solutions are fragmented and still bound to resource-centric models. Despite emerging convergence, they fail to provide the necessary conditions for seamless application lifecycle management. Consequently, achieving true transparent deployment and reconfiguration across the Continuum remains a significant scientific challenge.

This position paper introduces Nocher, an application-centric software approach designed to overcome the complexities of Computing Continuum. Nocher decouples an application–composed of services and datasets–from the underlying infrastructure layer, thanks to a Capsule: an autonomous unit endowed with orchestration capabilities that strictly separates business logic from lifecycle management. Deployment and reconfiguration objectives are defined through a Descriptor associated with each Capsule. The distributed Nocher Agent, deployed on each site, executes the necessary actions to satisfy these objectives and operates on three pillars: a local-first execution priority, a principle of subsidiarity that triggers inter-site collaboration only when necessary and on-demand extensibility towards neighboring sites.

The approach is analysed using two representative scenarios: In-Transit Computing and content-network-delivery-like architecture. By reifying this abstraction across all sites, Nocher provides a cohesive solution to the challenges of the Computing Continuum.

Keywords: Application-centric · Computing Continuum · Geo-distribution · Business-lifecycle decoupling · Principle of subsidiarity · Local-first · Transparent reconfiguration

---

Courtesy of Ariane Nicolas and Hannoun Moubarak for Figs. 1–4 and 8–9.

Published by Springer Nature Switzerland AG 2027
D. Balouek et al. (Eds.): ESOCC 2026, LNCS 16834, pp. 134–149, 2027.
https://doi.org/10.1007/978-3-032-37831-6_9

1 Introduction

Over the last decade, Cloud Computing has evolved from traditional centralized architectures to a fragmented ecosystem incorporating Fog and Edge computing. This transformation was driven by the stringent latency and bandwidth requirements of modern applications. More recently, the Continuum has emerged as a paradigm shift to consolidate these disparate and distributed environments. Its objective is to deliver a seamless, unified experience that abstracts the complexity of systems mainly characterized by geo-distribution, volatility of operational environments, and the extreme infrastructure heterogeneity.

However, realizing this paradigm faces major challenges. First, the volatility of execution environments complicates application lifecycle management, while infrastructure diversity imposes strict trade-offs between the low latency of the Edge and the scalability of the Cloud. Second, specialized technologies such as embedded AI and 6G tend to promote closed architectures that hinder interoperability. Finally, data management adds another layer of complexity, requiring distinct strategies for real-time versus historical processing while navigating conflicting regulatory frameworks (e.g., EU GDPR, California CCPA) across transnational clouds.

Several recent works have formalized the concept of the Continuum to address existing challenges [6] [13]. One approach defines the Continuum as an expansion of Cloud services towards peripheral entities, notably Edge and IoT, emphasizing the continuity of available resources and the principle of adapting the infrastructure to the application's needs. More recently, this perspective has been broadened by proposing a definition of the Computing Continuum as a global distributed system, explicitly integrating constraints related to geo-distribution, heterogeneity, and adaptability. However, although this framework establishes the fundamental principles of the Continuum, it has been highlighted that concrete abstractions remain lacking, and that operational models are still needed to fully realize this vision [6].

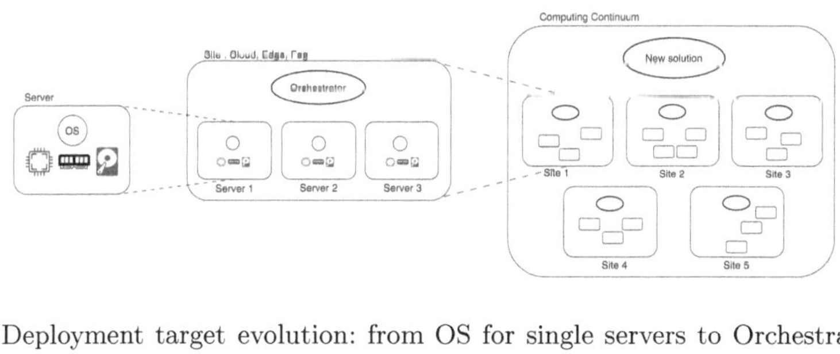

Fig. 1. Deployment target evolution: from OS for single servers to Orchestrators for clusters, now a new inter-site abstraction is required for the Computing Continuum.

To understand how to bridge this gap, it is useful to examine the historical evolution of system abstractions (Fig. 1). Historically, operating systems abstracted physical hardware, managing resources and time-sharing. Subsequently, orchestrators like OpenStack and then Kubernetes abstracted the infrastructure, automating cluster management and standardizing deployment. However, with the proliferation of Cloud, Edge, and Fog within the Computing Continuum context, the question of transparent deployment arises once again.

Kubernetes has emerged as the *de facto* industry standard container orchestrator. Although it excels in managing a homogeneous local cluster, its architecture was not natively designed for geo-distribution. To bridge this gap, numerous academic and industrial works have adopted a cluster-centric approach. They organize the management of clusters among themselves, rather than rethinking the deployment unit. In the industrial and open-source domains, recent solutions like Karmada [4] or Open-MCP [5] are emerging to unify the control of multiple clusters. While initiatives such as KubeEdge [15] and k3s [3] offer lightweight versions of native orchestrators for the Edge, they only partially address the problem by managing geo-distribution through distinct Cloud and Edge components. Extending this paradigm, works like Unbound [11] have pushed this logic to the concept of meta-federation, allowing the orchestration of complex topologies of physical and virtual clusters. Even though these solutions address fragmentation, they remain inherently limited by their granularity: the base unit remains the physical or virtual site. The application is thus managed as a resource to be distributed over a pre-existing topology, maintaining a strong dependency on the underlying infrastructure.

"The field of distributed systems is at a watershed and that new approaches are urgently needed" [7]. Our community should propose high-level abstraction paradigms, centred on the application domain and capable of self-assembling and dynamically adapting.

Application-centric orchestration has a rich research history. SeMaFoR [1] offers a step in this direction by replacing the site resource with a Fog Area—a flexible, consensus-managed logical resource grouping. However, this transition remains insufficient, as the approach is still fundamentally anchored-deeply rooted, in resource management. Concerto-D [2], while application-centric, offers only a partial response to the Continuum. It focuses primarily on network resilience but lacks support for infrastructure volatility management, placement decisions, and orchestration logic. It assumes the underlying heterogeneous infrastructure is already unified and delegates data management entirely to the application's functional design, without providing data lifecycle management capabilities. Cheops [10] introduces a more definitive application-centric solution. By externalizing geo-distribution management, Cheops gives the illusion of a single system through a local-first [12] strategy followed by inter-site collaboration (collaborative-then). While Cheops represents a significant advancement by placing the application at the core of the management system, its scope is largely restricted to DevOps requests. It lacks the automated, autonomous self-management logic necessary for the broader application lifecycle, a limitation acknowledged by its authors. Faced with the increasing complexity of distributed environments, a true conceptual breakthrough is needed.

Nocher completely decouples the application through:

- The **Capsule**, a fully application-centric deployment unit that encapsulates business logic, datasets, and lifecycle management rules, strictly separating them from infrastructure concerns.
- A **Descriptor**, a declarative blueprint that describes the application's desired states.
- The **Agent**, a runtime engine that provides the execution capability to the Capsule.

The relevance of this concept is empirically analysed in two representative scenarios.

The remainder of this position paper is organized as follows: Sect. 2 presents the background; Sect. 3 details the architecture of Nocher; Sect. 4 analyses our approach; Sect. 5 presents a comparative analysis with other state-of-the-art solutions; and Sect. 6 concludes the paper and outlines future works.

2 Background

To address the limitations of current resource-centric approaches and build upon the application-centric foundations laid by Cheops, this section establishes the theoretical background of Nocher paradigm by examining three key concepts: the Kubernetes Pod, the Jade framework [9], and the Fractal model [8].

In the **Kubernetes** architecture, the Pod constitutes the smallest deployable unit. It groups one or more containers within a shared execution context, including an IP address, a network namespace, and shared storage resources. This abstraction establishes a clear separation between application logic and infrastructure management mechanisms. However, the Pod remains a static entity, limited in its ability to express execution constraints, which can nevertheless be complex. The main control mechanism offered by Kubernetes relies essentially on the replication factor, adjusting the number of instances to ensure availability and scalability. This approach remains limited when it comes to expressing more complex requirements related to the application's internal business constraints (e.g. in a database failover scenario, if the primary pod dies, Kubernetes may restart it, but it cannot promote a replica to primary, update connection strings, or guarantee data consistency before services are restored). Ultimately, the Pod manages the application's container without understanding what's inside.

The lack of awareness of application internals, was addressed 15 years ago in the **Jade** paper [9], Just-in-time Autonomous Design Environment, which formalized the separation between application logic and lifecycle management. Jade targets the automated management of complex distributed systems (such as clusters and multi-tier architectures) and encapsulates software within Managed Elements to expose a common control interface. This approach isolates the business logic from non-functional properties and maintains a global system state through a *Managed Architecture*—a potential precursor to the digital twin—orchestrated by autonomic managers. Finally, the architecture supports "self-self" behaviours [9], where the management system is capable of managing itself, thereby ensuring its own reliability.

The architecture of Jade relies on the **Fractal** component model [8], which warrants further examination. It serves as an architectural pattern for designing modular software systems. It is based on three fundamental principles: a hierarchical and recursive organization of components, a separation of concerns, and reflective control, while also supporting component sharing. This hierarchical and recursive organization enables the construction of complex applications by assembling simpler foundational components. The Component abstract class (Fig. 2) serves as a common foundation for all elements: a component is either a Primitive (leaf) or a Composite (a node containing other components). Consequently, a Composite can itself contain subcomponents indefinitely.

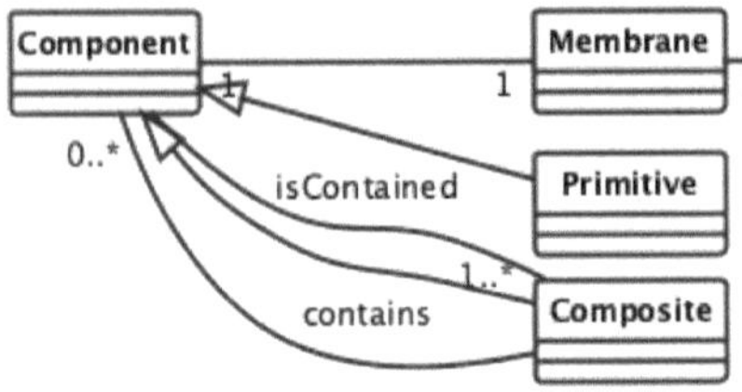

Fig. 2. Fractal software pattern

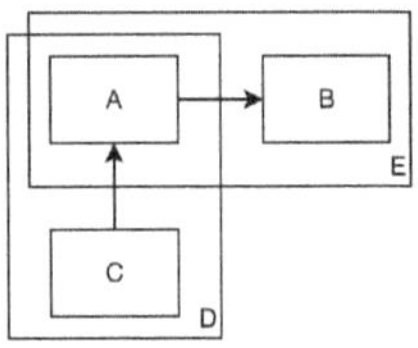

Fig. 3. Fractal shared components example

At the core of this model, the Membrane wraps each component to decouple its internal functional logic from the management of non-functional aspects. This Membrane, comprising dedicated Controllers—lifecycle, binding, introspection, security, synchronization, transactions, and logging—provides advanced reflective capabilities, enabling the system to observe and reconfigure itself at runtime. Furthermore, Fractal enables component sharing (Fig. 3) between multiple Composites, facilitating the fine-grained reuse of resources and cross-cutting features without compromising encapsulation.

From the perspective of the Fractal model, a Kubernetes Pod can be viewed as a very simple Primitive component that encapsulates functional logic. In Kubernetes, the Control Plane and operators collectively act as a huge membrane around the Pods. Consequently, the Pod does not fully exploit the Fractal model.

Nocher, through its Capsule concept, overcomes this limitation by internalizing the lifecycle. This extends the component's introspection, reconfiguration capabilities and provides hierarchical recursivity capability. In essence, the Capsule acts as a richer system that encompasses different types of workloads, including Pods, Containers or Virtual Machines, transforming it into a true autonomous Fractal component.

Ultimately, Nocher automates Cheops's application-centric approach to geo-distribution incorporating Jade's model-driven and "self-self" behaviours.

Together, these elements provide the comprehensive foundation required to build the Nocher system. A comparative analysis with other state-of-the-art solutions is presented later in Sect. 4.

3 Design and Development

This section details the Nocher architecture, centered on the **Capsule** abstraction that decouples business logic from the underlying infrastructure. It introduces the **Descriptor** used to define the Capsule and the event-driven execution engine powered by decentralized **Agents**. Furthermore, it details two kinematic processes that illustrate the mechanisms controlling initial deployment and the dynamic, constraint-driven geographic expansion of a Capsule.

The **Descriptor** serves as the declarative blueprint. It formalizes the applications' desired states and defines its services and datasets along with their respective lifecycles, operational constraints, and business rules. Written in YAML-like syntax that can extend standard Kubernetes manifests, the Descriptor functions as an actionable plan interpreted by the Nocher runtime rather than a static configuration file. Architecturally, it uses a recursive, hierarchical structure based on the Fractal component model allowing complex applications to be built from simpler blocks: a root Composite Component defines the application boundary; intermediate Composite Components group sub-systems; and Primitive Components represent the hierarchy leaves (such as specific services or datasets).

To enable autonomous behaviour, every component within the Descriptor, whether Composite or Primitive, is wrapped in a Fractal Membrane with distinct Controllers. These controllers handle non-functional operations like observation, control, instantiation, and dynamic reconfiguration for flexible lifecycle management. They enforce non-negotiable system invariants (constraints) that may be relaxed, encode continuous event-driven business logic and monitoring thresholds (rules), manage information linking internal components and network rules, and handle custom attributes. To provide granular control over operational behaviours, our architecture mandates a strict logical separation between computational services and stateful datasets. Each service and dataset is encapsulated as a distinct Primitive Component. This segregation is critical because it allows the system to apply divergent lifecycle policies to each component type; for instance, stateful datasets may require specific backup, consistency, or retention rules, while services may need scaling or update strategies independent of the data they process.

The **Capsule** emerges as the autonomous executor of the Descriptor once it is established as a declarative plan, serving as the logical deployment unit in Nocher. The abstraction decouples a single application, composed of services and datasets, from the underlying site infrastructure, by endowing it with orchestration capabilities, an independent lifecycle-instantiation, updates, suspension, and termination-thus ensuring operational autonomy.

Beyond orchestration, the Capsule acts as a modular framework that can be augmented with custom non-functional properties and mechanisms. These

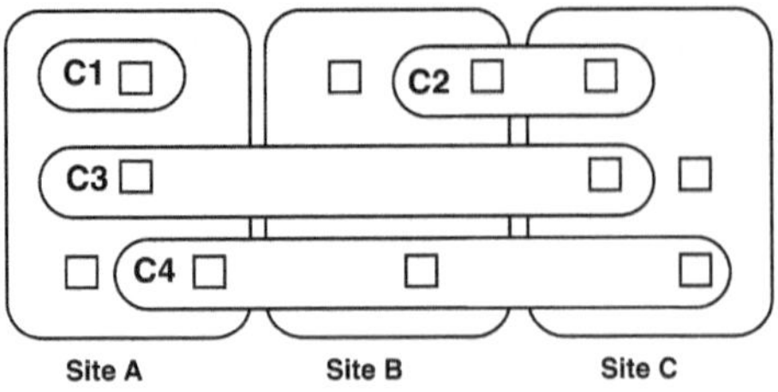

Fig. 4. E.g. One application per Capsule. A Capsule on 3 sites has 3 Agents, one on each site. Capsules don't share their Agents.

extensions address specific operational requirements such as geo-distributed error recovery, backup-restore, custom data transfer mechanisms, network routing, security policies, chaos engineering, and autonomous self-healing procedures. By embedding these functionalities directly within the deployment unit, the Capsule ensures that critical operational intelligence remains intrinsic to the application lifecycle. By isolating services and datasets in distinct Primitives, the Capsule ensures that lifecycle management actions (such as instantiation, migration, or termination) can be executed autonomously for each element without unintended side effects on the other. Figure 4 shows four Capsules, each containing one application. A Capsule on 3 sites has 3 Agents, one on each site. Capsules don't share their Agents.

Through Agents, a Capsule can be instantiated on a single site or span multiple geographically distributed sites.

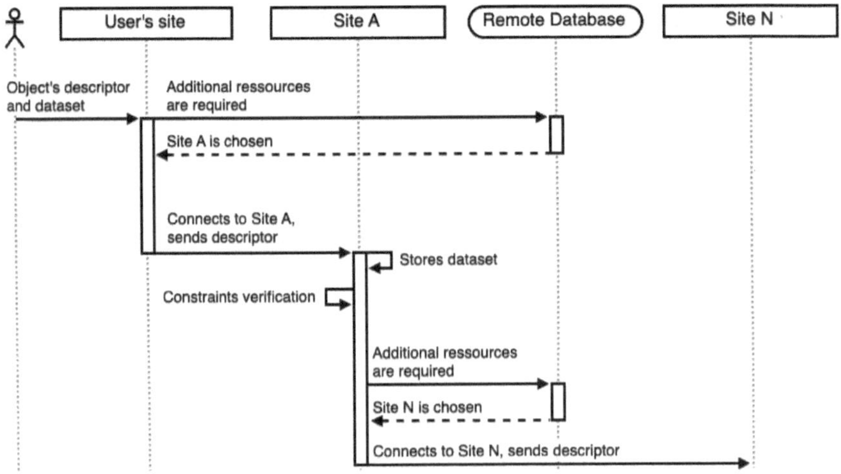

Fig. 5. Sequence bootstrap Capsule

Within the Nocher paradigm, the **Agent** acts as the distributed runtime engine responsible for instantiating a Descriptor into a live Capsule. Its characteristics include:

(i) autonomous decision-making: Agents deployed on every site, interpret the Descriptor and monitor states;

(ii) infrastructure agnosticism: Agents operate entirely at the application level. They schedule Capsule constituents transparently across sites without interfering with local resource managers (e.g., Kubernetes, virtual clusters, Fog Areas, or Linux hosts), which retain control over the physical hardware.

(iii) Event-Driven approach: The Agent relies on three kind of information, local data for the reconciliation loop, Agent-specific data, and information exchanged between Agents belonging to the same Capsule. If a **local-first** resolution fails, a **principle of subsidiarity** is applied: resolution is first attempted at the Agent level, then through intra-Capsule coordination ("collaborative-then"), and finally by **extending to neighboring sites** to acquire new resources, following the principles of the DVMS (Distributed Virtual Machine Scheduler) concept [14].

(iv) Scheduling logic: Agent provides a pluggable scheduling engine based on Constraint Programming. This module ensures compliance with constraints (affinity, regulations, energy, carbon, security, latency, data placement) and generates reconfiguration plans. To guarantee system responsiveness and minimum computational overhead, routine events are processed using pre-established business rules. The solver is invoked exclusively for complex scenarios, such as extension of the Capsule to new topologies or a major reconfiguration following a failure. For routine adjustments, the Agent applies pre-established business rules without querying the scheduling engine. Once a solution is determined, each Agent executes its designated portion of the plan.

Bootstrap Kinematics (Fig. 5): (1) The user site initializes the Capsule from the application Descriptor and an instance of the Nocher Agent. (2) This operation triggers a request to the remote distributed DataBase, which returns an available site (SiteA) to which the Capsule expands. (3) The user site then transmits the Descriptors to SiteA. (4) The Agent on SiteA verifies the constraints and, if necessary, requests a new resource (SiteN) from the remote distributed DataBase, triggering a further extension of the Capsule.

Capsule Extension Kinematics (Fig. 6) : (1) SiteN, previously solicited by the Agent, enters an iterative constraint verification loop. (2) If these are not satisfied, the Capsule extends its perimeter to a neighboring site (SiteN+1). (3) The process iterates on this new site until the constraints are satisfied. (4) Finally, the terminal site, having resolved the constraints, generates a global operational plan redistributed to all sites. Simultaneously, SiteA broadcasts the datasets within the Capsule.

4 Case Studies

This section evaluates the relevance and effectiveness of the Nocher paradigm through the implementation of two use cases representative of the challenges

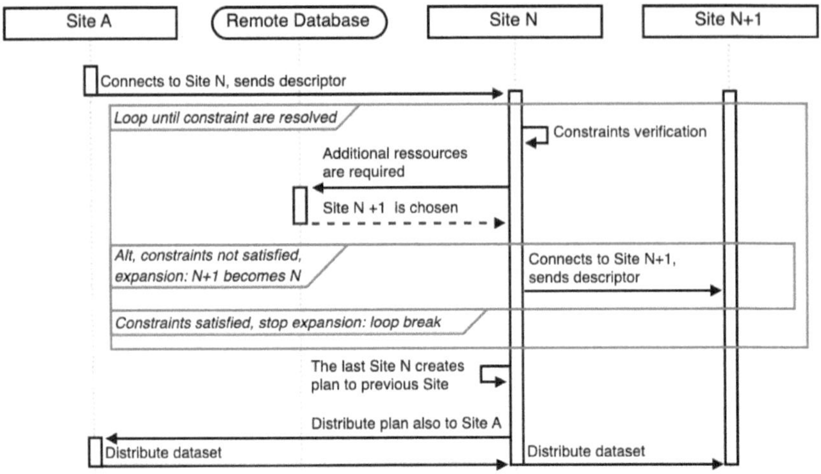

Fig. 6. Sequence expansion Capsule

inherent to the Continuum. The objective is to validate how the proposed abstraction enables transparent deployment and autonomous reconfiguration in the face of infrastructure heterogeneity and volatility. We demonstrate the system's ability to encapsulate operational complexity, transforming traditionally manual and complex incident management or scaling procedures into automated sequences driven by business constraints. The first scenario, dedicated to In-Transit Computing within a 5G context, illustrates the resilience of the approach against failures. It highlights the automatic reconfiguration mechanism in the event of a site failure, ensuring service continuity without human intervention. The second scenario, inspired by a Content Delivery Network (CDN) architecture, evaluates the versatility and elasticity of the Capsule. It demonstrates the joint lifecycle management of both applications and data through dynamic expansion and retraction operations.

In-Transit Computing, GPS-Free Geolocation (Signal Relay). Signals emitted by mobile devices are captured by cell towers, collected at the Edge level, and then forwarded to the Fog, where they are filtered in real-time according to business rules predefined by the Central (Cloud) layer. The Central layer aggregates the data to calculate the target mobile's location via trilateration using fixed antennas. However, the failure of a Fog element leads to a failure, leaving the Edge elements active (e.g., emergency calls to 18) but isolated. This blinds the Central layer, rendering the anomaly undetectable.

Figure 7 depicts our scenario organized into three geo-distributed levels: the Central Cloud (C) for the Position service, the Fog (F) for the Filter service, and the Edge (E) for the Collector service. Under nominal operation, each Collector connects to a single Filter, and each Filter is managed by the Central layer, which aggregates the data.

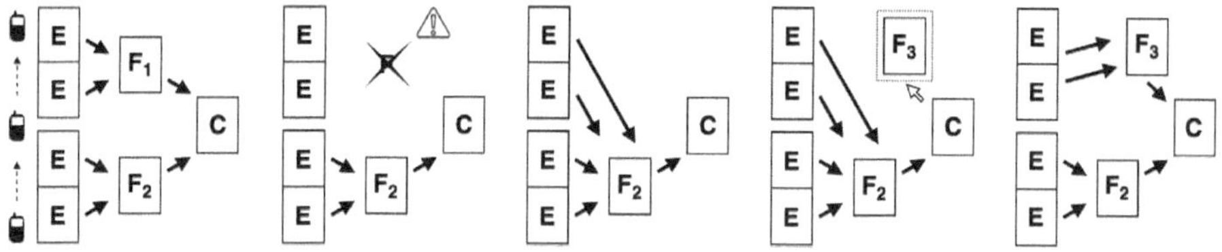

(a) Initial state (b) Fog crash (c) Edge reconfiguration (d) New Fog (e) New fog reconfiguration

Fig. 7. Sequential description of Fog issue for geo-localisation scenario.

Service deployment and configuration are contextual and performed manually by an operations team. This error-prone approach presents limitations that we will address subsequently by automating the entire process via a Nocher Capsule. In the nominal state (a), data flows from the Edge to the Central layer. The failure of a Fog site (b) causes a total data loss and triggers alerts. The manual repair procedure is carried out in three phases: the operator first redirects flows from orphaned Edge sites to a neighboring Fog site (c), instantiates a new Filter service on a replacement site (d), and finally reconfigures the Central layer to integrate the new Fog site (e), thereby restoring the nominal service.

Such a repair sequence involves cross-layer coordination (Edge routing, Fog instantiation, Central configuration) that exceeds the scope of standard Kubernetes operators or geo-distribution tools like KubeEdge, which cannot atomically manage business-level state transitions across heterogeneous sites.

The Nocher Capsule, defined by business constraints and rules, acts as a substitute for human intervention. The initial step consists of translating the application architecture into a formal Descriptor (Listing 1, Fig. 8 and Table 1) executable by the Nocher runtime. This hierarchical structure, inspired by the Fractal model, represents each service (Collector, Filter, Position) as a Primitive component as shown in lines 26 and 41 of Listing 1. These components encompass both technical configuration (cpu, ram, line 42–43) and placement constraints, along with associated business rules (e.g., failure handling procedures at the Fog level). The overall application is represented as a Composite component that aggregates these Primitives, thereby ensuring topology management and holistic orchestration.

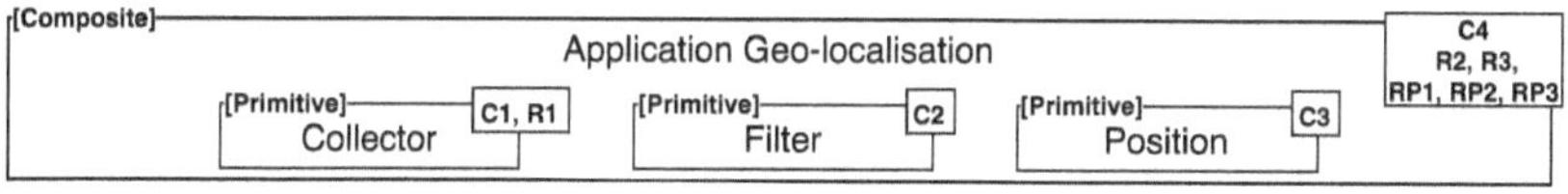

Fig. 8. Schematic view of the geo-localisation Capsule Descriptor, illustrating a Composite and its three Primitives services along with their constraints.

Once the Descriptor is generated, the Nocher system autonomously deploys the application across the infrastructure (Edge, Fog, Central) in compliance with the defined constraints (c1 to c4, line 8). The Capsule initializes on an initial site following the Bootstrap sequence (Fig. 5) and then automatically expands across all required sites (Edge, Fog, Central) according to the Extension sequence (Fig. 6). Configuration parameters (r1 to r3, line 14), such as the lists of Fog nodes for Collectors, are automatically injected during deployment or upon any subsequent change.

```
1  apiVersion: nocher.io/v1
2  kind: Capsule
3  spec:
4    componentType: Composite
5    membrane:
6      constraints:
7        - id: c_placement_hierarchy
8          expression: "children.node_type IN [Edge, Fog] MUST have
               parent in [Fog, Cloud]"
9        - id: c_resource_cardinality
10         expression: "count(active_primitives.filter) >= 2"
11     rules:
12       - id: r_initial_binding
13         trigger: "on_bootstrap"
14         action: "
               get_nearest_fog_list_and_inject_into_children_config"
15       ...
16     reaction_policies:
17       - id: rp_handle_resource_starvation
18         trigger: "constraint_violation(c_resource_cardinality)"
19         sequence:
20           - action: "query_remote-database_for_new_site(fog)"
21           - on_failure: "request_neighbor_capsule_degraded_mode()"
22       - id: rp_xxx
23         ...
24   children:
25     - name: generic-filter-service
26       componentType: Primitive
27       membrane:
28         constraints:
29           - id: c_proc_placement
30             expression: "site.type == Fog"
31         rules:
32           - id: r_proc_config
33             trigger: "on_parent_extension"
34             action: "apply_cpu_affinity(isolated_cores)"
35       containers:
36         - name: filter
37           image: filter:latest
38           ports:
39             - containerPort: 80
40           resources:
41             requests:
42               cpu: "100m"
43               memory: "64Mi"
44     - name: generic-collector-service
45       componentType: Primitive
46       membrane:
47         constraints:
48           - id: c_proc_placement
49             expression: "site.type == Edge"
50           ...
51     ...
```

Listing 1. Part of Descriptor example

Table 1. Business-level specification extracted from the Capsule Descriptor (constraints, routing, recovery) for the geo-localisation use case.

Rule	Description
c1	installation on Edge site
c2	installation on Fog site
c3	installation on Central site
c4	topology : 1 Central, 2 Fogs connected to Central, 2 Edges per Fog
r1	Connects by default on 1st Fog of the list or wait for a list
r2	create one list per Collector of the default Fog and the nearest backup Fogs computed by the system.
r3	create a filter on each available Fog
rp1	Controller configures Collector to switch on backup Fog
rp2	c4 constraint violation detected → Scheduler request → extension plan to a new Fog site
rp3	Central recreate a filter on each new Fog

The incident recovery workflow is the core of this demonstration, illustrating how the Capsule autonomously reacts to a Fog node failure (e.g., node crash, network partitioning, or hardware resource exhaustion). Upon detecting the failure, the Local Controller of the affected Edge nodes enforces its business rule rp1 (error recovery): it seamlessly switches its connection to a designated backup Fog from its predefined list. Simultaneously, the Agent observes that the global constraint (e.g., maintaining a minimum of two active Fog nodes) has been violated. It then triggers the Scheduler to identify and provision a new available site via the remote distributed DataBase. The recovery process concludes with the "Repair and Realignment" phase: a new Fog node is instantiated and configured with the required Filter service. Finally, the Agent updates the Central configuration to integrate the new participant, restoring the nominal state without any human intervention.

This scenario demonstrates Nocher's ability to ensure the transparent deployment of a complex application across the Computing Continuum while encapsulating operational complexity within rule based incident management. We will now proceed to the scenario detailing the dataset lifecycle.

Content Delivery Network - like. This scenario aims to demonstrate the agility and robustness of the Nocher Capsule concept in the face of complex and evolving use cases. Through a CDN system, it illustrates dataset lifecycle management and the versatility of the Capsule over time—reconfiguration, extension, retraction. This scenario relies on the telecom infrastructure from the previous scenario, composed of Edge, Fog, and Central sites, whose geographical distribution follows population density.

The application manages content for a television series, structured hierarchically into seasons and episodes. The system is responsible for governing both the placement of this content and the delivery service required to stream it to end-users.

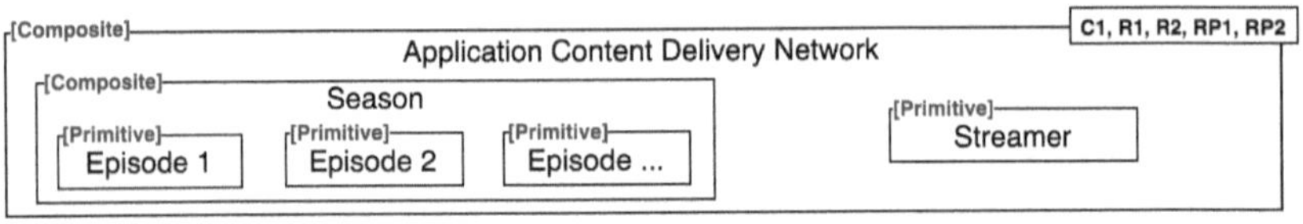

Fig. 9. Schematic view of the CDN-like Capsule Descriptor, illustrating a Composite and its N Primitives with dataset along with their constraints.

The application is encapsulated within a Nocher Capsule and modeled using a schema (Fig. 9, Tab. 2) inspired by the Fractal component model: Primitive components represent individual episodes and distribution services, while Composite components aggregate these elements to form the seasons to be delivered. This structure allows for a clear separation between dataset management—embodied by the video content—and the application logic, represented by the streaming service. At the onset of the scenario, the Capsule is deployed from the Central site across the Edge, Fog, and Central infrastructure using the Bootstrap and Extension mechanisms.

Table 2. Business-level specification extracted from the Capsule Descriptor (constraints, lifecycle rules and retraction policies) for the CDN-like use case.

rule	description
c1	Streaming Service, dynamic placement on all sites depending on demand.
c2	CDN application, hierarchical topology (Seasons/Episodes) and data consistency.
r1	Definition of a critical activity threshold (number of clients) to maintain instances.
r2	Non-interruption policy: ensure active sessions finish before releasing the site.
rp1	Retraction: if the threshold falls below the limit, redirect new clients to the parent site.
rp2	Archiving: at a defined date, merge Capsules and split to exclude the streamer.

Let us examine the reconfiguration and retraction steps of the Capsule following a decline in demand. The retraction process propagates from the Edge back to the Central site, following a logic of progressive resource release. It begins with continuous monitoring of activity on each Edge site. The system detects when the number of active users on an Edge site falls below a threshold defined by business rules. In response, the Capsule's decision-making mechanism updates the routing policy: new users requesting to start a playback are automatically redirected to the parent Fog site. The Capsule retracts once the final user disconnects from the Edge, thereby releasing the site's computing, storage, and bandwidth resources. This movement then propagates to the upper tier. As Edge sites retract, the Fog site experiences a decreasing load. When the number of users connected to the Fog also falls below its critical threshold, the same logic is applied. The Fog site ceases to accept new local requests and redirects new users to the Central site. Once all sessions are terminated, the Fog site releases its resources and detaches from the Capsule. Following these two phases, the Capsule's architecture has been significantly downsized. All residual traffic, corresponding to the final clients viewing the season, is now served by the Central site. The Capsule, which had extended across a geographically dispersed architecture during the peak-demand period, has fully retracted to its central core to optimize infrastructure utilization.

This progressive retraction based on session completion rather than resource metrics requires a business-aware lifecycle manager. Solutions like Karmada or SeMaFoR, focused on resource placement, cannot enforce "wait-for-session-end" policies coupled with data archiving logic without custom, external scripting (Table 3).

Table 3. Positioning of Nocher against state-of-the-art orchestration solutions.

Feature	k8s KubeEdge [15]	Karmada [4]	Unbound [11]	SeMaFoR [1]	Cheops [10]	Concerto-D [2]	Nocher (ours)
Abstraction Unit	Pod/Cluster resource-centric	Cluster site-centric	Meta-Federation physical/ virtual clusters	Fog-Area logical resource grouping consensus	Application local-first collaborative-then	Application network resilience focused	**Capsule service datasets orchestration logic**
Business Logic	No	No	No	No (Resource)	Partial/ limited (Routing)	Partial/ limited (Resilience)	**Native** (Full)
Geo-distribution	Partial/ limited (Manual)	**Native** (Site)	**Native** (Site)	**Native** (Area)	**Native** (Local-first)	**Native** (Network)	**Native**
Data-centric Lifecycle	No	No	No	No	No	No	**Native**
Autonomous Repair	No (Operator)	No	No	Partial/ limited Consensus	Partial/ limited DevOps	Partial/ limited	**Native**
Infra Agnostic	No	No	No	Partial/ limited	Partial/ limited	Partial/ limited	**Native**

This scenario demonstrates Nocher's ability to orchestrate the dataset lifecycle and reconfigure Capsule topology through time-sensitive business rules.

5 Positioning Against State-of-the-Art

These scenarios highlight a critical gap in current solutions. Standard orchestrators (Kubernetes, KubeEdge) and multi-cluster managers (Karmada, Unbound) remain resource-centric: they manage pods across sites but lack awareness of application business logic, making autonomous topology rewrites (e.g., promoting a backup Fog, updating Central configuration) impossible without external operators. Similar to existing application-centric approaches like Cheops, Concerto-D binds resource lifecycle to the application's topology and logic. Consequently, datasets lack an autonomous lifecycle independent of component states, limiting management based on independent business constraints.

Nocher is the only approach that encapsulates both orchestration logic and business rules within the deployment unit, enabling a data-centric reconfiguration.

6 Conclusions and Perspectives

This position paper addresses the limitations of traditional infrastructure-centric models by proposing Nocher, a holistic, application-centric approach for the Computing Continuum. By introducing the Capsule abstraction, Nocher decouples business logic and dataset lifecycle from infrastructure concerns, enabling transparent deployment and autonomous reconfiguration across geo-distributed environments.

We argue that Nocher's autonomous reconfiguration effectively supersedes traditional DevOps. This validates our architectural choices, specifically the use of Fractal Descriptors and subsidiarity principles. These scenarios highlight a critical gap in existing solutions. Nocher is the first to unify placement, business logic, and data lifecycle within a single Capsule abstraction, enabling fully autonomous, application-centric reconfiguration.

While this initial study focuses on core functionalities, security and governance policies remain outside its current scope, marking a clear boundary for our primary analysis.

Future work will focus on three main axes:

- Capsule composition to handle network partition.
- Autonomous Capsules coordination to handle extreme cases, including starvation modes and critical failure scenarios.
- Exploring the integration of Nocher with Concerto-D, taking advantage of the complementary strengths of both approaches.

By reifying the Capsule abstraction across geo-distributed sites, Nocher provides a cohesive solution to the challenges of the Computing Continuum. This approach establishes a solid foundation for a new generation of application-centric distributed systems.

References

1. Alidra, A., et al.: SeMaFoR - self-management of fog resources with collaborative decentralized controllers. In: IEEE/ACM 18th Symposium on Software Engineering for Adaptive and Self-Managing Systems (SEAMS). IEEE (2023). https://doi.org/10.1109/SEAMS59076.2023.00014
2. Arfi, F., Coullon, H., Loulergue, F., Philippe, J., Robillard, S.: An overview of the decentralized reconfiguration language concerto-d through its maude formalization. Electron. Proc. Theor. Comput. Sci. (2024). https://doi.org/10.4204/EPTCS.414.2
3. Author of project: K3s. https://k3s-io.github.io/
4. Author of project: Karmada and open cluster management two new approaches to the multicluster fleet management challenge (2022)
5. Authors of project: Open Managed Control Planes. https://github.com/openmcp-project
6. Bittencourt, L.F., et al.: The computing continuum: past, present, and future. Comput. Sci. Rev. (2025). https://doi.org/10.1016/j.cosrev.2025.100782

7. Blair, G.: Complex distributed systems: the need for fresh perspectives. In: 38th International Conference on Distributed Computing Systems (ICDCS). IEEE (2018). https://doi.org/10.1109/icdcs.2018.00142
8. Blair, G., Coupaye, T., Stefani, J.B.: Component-based architecture: the fractal initiative. Ann. Telecommun. (2009). https://doi.org/10.1007/s12243-009-0086-1
9. Bouchenak, S., Boyer, F., Claudel, B., De Palma, N., Gruber, O., Sicard, S.: From autonomic to self-self behaviors: the JADE experience. ACM Trans. Auton. Adapt. Syst. (2011). https://doi.org/10.1145/2019591.2019597
10. Cherrueau, R.A., Delavergne, M., Lèbre, A.: Geo-distribute cloud applications at the edge. In: Euro-Par 2021: Parallel Processing. Springer International Publishing (2021). https://doi.org/10.1007/978-3-030-85665-6_19
11. Huang, C.K., Pierre, G.: UnBound: multi-tenancy management in scalable fog meta-federations. In: IEEE/ACM 17th International Conference on Utility and Cloud Computing (UCC) (2024). https://doi.org/10.1109/UCC63386.2024.00029
12. Kleppmann, M., Wiggins, A., van Hardenberg, P., McGranaghan, M.: Local-first software: you own your data, in spite of the cloud. In: Proceedings of the 2019 ACM SIGPLAN International Symposium on New Ideas, New Paradigms, and Reflections on Programming and Software. Association for Computing Machinery (2019). https://doi.org/10.1145/3359591.3359737
13. Moreschini, S., Pecorelli, F., Li, X., Naz, S., Hästbacka, D., Taibi, D.: Cloud continuum: the definition. IEEE Access (2022). https://doi.org/10.1109/ACCESS.2022.3229185
14. Quesnel, F., Lèbre, A.: Cooperative dynamic scheduling of virtual machines in distributed systems. In: Euro-Par 2011: Parallel Processing Workshops. Springer (2012). https://doi.org/10.1007/978-3-642-29740-3_51
15. Xiong, Y., Sun, Y., Xing, L., Huang, Y.: Extend cloud to edge with KubeEdge. In: 2018 IEEE/ACM Symposium on Edge Computing (SEC). IEEE (2018). https://doi.org/10.1109/SEC.2018.00048

Balancing Personality and Technical Expertise in Microservice Teams: An Algorithmic Approach

Dario Amoroso d'Aragona[2(✉)], Fabio Calefato[1(✉)], and Davide Taibi[2(✉)]

[1] University of Bari, Bari, Italy
fabio.calefato@uniba.it
[2] University of Southern Denmark, Vejle, Denmark
{dariodaragona,taibi}@imada.sdu.dk

Abstract. Microservice architectures are commonly organized around small service-owning teams, making team composition a relevant architectural and human-factor concern. We propose an algorithmic approach for composing microservice teams by combining developers' Big Five personality traits, inferred from GitHub communication, with programming-language expertise extracted from contribution histories. The approach evaluates candidate assignments through a personality composition score grounded in organizational-psychology evidence and a technical-alignment score based on language coverage. A study on Spinnaker, HMDA-Platform, and Taskcluster shows that the method identifies higher-scoring candidate configurations and, more importantly, makes explicit how team size, contributor overlap, and technological diversity condition the feasible improvement space.

Keywords: Microservices · Team Composition · Big Five · Five Factor Model

1 Introduction

Microservices decompose systems into small, independently deployable services that are often owned by autonomous teams responsible for the full service lifecycle [7]. Because such teams are usually small, individual differences among developers may have stronger effects on coordination, communication, and conflict than in larger teams. Organizational psychology provides relevant evidence: high team-level *Conscientiousness* and *Agreeableness* are consistently associated with better team outcomes, while high *Neuroticism* is associated with poorer collaboration [1,3,13]; lower dispersion in key traits can also support coordination, although mean trait levels are usually more predictive than variance [13,15].

These findings have rarely been operationalized in microservice-oriented OSS settings, where membership emerges from contribution patterns rather than deliberate staffing. Li et al. [10] proposed personality-based collaboration

D. Balouek et al. (Eds.): ESOCC 2026, LNCS 16834, pp. 150–156, 2027.
https://doi.org/10.1007/978-3-032-37831-6_10

optimization for microservice projects, but empirical evidence on real projects remained limited. We address this gap by proposing and evaluating a team-composition approach that combines personality and programming-language expertise. We ask: **RQ1** whether algorithmic composition improves personality composition scores compared with existing configurations; **RQ2** how structural characteristics such as team size and developer distribution affect optimization; and **RQ3** how much technical alignment contributes to the combined score.

2 Background

This section summarizes the theoretical basis used to define the scoring function. The Big Five model describes personality through *Openness*, *Conscientiousness*, *Extraversion*, *Agreeableness*, and *Neuroticism* [6,8]. In software engineering, prior work has shown that Big Five traits can be estimated from textual traces such as mailing-list messages, issue comments, and pull-request discussions [2,4,5,16]. In team-performance research, meta-analyses identify *Conscientiousness* as the most robust predictor of team effectiveness and *Agreeableness* as the second most relevant trait for cooperation and cohesion [1,3,9,13]. Minimum *Agreeableness* is also relevant because one uncooperative member can disrupt group processes [1,15]. Effects for *Extraversion*, *Openness*, and *Neuroticism* are more context-dependent: *Extraversion* may support communication [3,12], *Openness* may support complex problem solving [13], and low *Neuroticism* may support emotional stability [1,14]. We operationalize these findings into an evidence-based composition quality score that allows alternative service-team assignments to be compared consistently.

3 Empirical Study Design

We evaluate the approach on three public GitHub microservice projects with different structures: *HMDA-Platform* (39 developers, 15 microservices, 2–4 developers per service, mean = 2.6), *Taskcluster* (27 developers, 12 microservices, 1–3 developers per service, mean = 2.25), and *Spinnaker* (273 developers, 12 microservices, 3–44 developers per service, mean = 22.75). This ordering is also used in the results to improve readability.

3.1 Data Collection and Personality Inference

For each microservice, we identified core developers from commit histories as the smallest contributor subset accounting for at least 80% of commits. If this produced too small a candidate pool, we added developers until reaching $3 \times k$ candidates, where k is the number of microservices. For each selected developer, we collected GitHub issues, issue comments, pull-request descriptions, and pull-request comments, and aggregated them into a developer-level textual corpus. Personality was inferred using seven pre-trained Big Five/OCEAN text models applied to three text variants: original text, regex-cleaned text with code/log artifacts removed, and grammar-corrected cleaned text. Rather than relying on a single classifier, the inference step explicitly tests cross-model stability: for each model, we compute the mean pairwise prediction difference against the others, retain the three most stable models, and use majority voting to assign the final OCEAN label for each trait. This makes the subsequent optimization depend on consensus personality labels rather than on one model's isolated prediction.

Technical expertise was estimated from contribution histories. For each developer, language skill $skill(d, l) \in [0, 1]$ was computed from the proportion of contributions in language l. For each microservice, language requirements were extracted from repository structure and file extensions, producing language weights w_l that sum to one.

3.2 Team Composition Algorithm

Let $D = \{d_1, \ldots, d_n\}$ be the developers and $MS = \{ms_1, \ldots, ms_k\}$ the microservices. A configuration $c = \{T_1, \ldots, T_k\}$ assigns a team T_i to each microservice ms_i. The generator first guarantees at least two developers per microservice by shuffling the candidate pool and assigning the first $2k$ developers across services. Remaining developers are then assigned randomly. When the candidate pool is smaller than required, the implementation allows developer overlap across multiple microservice teams to keep the configuration feasible. Duplicate configurations are removed using a canonical key based on sorted team memberships. Candidate configurations are evaluated by the scores below, and local search with random restarts improves assignments by swapping developers between teams; a swap is accepted when it improves the tuple (minScore, meanScore, − stdScore).

Traits are encoded as LOW=0, MEDIUM=1, HIGH=2. For each team, the personality score is:

$$Score_{pers}(T_i) = 3\mu_C(T_i) - \sigma_C^2(T_i) + 2.5\mu_A(T_i) - 0.5\sigma_A^2(T_i) + \min_A(T_i) - 2\mu_N(T_i) + \mu_E(T_i) + \mu_O(T_i).$$

The weighting reflects the relative support found in the literature: strong support for high average *Conscientiousness* and *Agreeableness*, moderate support for low variance in *Conscientiousness* and *Agreeableness*, explicit reward for minimum *Agreeableness*, negative weight for *Neuroticism*, and smaller positive weights for *Extraversion* and *Openness*. The support column indicates the strength of the literature evidence used to guide weighting; it is not a multiplicative factor in the formula. We normalize the raw score to $[0, 1]$ as

$$\widehat{Score}_{pers}(T_i) = \frac{Score_{pers}(T_i) - (-4)}{17 - (-4)}.$$

Technical alignment is computed as the best language coverage inside a team:

$$Score_{lang}(T_i, ms_i) = \sum_{l \in L(ms_i)} w_l \cdot \max_{d \in T_i} skill(d, l),$$

Table 1. How literature-supported rules are encoded in $Score_{pers}$. Support indicates the strength of the literature evidence used to guide weighting; it is not a multiplicative factor in the formula.

Rule	Encoded term	Support
High average *Conscientiousness*	$+3\mu_C$	5/5
Low variance in *Conscientiousness*	$-\sigma_C^2$	4/5
High average *Agreeableness*	$+2.5\mu_A$	5/5
Low variance in *Agreeableness*	$-0.5\sigma_A^2$	3/5
High minimum *Agreeableness*	$+\min_A$	4/5
Low average *Neuroticism*	$-2\mu_N$	3/5
Moderate/high *Extraversion* and *Openness*	$+\mu_E, +\mu_O$	3/5

and the combined score is

$$Score_{comb}(T_i) = \widehat{Score}_{pers}(T_i) + \lambda Score_{lang}(T_i, ms_i).$$

At configuration level, we report the minimum, mean, and standard deviation of team scores (Table 1).

Table 2. Baseline and generated-configuration results. "mean pers." is the normalized mean personality score; ranges summarize the ten generated configurations.

Project	Baseline	Baseline	Gen. team	Gen. mean	Mean lang	Mean comb.
HMDA	0.505	0.436	2–4	0.485–0.547	0.004–0.012	0.489–0.554
Taskcluster	0.520	0.395	2–4	0.429–0.566	0.620–0.662	1.066–1.227
Spinnaker	0.512	0.455	2–7	0.520–0.550	0.333–0.418	0.872–0.964

4 Results

Table 2 summarizes the main results. In **HMDA-Platform**, most generated configurations improve the normalized mean personality score over the baseline of 0.505, with the best reaching 0.547. Because baseline and generated teams have comparable size (2–4 developers per microservice), the improvement is attributable mainly to developer reassignment rather than to a team-size artifact. The best optimized minimum personality score is 0.441, slightly above the baseline minimum of 0.436. Language scores are close to zero (0.004–0.012), so the combined score mostly mirrors personality composition; this suggests a homogeneous technology stack rather than poor technical fit.

In **Taskcluster**, only the top configurations exceed the baseline mean of 0.520, with the best reaching 0.566. The project has the most constrained structure: original teams contain only 1–3 developers and the generated configurations use 2–4. Hence, improvements depend on specific reassignment decisions rather than on averaging. The low baseline minimum (0.395) confirms that very small service teams are highly sensitive to individual profiles; the observed spread in generated mean scores (0.429–0.566) shows that the algorithm is useful for surfacing viable high-scoring alternatives even when the search space is narrow.

In **Spinnaker**, all generated configurations improve the mean personality score over the baseline (0.512 to 0.520–0.550), but the baseline minimum (0.455) remains slightly above the best optimized minimum available in the detailed results (0.453). This reflects the effect of large-team averaging: the original project has up to 44 contributors per service, which naturally stabilizes scores, while generated teams are much smaller (2–7 developers). Language alignment differentiates Spinnaker configurations more than HMDA, suggesting that technical alignment becomes informative when the ecosystem is technologically diverse.

5 Discussion and Threats to Validity

The results answer **RQ1** positively at the level targeted by the paper: the algorithm identifies candidate configurations with higher average personality composition scores than the existing configuration in each project. This contribution is a decision-support mechanism for comparing alternative assignments under explicit personality and technical criteria. The result is strongest in HMDA, where baseline and generated team sizes are comparable, and more constrained in Taskcluster and Spinnaker, where structure respectively limits redistribution or creates strong averaging effects.

For **RQ2**, project structure strongly moderates the results. HMDA provides the cleanest case because baseline and generated team sizes are similar. Taskcluster shows that very small teams leave little room for redistribution. Spinnaker shows the opposite issue: large existing teams produce stable baseline scores through averaging, making optimized small-team configurations more variable. For **RQ3**, language alignment is project-dependent: it is negligible in HMDA, more discriminative in Spinnaker, and constrained by the small-team setting in Taskcluster.

Construct validity is mainly affected by indirect measurement. We mitigate personality-inference instability by combining multiple models, preprocessing variants, stability-based model selection, and majority voting; nevertheless, GitHub text primarily represents professional communication, and direct survey validation would further strengthen future studies. Language expertise is approximated through contribution proportions, which captures observed technical exposure but not necessarily depth of proficiency. Internal validity is limited by randomized generation and local search: the reported configurations are locally optimized candidates rather than guaranteed optima.

6 Conclusions

We proposed an algorithmic approach for composing microservice teams by combining Big Five personality composition and programming-language expertise. Across three OSS microservice projects, the approach identifies candidate configurations with improved average personality composition scores and explains when such improvements are feasible: they are clearest when teams are small enough for individual profiles to matter but flexible enough to allow reassignment. The study therefore turns personality-aware team composition from a conceptual proposal into an operational, auditable optimization procedure. Future work can extend this procedure by validating inferred traits against self-reported measures, relating composition scores to observable development outcomes, and adding explicit objectives for worst-case team quality.

References

1. Barrick, M.R., Stewart, G.L., Neubert, M.J., Mount, M.K.: Relating member ability and personality to work-team processes and team effectiveness. J. Appl. Psychol. **83**(3), 377–391 (1998)
2. Bazelli, B., Hindle, A., Stroulia, E.: On the personality traits of StackOverflow users. In: Proc. IEEE International Conference on Software Maintenance (ICSM), pp. 460–463. IEEE (2013). https://doi.org/10.1109/ICSM.2013.72
3. Bell, S.T.: Deep-level composition variables as predictors of team performance: a meta-analysis. J. Appl. Psychol. **92**(3), 595–615 (2007)
4. Calefato, F., Lanubile, F.: Using personality detection tools for software engineering research: how far can we go? ACM TOSEM **31**(3), 1–48 (2022). https://doi.org/10.1145/3491039
5. Calefato, F., Lanubile, F., Vasilescu, B.: A large-scale, in-depth analysis of developers' personalities in the Apache ecosystem. Inf. Softw. Technol. **114**, 1–20 (2019). https://doi.org/10.1016/j.infsof.2019.05.012
6. Costa, P.T., Jr., McCrae, R.R.: Revised NEO Personality Inventory (NEO-PI-R) and NEO Five-Factor Inventory (NEO-FFI) Professional Manual. Psychological Assessment Resources, Odessa, FL (1992)
7. Fowler, M., Lewis, J.: Microservices: A definition of this new architectural term (2014). https://martinfowler.com/articles/microservices.html Accessed 01 May 2025
8. Goldberg, L.R.: An alternative "description of personality": the Big-Five factor structure. J. Pers. Soc. Psychol. **59**(6), 1216–1229 (1990). https://doi.org/10.1037/0022-3514.59.6.1216
9. Hurtz, G.M., Donovan, J.J.: Personality and job performance: the big five revisited. J. Appl. Psychol. **85**(6), 869–879 (2000)
10. Li, X., Calefato, F., Lenarduzzi, V., Taibi, D.: Toward collaboration optimization in microservice projects based on developer personalities. In: Proc. 21st IEEE International Conference on Software Architecture – Companion (ICSA-C), pp. 95–99. IEEE (2024). https://doi.org/10.1109/ICSA-C63560.2024.00024
11. Mathieu, J.E., Maynard, M.T., Rapp, T., Gilson, L.: Team effectiveness 1997–2007: a review of recent advancements and a glimpse into the future. J. Manag. **34**(3), 410–476 (2008)

12. Neuman, G.A., Wagner, S.H., Christiansen, N.D.: The relationship between work-team personality composition and job performance. Group Organizat. Manag. **24**(1), 28–45 (1999)
13. Peeters, M.A.G., van Tuijl, H.F.J.M., Rutte, C.G., Reymen, I.M.M.J.: Personality and team performance: a meta-analysis. Eur. J. Pers. **20**, 377–396 (2006)
14. Prewett, M.S., Brown, M.I., Goswami, A., Christiansen, N.D.: Effects of team personality composition on member performance. Group Organizat. Manag. **43**(2), 316–348 (2018)
15. Prewett, M.S., Walvoord, A.A.G., Stilson, F.R.B., Rossi, M.E., Brannick, M.T.: The team personality-team performance relationship revisited. Hum. Perform. **22**, 273–296 (2009)
16. Rigby, P.C., Hassan, A.E.: What can OSS mailing lists tell us? a preliminary psychometric text analysis of the Apache developer mailing list. In: Proc. Fourth International Workshop on Mining Software Repositories (MSR'07). IEEE (2007). https://doi.org/10.1109/MSR.2007.35

Analytics Feature Space: a Novel Framework for Interoperable Edge Machine Learning Detection

Hong-Linh Truong[1](✉) and Ngoc Nhu Trang Nguyen[2]

[1] Aalto University, Espoo, Finland
linh.truong@aalto.fi
[2] Daienso Lab, Da Nang, Vietnam
nhutrang.nguyen@daienso.com

Abstract. In many application domains, complex scenarios require us to perform composable analytics for a collective of assets, spaces, and environments from different near real-time edge AI/ML-based detections. However, extensive metadata required for interpreting the results is not well supported, causing the difficulty when integrating and analyzing detection results from multiple pipelines and algorithms and when sharing data to third parties. We present Analytics Feature Space (AFS) as a novel, practical framework to support high-level analytics and integration for multiple types of AI/ML-based detections at the edge in a unified way. AFS supports key metadata related to edge AI/ML-based detections, changes in detection deployments, and metadata for the collectives of asset, space, and environment detection and analytics. We introduce techniques to manage relationships between analytics subjects, AI/ML detection models, and results. Different ways for integrating AFS with detection pipelines and improving data sharing are discussed.

1 Introduction

Although object detection [4] is widely used in many applications, in real-world complex systems, like Intelligent Operation Centers for industrial zones, Digital Twins, or smart seaports, we have many other types of detection, like anomaly detection, event detection, and hazardous material and surface detection. In the view of analytics for different purposes, we move away from single detections for single assets to the analytics of complex subjects encapsulating highly connected assets (e.g., pumps and pipes), related spaces (e.g., wastewater lakes), and environments (e.g., water and air) in a managed business (e.g., wastewater treatment factories in an Intelligent Operation Center) and in a global supply chain of assets and goods. We call entities abstracted in such a complex subject that must be managed together a Collective of Assets, Spaces, and Environments (CASE), depicted in Fig. 1. In complex operations and management involving multiple stakeholders and parties, to manage CASE, the analytics can leverage

Published by Springer Nature Switzerland AG 2027
D. Balouek et al. (Eds.): ESOCC 2026, LNCS 16834, pp. 157–165, 2027.
https://doi.org/10.1007/978-3-032-37831-6_11

many types of above-mentioned detections. Thus, there is a need to integrate results from different types of detection for a holistic analytics of CASE.

When examining the detections required for the downstream applications and data sharing of CASE, two key observations are drawn. First, the detection pipelines are diverse in terms of underlying AI/ML models (e.g., object detection models vs time series anomaly data detection models) and outputs (e.g., multiple object detection vs specific anomaly detection). Second, due to highly decoupling and management in software and system operations at the edge, these pipelines can be reconfigured and changed, w.r.t. runtime configurations, ML model updates, and data sources, without awareness of the downstream applications and consumers, affecting the results, quality of data, and explainability. Therefore, for downstream applications and consumers, which aggregate the results from various pipelines, there are many types of data that can be missed or inadequate and are not interoperable to support the analytics and integration of the outputs from these pipelines.

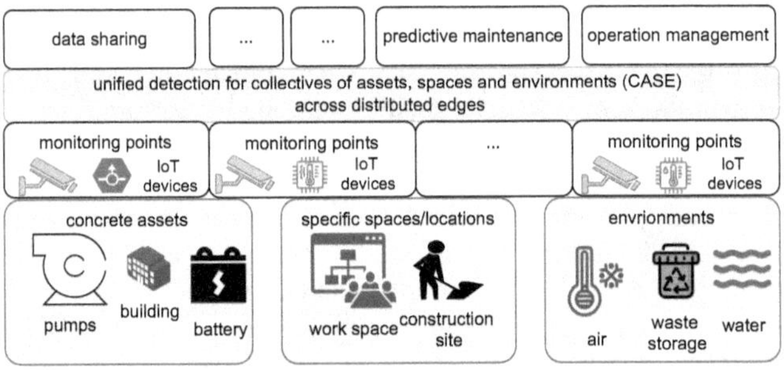

Fig. 1. Unified detection management for collectives of assets, spaces, and environments at the edge. Applications need to analyze multiple entities in a CASE.

In this paper, we address the above-mentioned issues by introducing the Analytics Feature Space (AFS) as a novel, practical framework to support the interoperability, integration, and explainability for multiple types of AI/ML-based detection at the edge in a unified way for CASE. The paper makes the following contributions:

- *making several types of metadata associated with edge detection pipelines for a CASE explicitly*: many types of metadata are implicitly hidden inside the implementation and need to be explicitly modeled for downstream applications and data consumers.
- *capturing important changes for downstream applications*: given the autonomous deployment and operation of edge pipelines, cloud-based downstream applications must be aware of the changes in order to make decisions.
- *providing a generic framework with functions and middleware for the enrichment of results and metadata*: usually such enrichment cannot be done at a

single place due to the complex deployment, thus various functions together with messaging middleware to support the enrichment are needed.

The rest of this paper is organized as follows: we present the Analytics Feature Space framework in Sect. 2, discuss related works in Sect. 3, and then conclude the paper in Sect. 4.

2 The Analytics Feature Space Framework

2.1 Defining an Analytics Feature Space

Unified Detection Management for CASE at the Edge. In existing work, typically there are multiple assets (e.g., pumps and pipes) located in a location, and each asset has a set of dedicated monitoring points, e.g., linked to sensors/cameras, for the asset. Then, analytics/detection is specifically applied to the asset by analyzing measurements and detection results from data provided by these monitoring points. However, due to the dynamic edge deployments, software, changes, and the concept of analytics/detection associated with the domain, several relationships are complex and changing. For example, a monitoring point at a specific location can provide data for a concrete asset, such as equipment, but it can also provide data for monitoring a specific space. Hence, a single monitoring point is for two separate analytics subjects.

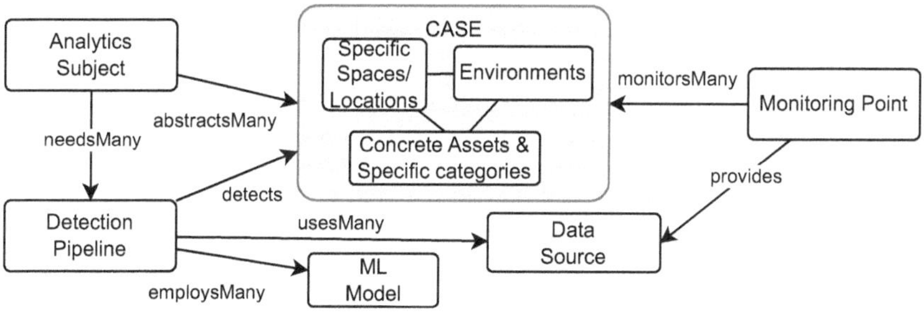

Fig. 2. High-level relationships of main elements in a unified detection view.

Figure 2 presents a unified view of relevant software and data components for dynamic, multiple types of detection. From the application viewpoint, a *Detection Pipeline* can be deployed for the detection of an asset, space or environment. A *Detection Pipeline* will rely on *Data Source* provided by *Monitoring Point.* An *Analytics Subject* is a high-level abstraction that indicates the subject to be analyzed in a CASE. The subject can include a concrete asset, a specific space, or an environment. Analytics subjects are usually defined in the application specific setting, e.g., a safety application. To analyze a subject, different AI/ML models with different data sources are deployed and integrated into a unified view.

In principle, the detection results can be associated with different classification labels (e.g., "person" for an object detection or "anomaly" for anomaly detection) defined in different naming classes. Moreover, a detection result includes many other types of data, covering (i) properties of the detection result such as `''count''` – a specific measurement for `''person''` or `''anomaly''` – an indicator of an anomaly and (ii) confidence of the detection associated with the detection object via `''hProbability''`. Besides the detection results, there are many other types of data characterizing and explaining the result, e.g. which AI/ML models or configuration are used. Therefore, in real-world situations, the detection results can be considered as part of a data product of which metadata and data properties must be explicitly expressed for downstream applications and data sharing.

Analytics Feature Space (AFS) and AFS-Aware Detection Systems. Overall, given a CASE, when using multiple AI/ML models for various detection tasks with multiple pipelines, we can consider that the results, changes, and associated metadata from these pipelines belong to an "Analytics Feature Space" (AFS), abstracting entities for the analytics of CASE. An AFS defines *a unified detection management for a collective of assets, spaces, and environments (CASE) at the edge*, supporting key metadata, changes, and detection results enrichment to address interoperability, integration, and explainability. AFS provides modeling for the results outputted from edge detections and their associated metadata in a generic way. This helps downstream applications improve the selection of detection results based on ML algorithms and their changes. AFS assists the use and composition of the detection results for further applications by providing feature instances. Besides, when configuring with right policies and connectors, detection results can be shared to other parties via Data Hub/Gateway and Connectors using data spaces techniques and frameworks [3]. A system supporting the AFS concept is called an *AFS-aware detection system*. Figure 3 presents a high-level view of an exemplified AFS-aware detection system.

2.2 AFS Data Modeling

Explicit Analytics Subject. An *Analytics Subject* is used to represent a CASE for complex detections and analytics. We assume that any AFS-aware detection system will integrate with *CASE Management Services* (e.g., asset management), which have detailed information about the subjects. AFS will use the identifier of the subject for discovering associated entities. Every analytics subject is unique in a system (based on naming convention) and for the purpose of integration and explainability, the analytics subject is explicitly modeled in AFS by tagging an identifier – `analyticsSubjectId`.

Explicit Detection Feature Instances. Outputs from an upstream, edge ML detection pipeline are *feature instances* or candidates for *feature instances*

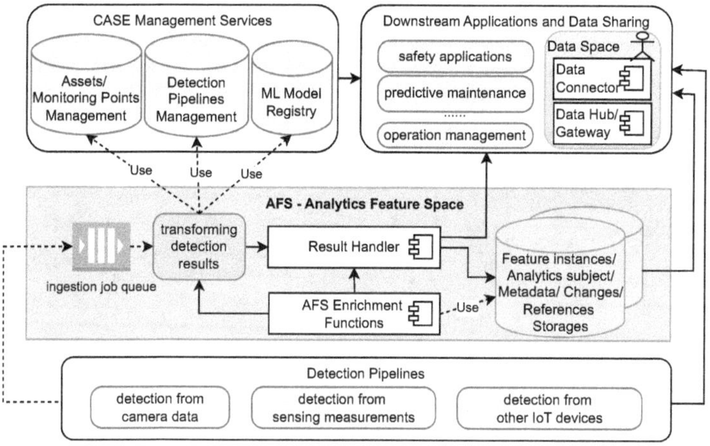

Fig. 3. An exemplified AFS-aware detection system including AFS components, edge Detection Pipelines, and Downstream Applications and Data Sharing.

to be used in downstream applications or in data sharing to third parties. Candidates for feature instances must be processed through *transformation/enrichment functions* to be *feature instances*. Feature instances must also be associated with information about domains and extension for enrichment. Besides, the schema for metadata associated with the feature instances is an important matter. Such metadata can be collected and enriched through the pipeline.

Domain Categories for Detection Purposes. Understanding the detection purpose and the application domain is important. Such purposes are *implicitly* hidden in the deployment of the pipelines. AFS supports a hierarchical domain category and models *the domain category hierarchy* explicitly. This is part of the metadata to associate the results to indicate different application categories. The category hierarchy can be implemented by using hierarchical naming mechanisms. For example, Fig. 4 gives a snapshot of the hierarchical category.

Explicit Naming Classes for Detection Results. Given a detection for a data stream, many different ML detection models can be used. However, different models may use different class names for a detected object and the confidence degree associated with the used model. Therefore, AFS proposes to map labels/class names from specific ML models to a common naming category for integration and interoperability purposes, while attaching the confidence degree together with metadata about ML models. Common prediction classes then can be used in pipelines. We use a common namespace way ``namingscheme.classname'' to specify information about the scheme where class names are based on.

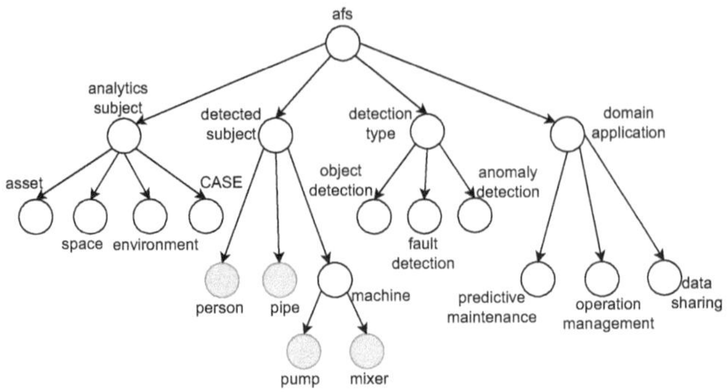

Fig. 4. Example of the hierarchical category, which can be defined and customized for specific deployment.

2.3 AFS Functions and Services

Transformation/Enrichment Functions. Feature instances may not be completed for downstream applications and consumers due to various reasons, such as the detection may decide to put only basic information for efficient purposes (e.g., to be fast or due to limited deployment) or information is not available at the detection pipeline and reference data resides in an external place. Therefore, functions can be used to transform/enrich detection results. Such functions can be deployed at various points to perform the enrichment at near real-time. Another aspect of enrichment is related to the reference sources for metadata. Because the edge detection deployment is lightweight, the results may include several references, instead of values. Given such references and sharing purposes, the specific results can be enriched with metadata obtained from reference sources.

Capturing Runtime Configuration Changes. Runtime information about an ML-based detection includes two main aspects. First, the ML models used in the pipeline have different runtime parameters, including the composition of multiple models like ensembles [2]. Second, given an ML model and its data sources, the configuration of several parameters, like data sampling rate, window length, and detection frequency, can be customized and configured based on specific deployments. AFS explicitly supports the capture runtime configuration based on a change lifecycle. At the deployment time, runtime configuration will be recorded, like a checkpoint, and sent to the downstream.

Capturing Data Source Changes. The information about data sources can be modeled based on existing information systems and schemas [8]. However, the change of such data sources cannot be detected by the downstream or it is challenging for the downstream to detect the change of data sources by knowing only the detection result. In AFS, we explicitly model the change of data sources by introducing a schema for sending changes about data sources. A basic lifecycle of a data source is given, covering states like `added, removed, unavailable, changed`. We can provide APIs for pipelines to checkpoint data sources inside the pipeline (during the deployment and runtime). If there is a change, the change information will be recorded and propagated.

Messaging Middleware for the AFS (MAFS). Since detection results are mostly delivered at near real-time to the downstream applications and data hubs, various messaging middleware can be used. We focus on MAFS atop common, well-established middleware (like MQTT, Apache Pulsar and Apache Kafka) for detection results. We mainly focus on added functions to support the exchanges of AFS-based feature instances and metadata, meaning the routing and enrichment, because techniques and software for bridging and integrating multiple messaging systems are well-developed. Messages encapsulating feature instances are propagated through a scalable middleware. Detection pipeline pushes results of feature candidates/instances to AFS via topics, supporting:

- *Context-aware result delivery:* Hierarchical category naming can be mapped to topics/subscriptions. Given the result constraints, detection pipelines can also support the concept of context-aware data sharing by fan-outing or routing the detection results to different topics.
- *Delivery of additional data:* Non message-based data, such as an image, a video or a CSV dataset, linked to feature instances can also be supported. They can be delivered via two mechanisms: pull from an edge storage or push to a cloud based storage.

2.4 Integration

Integration of Functions for Transforming/Enriching Results. The integration is based on two different deployment modes: the internal deployment mode explores serverless and streaming analytics of the messaging brokers and the external deployment mode allows functions to consume messages that can be implemented using docker-based microservices.

Integration with Pipeline Development. Metadata and results as well as AFS models can be used differently: (i) the pipelines do not use AFS but the downstream applications use AFS to transform non-AFS results. (ii) existing pipelines can be modified to add metadata into detection results, and (iii) the pipelines completely uses new schemas from AFS.

Integration with Data Spaces. The detected data and, if needed, raw monitoring data can be shared to relevant (global) third-party parties via data space concepts and frameworks [3]; such data is part of the data product. Besides required integration in terms of defining connectors, identity management, policies, etc., we note the important role of metadata covering data product description, catalog and policies, which can be enriched with AFS metadata. Currently, data space specifications have not explicitly support AI/ML software related information and compliance information w.r.t. the underlying AI/ML pipeline producing the detected result. With AFS and the focus on near real-time detection data, we integrate with data spaces on the two following aspects:

- information about AI/ML model software compliance together with AI/ML model information that help interpret and explain the detection results.
- information about changes affecting data products: (i) changes in runtime detection constraints and (ii) changes in AI/ML deployment.

To this end, enrichment functions are used for integrating data space frameworks.

3 Related Works

Edge ML Detection. A large number of works on object detection at the edge in various scenarios have been published [4]. They cover ML models and algorithms for detection, systems for integration of detection, and performance evaluation. In the industry, there are many tools and models available, like in [1]. However, the major problems that can be seen when utilizing them are specific data models and lack of metadata. Another problem is that these works do not address the detection and communication of changes in detection deployment to the downstream. Our work focuses on reducing such challenges.

Metadata and Data Transformation. J. de Oliveira et al. [7] focus on querying data to support adaptation. This is a kind of "downstream" applications based on multiple sources of data. Detection results with metadata help improve such a work. Shi et al. [9] focus on metadata and data modeling for assets and processes. Our work differs due to the focus on the integration of detection results. Although various researches have presented the importance role of AI/ML quality attributes, explainability information of AI/ML systems and the observability of changes [5,6], current metadata about the quality and changes of AI/ML detection models and pipelines for interoperability and trustworthiness purposes has not been included for downstream applications and data consumers.

4 Conclusions

Today and future's AI/ML detection relies on multiple AI/ML models and pipelines developed by different vendors, and is highly decoupling in terms of operations and management responsibility. Especially, various types of detected data are from different pipelines (data providers) and quality. We have introduced AFS as a novel framework to abstract individual detections and unified them for analytics of subjects associated with collectives of assets, spaces

and environments, presenting various schemas and techniques to link and enrich metadata for detection integration and interoperability.
Software prototype availability: The implementation of AFS data models is open sourced at https://github.com/daienso/fansipan-afs.

References

1. Computer Vision Tasks Supported by Ultralytics YOLO26. https://docs.ultralytics.com/tasks/#detection. Access 26 May 2026
2. Blaom, A.D., Vollmer, S.J.: Flexible model composition in machine learning and its implementation in MLJ. In: CORR. arxiv preprint arxiv:2012.15505 (2020)
3. Möller, F., et al.: Industrial data ecosystems and data spaces. Electron. Mark. **34**(1), 41 (2024)
4. Murshed, M.G.S., Murphy, C., Hou, D., Khan, N., Ananthanarayanan, G., Hussain, F.: Machine learning at the network edge: a survey. ACM Comput. Surv. **54**(8) (2021)
5. Nakagawa, T., Narita, K., Kim, K.S.: How provenance helps quality assurance activities in AI/ML systems. In: Proceedings of the Second International Conference on AI-ML Systems. AIMLSystems 22, Association for Computing Machinery (2023)
6. Nigenda, D., et al.: Amazon sagemaker model monitor: a system for real-time insights into deployed machine learning models. In: Proceedings of the 28th ACM SIGKDD Conference on Knowledge Discovery and Data Mining, pp. 3671–3681. KDD '22, Association for Computing Machinery (2022)
7. de Oliveira, J., Calle, C., Calvez, P., Curé, O.: Towards autonomous anomaly management using semantic technologies at the edge. In: 2023 IEEE International Conference on Edge Computing and Communications (EDGE), pp. 159–165 (2023)
8. Paton, N.W., Chen, J., Wu, Z.: Dataset discovery and exploration: a survey. ACM Comput. Surv. **56**(4) (2023)
9. Shi, H., Liu, S., Pan, L.: Domain modeling for scenario sensing and edge decision-making. In: 2023 IEEE International Conference on Edge Computing and Communications (EDGE), pp. 118–125 (2023)

PROPEL: Proactive Energy-Efficient Task Offloading at the Edge via Online Reinforcement Learning

Leo Wilhelm Lierse(✉), Francesco Daghero, Mahyar Tourchi Moghaddam, and Mikkel Baun Kjærgaard

University of Southern Denmark, Odense, Denmark
{leoli,fdag,mtmo,mbkj}@mmmi.sdu.dk

Abstract. In edge computing, heterogeneous computing nodes enable opportunities to improve energy savings through resource-aware offloading policies. Existing task offloading approaches typically rely on hardcoded energy profiles or require offline-trained models and pre-deployment benchmarking. Furthermore, in high-throughput scenarios, offloading decisions must be made under delayed feedback, as failures (e.g., timeouts) and energy effects are observed only after subsequent tasks have already been offloaded. This is compounded by coarse-grained energy telemetry from external sources that cannot be attributed to individual requests. We propose an architecture that integrates an online reinforcement learning agent into a MAPE-K control loop to enable energy-aware task offloading without offline training or manual benchmarking. The agent deals with delayed rewards and observations, facilitating proactive decision-making. The results demonstrate that the agent robustly maintains performance and latency constraints while reducing total energy usage by 12%. Furthermore, the agent requires no offline calibration or training. This work contributes by presenting a reusable MAPE-K-integrated RL architecture for energy-aware offloading that accounts for delayed and aggregated energy/timeout feedback applied to edge computing.

Keywords: Energy-Aware Computing · Sustainable Computing · Edge Computing · Task Offloading · Self-Adaptive Systems · MAPE-K · Reinforcement Learning

1 Introduction

Task offloading is critical for computationally intensive applications running on resource-constrained edge devices, as local execution is often unfeasible due to compute [8] or battery constraints [11]. These scenarios are common in industrial systems, where multiple low-power sensing units continuously collect data that has to be rapidly processed to enable smart decision-making. The required processing often involves the execution of Machine Learning (ML)-based workloads,

Published by Springer Nature Switzerland AG 2027
D. Balouek et al. (Eds.): ESOCC 2026, LNCS 16834, pp. 166–173, 2027.
https://doi.org/10.1007/978-3-032-37831-6_12

processing the transmitted data, and responding within tight deadlines. This context also requires management of power usage, which directly affects operational costs and environmental sustainability.

Offloading to the cloud suffers from latency and privacy limitations due to data transmission and network variability. Edge computing alleviates these issues by placing moving computations closer to edge devices, but relies on heterogeneous hardware. Heterogeneity enables energy-performance trade-offs [1,2,7], but complicates offloading decisions, and existing solutions require extensive node profiling or large datasets [3,4,10], making them unsuitable for varying edge environments. Reinforcement Learning (RL), on the other hand, enables learning an offloading policy online, without prior knowledge of the nodes in the cluster. However, prior RL-based solutions [5] often assume synchronous request offloading, even though real-world scenarios may deal with high-throughput, asynchronous requests, resulting in delayed observations and feedback.

In order to address these challenges, we propose PROPEL, an architecture that extends the Monitor-Analyze-Plan-Execute over a shared Knowledge base (MAPE-K) feedback loop with an RL agent. The RL agent learns a cluster-specific policy to reduce power draw directly from the environment without prior knowledge of the cluster. PROPEL integrates techniques for handling delayed observations and feedback in the RL agent to ensure adaptation in high-throughput environments [13]. We evaluate PROPEL by implementing an offloading system based on it and achieve energy savings of 12%.

Our code is available on Github[1].

2 Background

Offloading tasks from constrained edge devices to more powerful nodes is a common pattern, especially in mobile ML inference [8], because edge devices (e.g., robots and phones) often lack the necessary resources to handle the tasks. However, when offloading to the cloud, we contend with wide-area network latency and congestion. Offloading instead to nearby edge clusters mitigates these problems [11].

Edge clusters are often heterogeneous, featuring nodes with wide differences in computational resources and power usage [2]. Leveraging this heterogeneity is the key to energy efficiency, even though operating all nodes in an optimal regime is not trivial [1,7]

Naive strategies such as round-robin scheduling or opportunistic offloading may yield suboptimal results in terms of latency and energy [10]. Thus, a suitable offloading policy must balance latency and energy usage by tracking each node's performance, workload, and power draw. Rule-based systems [3] use pre-measured node profiles that require upfront effort; if the environment drifts from these profiles, re-profiling and adjustment are necessary. Data-driven methods such as supervised learning [4] perform well but require large training datasets

[1] https://github.com/sdu-deco-lab/propel.

and struggle with unpredictable environmental shifts. Given these dynamics, online adaptation is essential. An ideal offloading policy should continuously adapt to live conditions rather than rely on static design-time knowledge, making RL highly appealing.

In RL, an agent learns a policy mapping states to actions to maximize cumulative reward [6]. Unlike supervised learning, it relies on trial-and-error to discover policies that yield high long-term rewards. Double Deep Q-Networks (DDQN) is an adaptation of the foundational Q-learning method [6], and features two Neural Networks (NNs) that are exploited to deal with large and continuous state and action spaces [9]. Two networks prevent the action value overestimation of single Deep Q-Networks, by decoupling action selection and evaluation [12]. To deal with delayed observations, strategies like Delay Reconciliation (i.e., fixing delayed observations for training) or State Augmentation (i.e., providing insights on unobserved behavior) can be used [13].

Prior work [5] explored RL for energy-performance trade-offs but assumed instantaneous feedback and fixed node frequency, which is unrealistic in edge settings where monitoring is delayed, and requests arrive so frequently that outcomes manifest after subsequent decisions. Consequently, energy-efficient offloading under high request rates and delayed feedback remains underexplored.

We address the requirements of online learning, the complexity of the task, and the high-throughput nature of the use case by embedding a DDQN RL agent within a MAPE-K architecture, enabling adaptation to unfamiliar environments without extensive pre-deployment benchmarking.

3 Approach

We propose PROPEL, a framework for energy-aware task offloading based on the MAPE-K control loop, shown in Fig. 1. This framework adapts the computing infrastructure, specifically the offloading policy, for self-adaptive edge applications. Such an application consists of sensors and actuators interacting with the environment. Environmental stimuli or periodic triggers generate computational tasks that must be processed within strict deadlines and enable adaptation. If such a process fails, the system will either trigger a fail-safe or become unsafe, both undesired states.

The computing infrastructure is a heterogeneous edge computing cluster, ranging from embedded devices to powerful servers. To exploit the heterogeneous nature of the nodes for energy efficiency, an offloading controller determines to which node to dispatch application tasks. Within the MAPE-K loop, the *Monitor* phase tracks resource utilization, performance, and power usage of the cluster. During the *Analyze* phase, the system preprocesses the most recent observations alongside internal state data (e.g., in-flight requests). All inputs are normalized and standardized for the state representation used by the RL agent.

PROPEL's core is a DDQN-based RL agent that merges *Analyze* and *Plan* phases by directly mapping the cluster state to a target node. Operating via continuous online learning, it eliminates the need for offline training or prior benchmarking. The agent updates its Q-networks continuously, adapting to changes in

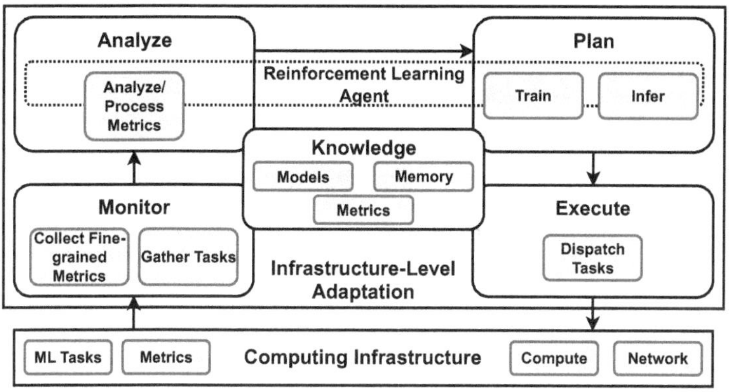

Fig. 1. Architecture of the proposed PROPEL framework.

the workload and node characteristics. Proper design of the state of reward function allows PROPEL-based systems to tolerate stale observations and delayed rewards [13].

In the *Execute* phase, the task is dispatched to the selected target. The system continues processing new requests concurrently. Upon completion, the result, request metrics, and power metrics are fed back to the knowledge base, together with other system metrics, such as in-flight requests. The result is returned to the application, while latency, success/failure, and power usage produce the reward signal for the RL agent, closing the MAPE-K adaptation loop.

RL-based Offloading Policy. In this section, we detail the minimum requirements for the state representation, reward formulation, and decision-making process. Upon task arrival, the state s_t is constructed using the most recent observations of the edge cluster. It comprises at least: *i)* per-node power draw, *ii)* the in-flight tasks per node, *iii)* average latency per node, and *iv)* the last N offloading decisions and their age. The in-flight information and action history are a state augmentation providing information on unobserved effects.

The reward r_t is formulated to incentivize low latency and low power draw while penalizing failures and deadline misses. r_t increases with low execution time and power draw. Deadline violations or task failures incur a substantial negative penalty. This formulation explicitly trades off latency against power draw, with weighting configurable to domain requirements. In our experiments, latency and energy are weighted equally (see Sect. 4).

Algorithm 1 details the per-task interaction. Upon arrival at time t, the agent constructs state s_t and a history of recent actions A. The agent evaluates $Q(s_t, A)$ and selects a target node a_t either greedily or via exploration. The task is dispatched, and the execution latency L_t is recorded. To address asynchronous execution, reward processing is deferred until the task deadline D_T by waiting $W_t = D_T - L_t$. This ensures state transitions and reward assignment occur with the same delay for all tasks. Afterwards, the agent gets the new state s_{t+L_t},

Algorithm 1: PROPEL procedure for each task

```
Input: Set of targets P; empty replay_buffer R; RL agent Q
foreach incoming task T with deadline D_T at time t do
    s_t ← get_environment_state()
    A ← get_recent_actions()
    a_t ← arg max_a Q(s_t, A)    // select action (greedy or random)
    offload task T to target P[a_t]
    monitor task latency L_t;
    return results to task issuer;
    wait for W_t seconds, such that W_t + L_t = D_T;
    s_{t+L_t} ← get_environment_state()
    r_t ← compute_reward(L_t, s_{t+L_t})
    R.add(s_t, a_t, r_t, s_{t+L_t});
    if enough transitions since last training then
        batch ← R.sample(batch_size);
        perform_TD_update(Q, batch);
    end
end
```

computes r_t from observed latency and power draw, and stores the transition $(s_t, a_t, r_t, s_{t+L_t})$ in the replay buffer.

4 Implementation

We evaluate our framework on a heterogeneous edge cluster composed of two Raspberry Pi 4Bs (RPi), a NUC equipped with an AMD Ryzen 5 7535HS (NUC), and a server with an AMD Ryzen 9 9950X (Server). Each hosts a containerized instance of an ML inference service and a metrics collector. The Server additionally hosts the offloading system and load generator. Power draw is measured using an Eaton EVMAFC20A Power Distribution Unit (PDU), which provides power measurements at a sampling frequency of 0.33 Hz with a resolution of 0.1 W.

The PROPEL-based offloading system is implemented with a DDQN-based RL agent comprising two Multi-Layer Perceptrons (MLPs) with three fully connected layers. We benchmark the system against Round-Robin (RR) and Inverse Response Time and Energy (IRTE) offloading, in terms of power draw and latency. RR requires no runtime metrics or dynamic state, so it has minimal overhead and is well-suited for homogenous clusters. The IRTE strategy computes a weight for every candidate node based on its recent mean response latency and latest power draw, but does not account for observation delays.

5 Evaluation

We assess PROPEL concerning energy efficiency and latency. All results are reported without the idle energy of the cluster, as it is identical for all benchmarked policies. Table 1 summarizes the power, energy, latency, and timeouts for each strategy, computed over the final two hours of our three-hour experiments following an initial 1-hour learning period. The experiments answer three research questions:

- **RQ1.** Does PROPEL reduce cluster power draw without missing deadlines?
- **RQ2.** How do PROPEL offloading policies adapt in a heterogeneous cluster under frequent, asynchronous task arrivals?
- **RQ3.** What impact does PROPEL have on latency and deadlines?

Table 1. Power Usage, Latency and Timeout Statistics

	Power [W]				Latency [ms]			
Experiment	Avg	Median	P95	Energy [kJ]	Avg	Median	P95	Timeouts
RR	44.61	44.69	47.66	321	860.2	732.09	1500	50%
IRTE	54.77	54.97	65.94	394	80.99	40.35	308.44	0%
DDQN	48.3	47.93	52.76	347	49.39	45.4	53.26	0%

RQ1. The RR baseline proved infeasible in our use case as it consistently overloads the slower RPis, resulting in about 50% of requests timing out. In contrast, both the IRTE heuristic and the PROPEL-based system completed 100% of requests without timeouts. Figure 2 shows how the total cluster power draw for IRTE and PROPEL. IRTE drew an average of 54.8 W, amounting to 394 kJ total energy, whereas PROPEL used only 48.3 W on average and 347 kJ in total. This corresponds to a 12% reduction in average energy usage relative to the baseline. Notably, RR's average power was lowest (44.61 W) simply because not all tasks were completed. These results demonstrate that the PROPEL-based system adjusts its offloading policy to minimize power draw and prevent deadline misses.

RQ2. Figure 3 provides a breakdown of power usage per node. PROPEL quickly reallocates almost all tasks towards the NUC. The server seems to incur a higher power draw, while the RPi nodes suffer from slow response times. The result is that the cluster operates mostly with the NUC under load and with the other nodes nearly idle. However, using IRTE, all nodes continue to receive a share of the tasks. Furthermore, delayed observations prevent the IRTE policy from converging to a stable equilibrium, causing oscillations in the cluster's power usage. To summarize, PROPEL-based systems adapt quickly and can learn cluster-specific policies to exploit the heterogeneity for energy savings; They learn to use the most energy-efficient node and cease requests to the other nodes, a behavior that baselines cannot replicate.

RQ3. Figure 4 shows the latency distribution under PROPEL and IRTE. It shows that the PROPEL-based systems' prioritization of energy efficiency results in a 12.5% increase in median latency. This latency increase reflects the decisions to sacrifice some performance to save energy. However, this trade-off provides an upside in this environment: It greatly improves the stability and tail

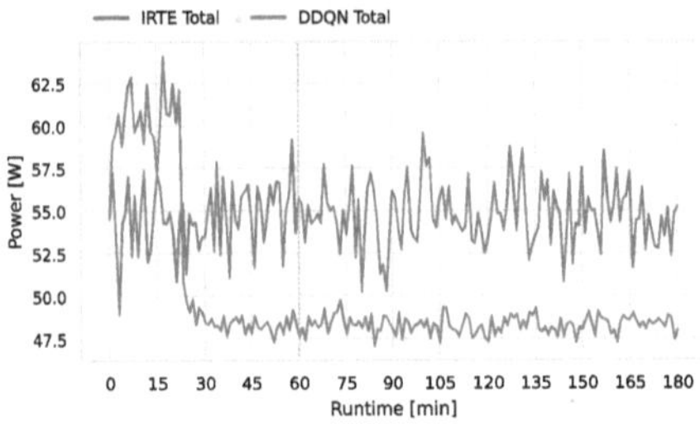

Fig. 2. Total Cluster Power Draw over time for the IRTE and PROPEL policies.

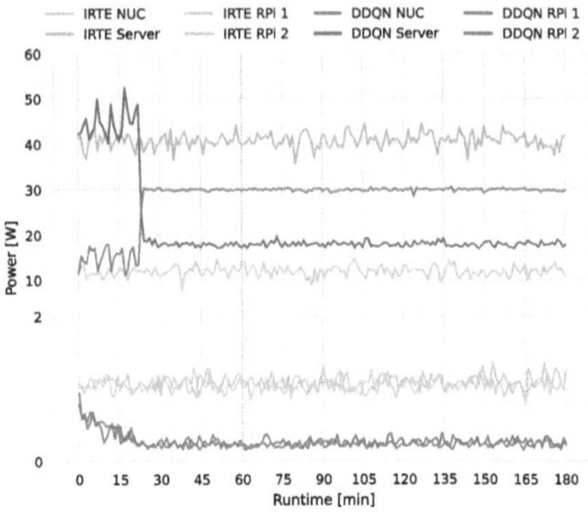

Fig. 3. Per Node Power Draw over time for the IRTE and PROPEL policies.

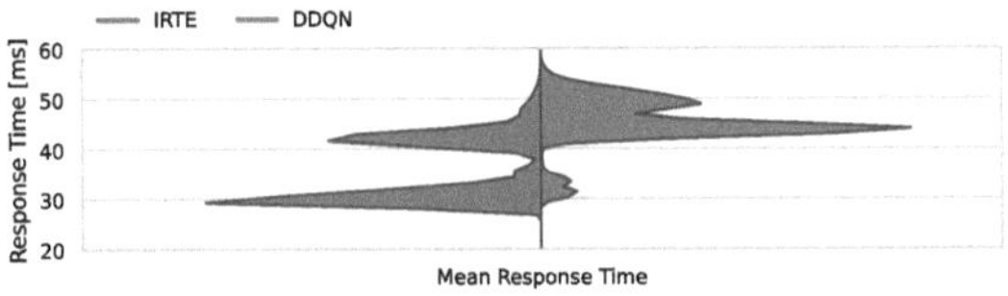

Fig. 4. Distribution of request response times.

latency. IRTE's 95th-percentile latency reached 308 ms, whereas PROPEL's 95th percentile was only 53 ms, a six-fold reduction in tail latency.

PROPEL-based systems can sacrifice performance for energy efficiency. As a result, they can consolidate requests on the most energy-efficient nodes, even if they are less performant. This consolidation also results in less latency variance.

6 Conclusion

We introduced PROPEL, a framework that integrates an RL agent within a MAPE-K loop to enable learning energy-efficient offloading policies in high-throughput environments, where feedback and state updates are delayed. We evaluated PROPEL by implementing an agent based on it that learns an offloading policy to improve energy efficiency in heterogeneous edge clusters. We demonstrate an energy usage reduction of 12% and highlight the potential of combining RL with self-adaptive architectures to address sustainability concerns in high-throughput edge environments.

References

1. Barroso, L.A., Hölzle, U.: The case for energy-proportional computing. Computer **40**(12) (2007)
2. Blem, E.: Power struggles: revisiting the RISC vs. CISC debate on contemporary ARM and x86 architectures. In: IEEE 19th International Symposium on High Performance Computer Architecture (HPCA) (2013)
3. Guzek, M.: HEROS: energy-efficient load balancing for heterogeneous data centers. In: IEEE 8th International Conference on Cloud Computing, IEEE, New York City, NY, USA (2015)
4. Hussain, B.: Mobile edge computing-based data-driven deep learning framework for anomaly detection. IEEE Access **7** (2019)
5. Hussin, M.: Efficient energy management using adaptive reinforcement learning-based scheduling in large-scale distributed systems. In: 2011 International Conference on Parallel Processing (2011)
6. Kaelbling, L.P.: Reinforcement learning: a survey. J. Artif. Intell. Res. **4** (1996)
7. Khokhriakov, S.: Multicore processor computing is not energy proportional: An opportunity for bi-objective optimization for energy and performance. Appl. Energy **268** (2020)
8. Li, E., et al.: Edge AI: on-demand accelerating deep neural network inference via edge computing. IEEE Trans. Wireless Commun. **19**(1), 447–457 (2020)
9. Mnih, V., et al.: Human-level control through deep reinforcement learning. Nature **518**(7540), 529–533 (2015)
10. Shahid, M.A.: A comprehensive study of load balancing approaches in the cloud computing environment and a novel fault tolerance approach. IEEE Access **8** (2020)
11. Shi, W.: Edge computing: vision and challenges. IEEE Internet Things J. **3**(5) (2016)
12. Van Hasselt, H., et al.: Deep reinforcement learning with double Q-learning. Proceedings of the AAAI Conference on Artificial Intelligence, vol. 30 (2016)
13. Wang, W.: Addressing signal delay in deep reinforcement learning. In: The Twelfth International Conference on Learning Representations (2024)

Analyzing the Evolution of Structural Communities Within Microservice Architecture

Alexander Bakhtin[1(✉)], Matteo Esposito[1,2], Valentina Lenarduzzi[1,2], and Davide Taibi[1,2]

[1] University of Oulu, Oulu, Finland
alexander.bakhtin@oulu.fi
[2] University of Southern Denmark, Vejle, Denmark
{esposito,lenarduzzi,taibi}@imada.sdu.dk

Abstract. In recent years, the detection of anti-patterns in microservice architecture has gained traction, particularly to identify instances of Microservice Architectural Degradation. In such tasks, the microservice architecture is often modeled as a network of microservice dependencies.

Temporal community detection methods have been proposed to analyze the community structure of networks that evolve in time. We performed temporal community detection within the microservice architecture of six releases of the *train-ticket* benchmark and analyzed the composition of the discovered communities and their activities over time. We observed a stable architecture with a clear separation of services into two communities, which we could identify with two business processes performed by the system.

Keywords: Microservices · Community detection · Temporal networks · Wrong cuts · Knot service

1 Introduction

Over the past decade, the adoption of Microservice Architecture (MSA) has led to the identification of various architectural patterns and anti-patterns to prevent Microservice Architectural Degradation [2]. Specific anti-patterns include Wrong cuts, when different responsibilities and business processes are incorrectly divided among the services, and Knot services, when services are too coupled to each other and communicate with too many other services [8]. Detecting such anti-patterns often involves modeling the microservice system as a network of connected services [3,4]. Moreover, in the context of architectural degradation, it is the *evolution* of such networks that is of interest [5].

In the field of network science, the study of ***temporal networks*** (TNs) has gained traction as a powerful way to model and analyze networks that evolve [5,12]. Specifically in MSA, Bakhtin et al. have applied temporal network methods to networks of microservice architecture [5] and developer collaboration

Published by Springer Nature Switzerland AG 2027
D. Balouek et al. (Eds.): ESOCC 2026, LNCS 16834, pp. 174–182, 2027.
https://doi.org/10.1007/978-3-032-37831-6_13

[6]. In particular, temporal community detection allows to identify communities that persist or re-emerge through time [10]. In MSA networks, community detection can help us identify groups of services that communicate a lot and assess whether such groupings correspond to business processes [9], or if their dependencies are the result of improper division of responsibilities or unoptimized behavior [11,13].

Therefore, leveraging the promising results obtained previously [5,6], in this work, we analyze the temporal community structure [10] of several releases of *train-ticket* OSS benchmark. Our contributions include the following: **(i)** we performed temporal community detection in the reconstructed MSA; **(ii)** we analyzed the temporal activity of the discovered communities and noted stable community structure; **(iii)** we observed the composition of microservice communities and how they reflect the business processes of the system.

Due to space constraints, background is provided in the Online Appendix[1].

2 Related Work

Community detection among microservices within MSA is an unexplored direction. The only works that we could identify are due to Khodabandeh et al. [13], analyzing the community structure of microservice clusters in the Alibaba production environment, and Gaidels and Kirikova [9], who analyzed an MSA network with several community detection algorithms and identified the context of each community. Crucially, *temporal* community detection has not been leveraged for the assessment of microservice architectural evolution, while Bakhtin et al. [5] only applied temporal centrality for this purpose. Abufouda and Abukwaik [1] argued for properly adopting TN methods in Empirical Software Engineering. However, their review focused only on applications of TNs for developer collaboration networks. Bakhtin et al. [6] have leveraged temporal community detection to analyze the structure and trends of TN of developer collaboration on microservices in an OSS benchmark, determining the groups of collaborating developers at each release. To our knowledge, this is the first attempt to apply temporal community detection to reconstructed microservice architecture networks in the context of Microservice Architectural Degradation.

3 Empirical Study Design

The **goal** of our study is *to **analyze** how the **temporal community structure** of microservices **evolves over time** and on what basis the microservices **communities are formed***. Therefore, we defined the following **Research Questions (RQs)**:

***RQ*$_1$*: Do the structure and activity of the microservice communities evolve?*

Since microservice architecture strives for *high cohesion, low coupling* design of the system, the presence of strongly coupled groups of microservices in

[1] https://doi.org/10.5281/zenodo.19253698.

the MSA network could indicate improper decomposition of the system into microservices or the presence of certain anti-patterns. Moreover, temporal variations in the community structure indicate that microservices change their dependencies from one release to the next, suggesting the instability of the architecture. Observing the trends in community activity and structure over time thus allows us to judge the stability of the architecture. Since the approach of Gauvin et al. [10] provides us with the communities' activity profiles over the analyzed time-span, we can observe if communities have near constant activity in the analyzed releases or if their activity varies a lot. We can leverage standard deviation for this analysis, and thus formulate the following null and alternative hypotheses: *($\boldsymbol{H}_{01}$) the activity values of each community stay within a 3-sigma interval around the mean; ($\boldsymbol{H}_{11}$) at least one community activity exceeds a 3-sigma interval around the mean.*

While the activity patterns of the discovered communities show the stability of the overall system, membership of particular services in different communities could serve as an indicator of Wrong cuts or Knot-like behavior:

$\boldsymbol{RQ}_2$: *Do microservices form communities based on business processes?*

Once we have determined the composition of each community, we can analyze whether these communities consist of microservices performing related business processes. For example, in the case of the *train-ticket* benchmark [16], we could assume the services for booking a ticket, reserving a seat, and checking the timetable would be in the same community, since they would all be invoked when purchasing a ticket. Moreover, since the method by Gauvin et al. [10] provides overlapping communities, i.e., the same service can belong to several communities, we can check if there are microservices that simultaneously belong to different communities focused on different business processes. If this is the case, it could hint at an improper service decomposition and responsibility allocation within the microservice system. We thus formulate the following hypotheses: *($\boldsymbol{H}_{02}$) all microservices belong to exactly one community; ($\boldsymbol{H}_{12}$) at least one microservice belongs to several communities.*

Data Collection. We have previously compiled a dataset of OSS MSS projects suitable for network analysis by reconstructing their architectures the Code2DFD tool [4,14]. In a follow-up study [5], we determined the OSS MSS projects whose architecture evolved throughout development. We discovered that the *train-ticket*[2] microservice benchmark project is the only available and reconstructed system that shows significant structural evolution. We thus leveraged the networks of all the train-ticket releases reconstructed in our previous work [4,5] as the TN for our analysis.

Data Analysis. We performed temporal community detection in the TN of *train-ticket*, applying the method by Gauvin et al. [10] with our previously developed implementation [6].

[2] https://github.com/FudanSELab/train-ticket/.

To determine the best number of communities to fit, we leveraged the core consistency metric [7] similar to [6,10]. According to the original authors, the core consistency values between the maximum of 100 and 90 are considered a good fit [7,10]. For each choice of the number of communities from 2 to 6, we reconstructed the community structure 20 times with random initialization of PARAFAC decomposition, measured core consistency, and computed their mean and standard deviation to determine the most stable results. In our case, the only instance in which we obtain values above 90 is for the fit of **two communities** to the TN of **releases *v0.0.1-v0.2.0***. This choice has an average core consistency of 99.05 and a standard deviation of 0.40. We used this community detection result for our analysis. All the used scripts and data of all the tested values are available in the Online Appendix[3]

We obtained the temporal activities of the two communities, as well as the membership strengths of microservices within these communities, based on incoming and outgoing connections. We scaled all three outputs to the interval [0.0; 1.0] by dividing by the maximum value in each case.

4 Results

In this section, we report the results of temporal community detection in the TN of *train-ticket* architecture and answer the **RQs**. The two detected communities are denoted consistently as *blue* round, solid stems and *orange* crossed, dashed stems in Fig. 1.

Looking at the **temporal activity** of the communities (**RQ**$_1$, see Fig. 1 in the Online Appendix), we observe that both *blue* and *orange* communities have **high activity**, consistently above 0.8 in all the releases. The activity on the interval *v0.0.2 - v0.1.0* is constant, indicating **identical, unchanging architecture**, as noted by Bakhtin et al. [5]. On this interval, *blue* community **appears to be dominating** the *orange* community, since the former increased its activity while the latter decreased compared to release *v0.0.1*.

To answer **RQ**$_1$, we computed the mean and variance of the temporal activities of each community. The exact temporal activity values of the *blue* community are 0.99, 1.0, 1.0, 1.0, 1.0, 0.97, providing a mean of 0.993 and standard deviation of 0.012. Thus, the 3-sigma interval is [0.956; 1.000]. For the *orange* community, the values are 0.84, 0.82, 0.82, 0.82, 0.82, 0.81 with the mean 0.822, standard deviation 0.0098, and the 3-sigma interval [0.793; 0.851]. Thus, for both communities, we **fail to reject the null hypotheses H**$_{01}$, since all temporal activity values stay within the respective 3-sigma intervals.

RQ*$_1$ *answer*:** *We observe* ***stable community structure *across the releases of train-ticket, with all activity values within 3-sigma interval around the mean.*

Considering the **composition of the temporal communities** (**RQ**$_2$), we determined the membership of microservices in the communities by setting a neutral threshold of 0.5 on the computed membership strength (Fig. 1).

[3] https://doi.org/10.5281/zenodo.19253698.

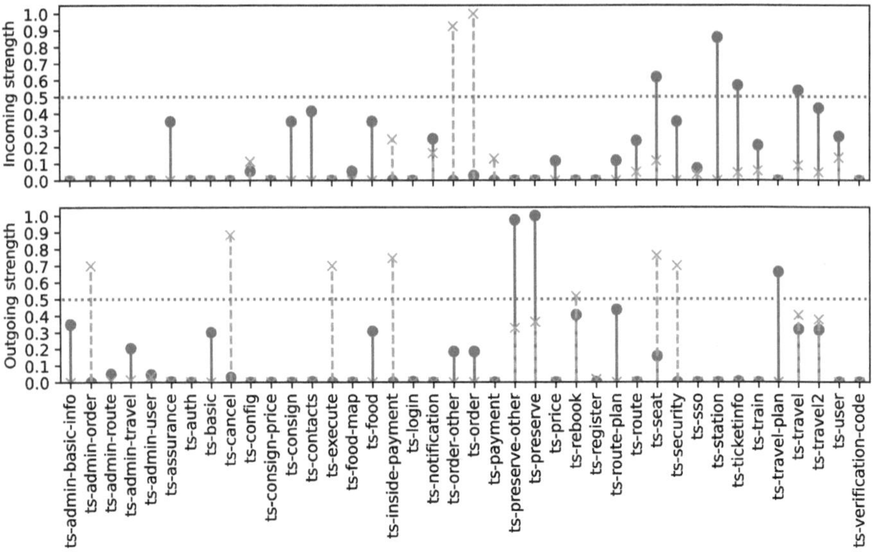

Fig. 1. Incoming and outgoing community membership, normalized by the maximum value. The horizontal lines show the membership cutoff threshold of 0.5.

Observing the *blue* community, we notice that it corresponds to *preserve*, *preserve-other*, and *travel-plan* services making calls to services like *seat*, *station*, *ticketinfo*, and *travel2* services. The aim of the *preserve* service is to preserve the ordered ticket data in the database, thus this community seems to correspond to the process of saving the different aspects of the order information, like stations mentioned in the ticket or the reserved seat, from respective services.

Furthermore, the *orange* community consists of several services like *admin-order*, *cancel*, *rebook*, and *seat* sending calls to *order* and *order-other* services. The *order* services stores the information on the made orders, thus this community seems to correspond to the business process of modification of the orders, such as rebooking or cancellation.

Concerning our hypothesis, we have to **reject the null hypothesis** in favor of the alternative hypothesis H_{12} since the *seat* service is a member of both communities, *blue* as a callee and *orange* as a caller.

***RQ_2* answer:** *Microservices participate in different communities associated with different business processes.*

5 Discussion

In this section, we discuss the results of our **RQs**, their implications for practitioners and researchers, as well as address the threats to validity.

Stability of the Temporal Community Reconstruction. Overall, we have observed a **stable architecture** of the *train-ticket* project, as indicated by the stable, almost **constant temporal activity** of the communities ($\mathbf{RQ}_1$) and **clear separation of the microservices** into communities ($\mathbf{RQ}_2$). However, the fact that we could only fit a community structure to the TN of releases *v0.0.1-v0.2.0*, excluding the latest release *v1.0.0*, could itself indicate problems with the architecture stability due to sudden changes in the MSA network. The change between releases *v0.2.0* and *v1.0.0* includes the refactoring of food-related services, which could have resulted in **noticeable changes in microservice dependencies** in that region of the MSA, and since the whole MSA consists of "only" 42 services, this could have had a **significant effect on the performance** of the community detection algorithm. We believe we would see more robust results if we considered an industrial-scale system with a long history of releases, since in an Agile environment, releases occur frequently and incrementally. On the other hand, temporal activity was constant between the releases *v0.0.2* and *0.1.0*, which is the interval which we previously identified as having no modifications in the architecture [5]. Thus, the **leveraged method is robust** to constant data and produces stable, non-fluctuating results when given a temporal network with identical snapshots.

Membership Strength Paints a Nuanced Picture. While we resorted to setting a threshold on the membership strength to interpret microservice communities and test our hypothesis, we also noticed that many services have non-zero membership strength below the 0.5 threshold (Fig. 1), and such observations could still provide value to architects and developers. Thus, the raw membership strength values can **enable more fine-grained interpretation**. For example, *rebook* and *route-plan* services have membership strength in the *blue* community close to 0.5. Moreover, services belong to several communities, suggesting that they **participate in several business processes**. This could indicate an inappropriate division of responsibilities between the services. Furthermore, some services have both the incoming and outgoing membership strength in the same community , like *food*, *travel*, and *travel2* services in the *blue* community. This could indicate instances of **Wrong cuts, Knot-like, or Hub-like behaviour** [3], since these services appear to be both called by and to call many other services. We believe that performing this kind of analysis on a large industrial system will enable more detailed observation of communities and their identification with the business process. Moreover, with more communities detected overall, the membership of a microservice in several communities would be easier to connect to bad practices or anti-patterns, with many overlapping communities potentially indicating higher severity.

Implications for Researchers and Practitioners. The proposed temporal community analysis can provide valuable **insights to practitioners** who wish to analyze how their MSA is evolving. It could highlight **positive trends**, e.g., architecture remaining stable, or **negative trends**, e.g., services not related by a business process or function forming a community or a community significantly increasing its activity. **For researchers, future directions** could include considering more closely what kinds of insights could be extracted from such an approach, in particular when analyzing a system that contains more communities that show sudden changes in activity, and how they relate to anti-patterns such as Hub-like or Knot services or Wrong cuts [3,8]. Moreover, the applicability of **other temporal community detection approaches** with different parameters, constraints, and outputs could be considered.

Threats to Validity. We discuss the threats to the validity following the guidelines by Wohlin et al. [15]. ***Construct validity:*** we leveraged the dataset of several versions of the *train-ticket* benchmark as reconstructed in our previous work [4,5] with the Code2DFD tool [14] as well as our own implementation of the community detection methods [6]. These tools have their limitations as research prototypes. ***Internal validity:*** we had to rely on *train-ticket* as the only MSA that is reconstructed for only seven releases with some architectural variability. However, even this variability is limited, with several releases having an identical architectural structure. Moreover, since the system contains only 42 microservices with many dependencies among them, we could only identify two communities, where a lot of services belong with a small, but non-zero strength. ***External validity:*** the *train-ticket* benchmark project is one of the biggest OSS MSA projects, and the only one that we could analyze in this work. However, it still does not represent an industrial-scale, in-production microservice system. We were thus careful not to overgeneralize our observations and conclusions , aiming instead to showcase the leveraged community detection algorithm. ***Conclusion validity:*** we are not closely familiar with all the services, functionalities, and business processes of *train-ticket*, so the mapping between the communities and business processes is subject to interpretation bias.

6 Conclusion

In this work, we performed temporal community detection within a temporal MSA network of six releases of the *train-ticket* benchmark project and identified two communities with near-constant temporal activity. Several services have incoming and outgoing memberships to several communities, which we identified with distinct business processes. For **practitioners**, the proposed methodology could highlight positive and negative trends in MSA evolution, such as architecture remaining stable or services not related by a business process forming a community. **For researchers**, this work opens up future directions for studying how MSA community structure and service membership interplay with bad practices and anti-patterns. Furthermore, different community detection algorithms could be analyzed and compared.

Acknowledgment. This work has been funded by the Research Council of Finland (grants n. 359861 and 349488 - MuFAno) and Business Finland (6GSoft).

References

1. Abufouda, M., Abukwaik, H.: On using network science in mining developers collaboration in software engineering: a systematic literature review. Int. J. Data Min. Knowl. Manag. Process (IJDKP) **7**(5/6), 17–34 (2017). https://doi.org/10.5121/ijdkp.2017.7601
2. Al Maruf, A., Bakhtin, A., Cerny, T., Taibi, D.: Using microservice telemetry data for system dynamic analysis. In: 2022 IEEE International Conference on Service-Oriented System Engineering (SOSE), pp. 29–38 (2022). https://doi.org/10.1109/SOSE55356.2022.00010
3. Bakhtin, A., Esposito, M., Lenarduzzi, V., Taibi, D.: Leveraging network methods for hub-like microservice detection. In: 2025 IEEE International Conference on Service-Oriented System Engineering (SOSE), pp. 27–38 (2025). https://doi.org/10.1109/SOSE67019.2025.00008
4. Bakhtin, A., Esposito, M., Lenarduzzi, V., Taibi, D.: Network centrality as a new perspective on microservice architecture. In: 2025 IEEE 22nd International Conference on Software Architecture (ICSA), pp. 72–83 (2025). https://doi.org/10.1109/ICSA65012.2025.00017
5. Bakhtin, A., Esposito, M., Lenarduzzi, V., Taibi, D.: Centrality change proneness: an early indicator of microservice architectural degradation. In: Andrikopoulos, V., Pautasso, C., Ali, N., Soldani, J., Xu, X. (eds.) Software Architecture, pp. 243–259. Springer Nature Switzerland, Cham (2026). https://doi.org/10.1007/978-3-032-02138-0_16
6. Bakhtin, A., Li, X., Taibi, D.: Temporal community detection in developer collaboration networks of microservice projects. In: Galster, M., Scandurra, P., Mikkonen, T., Oliveira Antonino, P., Nakagawa, E.Y., Navarro, E. (eds.) Software Architecture, vol. 14889, pp. 174–182. Springer, Cham (2024). https://doi.org/10.1007/978-3-031-70797-1_11
7. Bro, R., Kiers, H.A.L.: A new efficient method for determining the number of components in parafac models. J. Chemom. **17**(5), 274–286 (2003). https://doi.org/10.1002/cem.801
8. Cerny, T., Abdelfattah, A.S., Al Maruf, A., Janes, A., Taibi, D.: Catalog and detection techniques of microservice anti-patterns and bad smells: a tertiary study. J. Syst. Softw. **206**, 111829 (2023). https://doi.org/10.1016/j.jss.2023.111829
9. Gaidels, E., Kirikova, M.: Service dependency graph analysis in microservice architecture. In: Perspectives in Business Informatics Research: 19th International Conference on Business Informatics Research, BIR 2020, Vienna, Austria, Proceedings 19, pp. 128–139. Springer, Cham (2020). https://doi.org/10.1007/978-3-030-61140-8_9
10. Gauvin, L., Panisson, A., Cattuto, C.: Detecting the community structure and activity patterns of temporal networks: a non-negative tensor factorization approach. PLoS ONE **9**(1), e86028 (2014). https://doi.org/10.1371/journal.pone.0086028
11. Genfer, P., Zdun, U.: Using guided community detection to improve existing microservice designs. In: Aiello, M., Deng, S., Murillo, J.M., Georgievski, I., Benatallah, B., Wang, Z. (eds.) Service-Oriented Computing, pp. 205–220. Springer Nature Singapore, Singapore (2026). https://doi.org/10.1007/978-981-95-5012-8_15
12. Holme, P., Saramäki, J.: Temporal networks. Phys. Rep. **519**(3), 97–125 (2012). https://doi.org/10.1016/j.physrep.2012.03.001

13. Khodabandeh, G., Ezaz, A., Ezzati-Jivan, N.: Network analysis of microservices: a case study on alibaba production clusters. In: Companion of the 15th ACM/SPEC International Conference on Performance Engineering, pp. 67–71 (2024). https://doi.org/10.1145/3629527.3651842
14. Schneider, S., Scandariato, R.: Automatic extraction of security-rich dataflow diagrams for microservice applications written in java. J. Syst. Softw. **202**, 111722 (2023). https://doi.org/10.1016/j.jss.2023.111722
15. Wohlin, C., Runeson, P., Höst, M., Ohlsson, M.C., Regnell, B., Wesslén, A.: Experimentation in Software Engineering (2024 edition). Springer Berlin Heidelberg, Berlin, Heidelberg (2024). https://doi.org/10.1007/978-3-662-69306-3
16. Zhou, X., et al.: Benchmarking microservice systems for software engineering research. In: Proceedings of the 40th International Conference on Software Engineering: Companion Proceeedings, pp. 323–324. ICSE '18, Association for Computing Machinery (2018). https://doi.org/10.1145/3183440.3194991

Project Track

The UK National Edge AI Hub

Omer Rana[1(✉)], Rajiv Ranjan[2], and Gaurav Kaushik[2]

[1] School of Computer Science and Informatics, Cardiff University, Cardiff, UK
ranaof@cardiff.ac.uk

[2] School of Computing, Newcastle University, Newcastle, UK
{raj.ranjan,gaurav.kaushik}@newcastle.ac.uk

Abstract. The UK National Edge AI Hub is a large-scale initiative advancing the design and deployment of artificial intelligence systems at the network edge, with strong alignment to service-oriented computing. The Hub integrates academic, industry, and public-sector stakeholders to develop modular and interoperable AI capabilities that can be orchestrated across heterogeneous, resource-constrained environments. It promotes distributed intelligence through federated learning and adaptive lifecycle management, enabling decomposition and dynamic composition of AI functionalities close to data sources. This supports low-latency, privacy-preserving, and resilient service delivery across sectors such as transport, healthcare, and energy. The research addresses key challenges in service-oriented computing systems, including coordination under intermittent connectivity, quality-of-service trade-offs, and integration of AI-driven services into critical infrastructures. Trust, security, and governance are treated as first-class concerns, aligning with the principles of reliability, accountability, and policy compliance. Through co-design with stakeholders and validation in real-world testbeds, the Hub demonstrates how Edge AI can be realised as a scalable ecosystem of intelligent services, supporting flexible, context-aware, and sustainable digital infrastructure.

Keywords: Cyber-disturbances · systems resilience · energy preservation · federated learning

1 Introduction

The UK National Edge Artificial Intelligence (Edge AI) Hub is a UK-wide initiative focused on AI algorithms that operates close to data sources such as sensors, devices, and embedded systems. By bringing together leading academic institutions, industry partners, and public-sector stakeholders, the Hub addresses the technical, organisational, and societal challenges associated with deploying AI in real-world, resource-constrained edge environments. The Hub brings together 15 Universities and 50+ industry partners.

Edge AI represents a strategic transition from cloud-centric intelligence towards systems that are low-latency, privacy-preserving, resilient, and energy-efficient. The Hub's mission is to deliver foundational research, translational

Published by Springer Nature Switzerland AG 2027
D. Balouek et al. (Eds.): ESOCC 2026, LNCS 16834, pp. 185–188, 2027.
https://doi.org/10.1007/978-3-032-37831-6_14

solutions, and skills development that enable the next generation of intelligent edge technologies across sectors including manufacturing, transport, healthcare, energy, and digital infrastructure.

2 Advancing the Foundations of Edge Artificial Intelligence

Research at the National Edge AI Hub is centred on the design, training, deployment, and governance of AI systems that operate reliably outside centralised cloud environments. As AI becomes embedded within physical systems and critical infrastructure, the Hub's research programme re-examines foundational assumptions in machine learning, systems engineering, and governance to reflect the realities of edge deployment.

A defining feature of the Hub's research is its emphasis on resource-constrained intelligence. Edge environments differ fundamentally from data centres, involving limited power budgets, intermittent connectivity, stringent latency requirements, and highly heterogeneous hardware. Hub researchers explore new algorithmic paradigms that balance accuracy, energy use, memory footprint, and responsiveness, challenging trends toward increasingly large and computation-intensive models in favour of approaches that are efficient, adaptive, and deployable at scale.

The Hub also undertakes substantial work on distributed and federated learning at the edge. Many applications require collaborative learning across networks of devices without centralising raw data, whether due to privacy, bandwidth, or regulatory constraints. Research in this area examines how learning can be coordinated across diverse edge nodes, how local adaptation can be reconciled with global model performance, and how robustness can be ensured in the presence of unreliable or adversarial participants. Another key aspect is the focus on cybersecurity challenges in this context – and area referred to as "cyber disturbances" in the Hub.

Adaptation and robustness in dynamic environments form another core strand of the research programme. Edge AI systems are often deployed in settings that evolve over time, with changing operating conditions, degrading sensors, and shifting patterns of use. The Hub investigates techniques for continual and online learning, concept drift detection, and safe model updating, ensuring that deployed systems remain dependable without introducing unacceptable risks.

Trustworthy and responsible AI is a cross-cutting theme throughout the Hub's research. Deploying AI at the edge intensifies concerns around explainability, accountability, fairness, and safety, as decisions may be taken autonomously and in close proximity to people and critical infrastructure. The Hub explores approaches to interpretable modelling, runtime assurance, and post-deployment monitoring that embed trustworthiness directly into system design.

The Hub's research agenda is closely aligned with emerging policy and regulatory priorities. Advances in privacy-preserving and federated approaches inform debates on data protection and data sovereignty, while work on robustness and assurance contributes evidence relevant to AI safety standards and governance frameworks. Through its engagement with policymakers and public-sector stakeholders, the Hub helps translate technical insights into practical guidance for infrastructure planning, procurement, and long-term digital strategy.

3 Stakeholder Engagement

The National Edge AI Hub places strong emphasis on translating research into deployable solutions. Working closely with industry and public-sector partners, the Hub supports the co-design of Edge AI applications that address real operational challenges, from real-time monitoring and predictive maintenance to intelligent control and decision support.

Through pilot projects, demonstrators, and experimental testbeds, the Hub enables validation of Edge AI systems under realistic conditions, helping partners understand performance trade-offs, deployment risks, and lifecycle management considerations. This translational activity ensures that research outputs are directly informed by, and relevant to, the needs of end users.

4 Long Term Engagement

Looking ahead, the National Edge AI Hub is positioned to play a sustained national role in shaping how artificial intelligence is embedded within future digital and physical infrastructure. As edge computing matures from isolated deployments into a core component of large-scale systems, long-term research priorities increasingly centre on scalability, resilience, sustainability, and governance, as well as on the integration of AI into environments where failure carries significant operational or societal consequences.

One major area of long-term interest lies in the development of sustainable and ultra-low-power Edge AI systems ("frugal AI"). As the number of connected devices continues to grow, energy efficiency becomes a defining constraint rather than an optimisation goal. Future research will increasingly focus on co-design approaches that span algorithms, hardware architectures, and operating systems, enabling AI to operate within strict power and thermal envelopes. This direction aligns closely with national and global sustainability goals, particularly as edge intelligence becomes embedded in large-scale sensing infrastructure and environmentally monitored systems. Supporting energy efficiency also impacts provision of services hosted on edge systems – as the quality of service may vary depending on imposing a power cap or constraints on overall execution time of an ML model.

A closely related priority is Edge AI for critical national and industrial infrastructure. Sectors such as transport, energy, manufacturing, and water systems are increasingly reliant on distributed digital control and monitoring. In these contexts, AI systems must be robust to faults, cyber threats, and unforeseen interactions, and must continue to operate even in degraded or disconnected modes. Long-term research in this area will involve developing architectures and assurance approaches that support resilient, fail-safe intelligence at the edge, while enabling human operators to maintain oversight and control.

The Hub also anticipates growing importance in research on secure and sovereign AI deployments. As concerns around data governance and supply-chain dependency intensify, edge computing offers opportunities to retain sensitive data and decision-making capability within local or national boundaries. Research into privacy preserving learning, secure execution environments, and verifiable system behaviour will be central to enabling AI systems that meet both operational and policy requirements, particularly in public sector and regulated domains. Another strategic direction is the integration of Edge AI with next generation communication networks, including 5G, emerging 6G concepts, and future satellite and hybrid networks. These technologies blur the boundary between computation and communication, enabling dynamic placement of intelligence across devices, edge servers, and network infrastructure. Research in this domain will explore how AI models can adapt to variable connectivity, exploit network awareness, and support time critical applications such as autonomous systems and real-time control. Understanding how edge systems can detect drift and adapt under a continuous learning process, safely, also remains an important challenge.

Human-centred teaming also represents a long-term focus. As intelligent systems operate closer to people—in workplaces, public spaces, and homes—issues of interpretability, usability, and trust become increasingly salient. Research will need to address how humans understand, supervise, and intervene in distributed AI systems, particularly when decisions are made autonomously and at scale. This includes developing explanation mechanisms appropriate for non-expert users and designing systems that support meaningful human oversight. Finally, the Hub recognises the growing importance of lifecycle management for deployed AI systems. Unlike static software, Edge AI systems must evolve over time in response to changing environments, regulatory expectations, and societal norms. Long-term research will address how models can be updated, audited, validated, and ultimately retired in a safe and transparent manner. This work directly informs emerging practices in AI assurance and contributes to the development of standards and guidance for long-term AI governance.

Collectively, these strategic areas position the National Edge AI Hub not only as a centre for technical innovation, but as a critical contributor to the responsible evolution of AI-enabled infrastructure. By aligning cutting-edge research with long-term societal and policy needs, the Hub supports a vision of Edge AI that is resilient, sustainable, and worthy of public trust.

Author Index

Published by Springer Nature Switzerland AG 2027
D. Balouek et al. (Eds.): ESOCC 2026, LNCS 16834, p. 189, 2027.
https://doi.org/10.1007/978-3-032-37831-6

FSC
www.fsc.org
MIX
Papier | Fördert
gute Waldnutzung
FSC® C083411

Kolibri 360 GmbH
Ferdinand-Jühlke-Straße 7
99095 Erfurt, Deutschland
produktsicherheit@kolibri360.de